MW01171624

IT AIN'T JUST ABOUT PLANES

When your life has totally fallen apart;
There can be a new beginning.

BILL BLACKFORD

Special "First Printing" Collector's Edition
CITATION PRESS
LAUREL, MISSISSIPPI

Published by:
Citation Press
3 Southern Place
Laurel, Mississippi 39440-1276
Copyright @2019 by Bill Blackford
Printing History: First Edition – 2024
ISBN: 979-8-9909361-5-7

ACKNOWLEDGMENTS

Appreciated thanks goes to my wife, Lynne, who was the love of my life for thirty-three years. She opened my eyes and my heart. She also endured many late nights and put up with a lot of craziness from me over the years. Lynne passed away October 12, 2006, and there will always be an emptiness in my heart and in my thoughts.

Special thanks go to Marty Sinker who has stood with me through thick and thin, and most importantly taught me what true customer service is all about; that FBO's are not just turnpike gas stations for aircraft but were in the hospitality business and so much more.

For years and years, many of my customers, acquaintances and employees have said that I needed to write a book about my life and experiences. It wasn't until I went back to my 50th high school reunion that I began to recall so many of my life's experiences and realized how unusual my life had actually been. In retrospect, I was pretty sure that most of my classmates wouldn't believe how my life had turned out, so I decided not to even bring most of my experiences into my conversations, some of which I couldn't really go into detail about anyway. I did, however, mention that I had arrived in a Citation Jet for the reunion.

The writing of this book could not have been possible without the help of friends, former employees, customers and fellow pilots too numerous to include here. For that glaring omission, I ask not for their forgiveness, but at least for their understanding. I would be remiss if I neglected to mention those individuals without whose help this book would be nothing more than a project unrealized or a paperweight sitting on my bookshelf in manuscript form.

To start at the beginning, I wish to thank my good friend Matt Jones, who listened so often to my ideas about someday writing a book about my life's experiences. He finally told me to quit talking about it, and just write a book.

I give my special thanks to Robert Kiss my editor/copyeditor for his patience and whose creative criticism kept *IT AIN'T JUST ABOUT PLANES* a viable project. A special thank you for taking on such a challenging task.

Table of Contents

CHAPTER ONE: GENESEO
1946 – 1964

It has been over 75 years since the story of my life began. I was looking forward to my 50th class reunion and recalling my personal history. It was the first class reunion I had gone back for; there was a reunion every five years. When I left Geneseo in 1964, I did not return for 50 years, with the exception of two funerals and one trip passing through town with a stop for dinner at The Cellar. Each time was an overnight stay. The next morning, my wife and I stopped at the house (it was never a home for me) that my parents were living in; however, we were denied entry. "Don't you remember what I told you when you left, that you could NEVER come back?" That's a pretty good example of my first sixteen years of life.

In recalling the previous fifty years as they were unfolding, they seemed very normal to me. But when I recalled all of the remarkable, unexpected, or unusual things that I had experienced or participated in since I left Geneseo, it was quite a collection of events. Especially for a very unpopular kid growing up in a small town with very few friends and absolutely no support from parents or teachers.

So here it goes, my journey through my life (so far). As far back as I can remember, I was about four years old, in the little town of Geneseo, Illinois. It is a relatively small town with a population of

5,000, named by the settlers from New York after their original city of Geneseo, New York. I heard the reason they left New York was because of religious differences. I did visit the other Geneseo, and strangely enough, the original layout of the town is exactly the same in the sister city. The Congregational Church, the business district, and the city park are in exactly the same location in both towns, and the streets also have identical names.

Geneseo is a beautiful town with its tree-lined streets and very well-maintained homes, and many original Victorian structures, which are now over 150 years old, lining the streets. Figure 1 – 1 shows Geneseo's downtown area. This is why it is also known as "Victorian Geneseo." Figure 1 – 2. Geneseo is located 18 miles east of the Quad Cities (Moline, East Moline, Rock Island, Davenport, and Bettendorf).

Geneseo was, and mostly still is, a farming community. However, there were several residents who worked for John Deere; their world headquarters is just a few miles northwest of town (Figure 1- 5), the Rock Island Arsenal, and A J Case in the Quad Cities. There were few scenic wonders unless you count Geneseo Creek or endless miles of cornfields as scenic wonders. There was one traffic light, located in the center of the "business district" if you can call a five-block area a business district. The traffic light was referred to by most as a "stop and go" light. There were two banks, three grocery stores, one meat market, three barbershops, a hardware store, one drug store (later another opened in a vacant building), a few bars, a bakery, three clothing stores, a century-old hotel that in 1960 was purchased by the owners of the Pontiac-Cadillac dealership (more about that later) and various other nondescript businesses. There were several grain silos and two lumber yards and a chicken processing plant that were also located in the same area. There were no strip malls, but there was a bowling alley with twelve lanes with automatic pin setters (that was a big thing at that time) on the south end of town. One of the grocery stores, the A & P, moved out of the business district into a new building on US 6 on the west end of town. It soon went out of business at their new location. Springfield Armory, the manufacturer of handguns, has moved their home base into that location.

There were several locally-owned bars in town. However, no package-style liquor stores were allowed within the city limits. As unusual as it may seem, there was a local ordinance that tied the number of liquor licenses to the number of churches within the city limits. The bars had to have clear glass windows with no obstructions such as curtains or shutters so that "Miss Priscilla Goodbody" could walk by and see who the patrons were using the facility. That wasn't her real name; it's the one that I gave her. For some reason, she believed that it was her duty to be the town's busybody. It just so happened that she went to the Methodist church, so she also took it upon herself to report what she believed was inappropriate behavior by the members of the church, especially me.

The Christmas Walk, also known as a Victorian Christmas, and The Cellar, which is a fine restaurant, are about the only reasons folks from the surrounding cities and towns would come to Geneseo. This holiday event is very well attended, with many people, in the thousands, coming from the Quad Cities and other nearby towns to take part in this holiday event.

Victorian Christmas was quite an event, kicking off in the morning with a 5K run. Sleigh rides are also offered throughout the day. Most of the guests spend their time shopping in downtown Geneseo. Children's activities fill the afternoon with special crafts and much more. Children's choirs are also featured at various times throughout the afternoon.

As the sun goes down, people line the streets as music and Christmas lights fill the landscape. Numerous floats, marching musicians, and animals parade northward up State Street into the downtown district. After the parade, visitors look into the storefront windows where living scenes depicting life and holiday traditions from the 1800s are on display, celebrating the Christmas season.

There was a country club (and golf course) just outside the city limits. It had two tennis courts and a boat launching ramp located at the Hennepin Canal, which runs parallel to the club, and a nine-hole golf course. The club's drive is where the final for the high school driver's ed course was held; you had to back along their long and winding road. Back then, this course was mandatory, and I wish it still was in all schools.

On the first day of driver's ed, a State Policeman came into the classroom and gave a "pep" talk. His first item was to have every other student stand; he told us that one-half of us would be involved in an accident within the next five years. I told the two that were standing closest to me to sit down because I had already had their accidents. I had been driving since I was thirteen, and another person in the driver-ed car was also proficient at driving. There was a third person in the car who was a slow and poor driver with absolutely no driving experience. If we could arrange it, she would be the last one to drive, then we would not get back before the end of the period. However, our instructor was onto our plan after a few sessions. Our actual "on the road" part of the course was in the winter. She was so unfamiliar with driving that when she would go around a corner, she would not neutralize the steering wheel, kept turning, and would drive right into the snowbanks along the edge of the road. The local Chevrolet dealer donated a 1963 Impala for the course. It just happened that later I purchased a 1963 Impala; however, mine was a convertible. Figure 1 - 3 My first car was a 1953 Cadillac; it had been abandoned at a local gas station, and I filed for a lost title; my total cost was $75.00, Figure 1 - 4.

A few years before I left Geneseo, a radio station opened, WGEN-Clear Channel 1500, not to be confused with WGN – 890 in Chicago. I did the Sunday church remotes for them. Attending the various churches in town got me thinking about the various doctrines that each religion has, and most interesting is that if you were not baptized in their church, you were not going to get into heaven – really! However, I had already made up my mind that there must not be an all-loving God because if there was a God, he would not allow any child to endure what I had endured. As an aside, I happened to be doing the remote broadcast from the Methodist church when Jack Ruby murdered accused Presidential assassin Lee Harvey Oswald. The same person who owned the radio station also had a contract with Motorola to install nurse call stations and televisions in hospitals across the United States. I worked for him the summer between high school and college; that was my first venture when I was truly on my own. More on that in a later chapter.

Geneseo, like most small towns, had advantages for its residents. Everybody knew everyone within their neighborhoods and would rat out any of the kids who were believed to be "up to no good." In other words, you couldn't get away with anything. However, it fostered a genuine caring attitude among most neighbors, and that's a good thing. Unlike living in large cities where you don't even know your next-door neighbor.

Downtown Geneseo - Figure 1-1

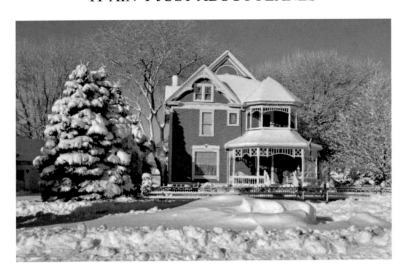

Typical Victorian Home - Figure 1 – 2

This is the house I grew up in, (just two houses from the upper picture) I planted the maple tree, front right.

Two homes north of where I grew up on Center Street.

Figure 1 – 3

My first car a rusty 1953 Sedan DeVille - Figure 1 – 4

John Deere World Headquarters

Figure 1 – 5

Where you came from does not determine where you are going.

When you are through changing,

You are through.

CHAPTER TWO:
MEET THE FARKLES
1950 - 1964

"Your hometown usually includes your family. Family means no one gets left behind or forgotten." If family life was only as simple as this popular quote from the Disney movie Lilo & Stitch. Although some people stress the importance of family and the love and bond that surrounds them, my experience was quite different. As the youngest, I know firsthand what it's like to be left behind and forgotten. And some days it went far beyond that. So, what was it like exactly? For me, that depended on the stage of life that I was in or the mood the Farkles were in.

I have no memory of anything before I went to kindergarten; I believe I was four at that time. I eventually figured out that I had to be adopted, and that my brother, Ken, was not my biological brother. As a young child, I didn't understand that things weren't great. I idolized Ken; he was eight years older than I was, and thought we were all one happy family. I put him on a pedestal and felt extremely happy to be his little brother. But as I got a little older, I started to realize that I didn't exactly fit in. The impact of that throughout my teenage years was very damaging.

Realizing that I didn't fit in with my own family was difficult for me to handle emotionally. But figuring that out as a teenager can be life-changing. For me, it translated into low self-worth, no self-esteem, and reckless behavior. I yearned for acceptance, so I spent much of my time trying to be someone I wasn't. And it didn't change the situation regardless; I still didn't fit in.

I would try really hard to be who I thought Ken and parents wanted me to be, and when I came up short, I blamed myself. There were times when I was suicidal. It seemed that I had a different mother than Ken had. There were three of them and one of me, so I always felt left out. I didn't fit in anywhere. Watching their close bond, having it in front of my face every day, made it even more difficult to accept the fact that I never felt like one of them. There were days I just wanted to die; I felt I would rather be dead than be a part of this dysfunctional family.

Near the end of WWII, the Catholic Churches, especially in the Chicago Area, would find babies on their doorsteps each morning. It got to the point that the church arranged for trains to head west with a load of these babies. The train would stop at the small towns along the route and offer these children to anyone who wanted one or more of them. Also, they came with blank birth certificates. After I learned about this practice, I came to believe that I had been a passenger on one of these trains.

With that being said, I was shunned from second grade through high school. At lunchtime in the second grade, four of us went downtown (about three blocks) to The Book Store. The other three were shoplifting small items. After school that day, I told my teacher about what had happened. I am not sure how the other three heard about my conversation with her, but they had. From that point on, I was an outcast. I really dreaded going to school every day; it was not much better than being home.

Entering early adulthood with this family dynamic, life was still difficult, but I came to believe that one day I would have the ability to make my own choices. That was the turning point for me. To follow that up, at this time my mother told me that I would have to pay for room and board. I was fourteen at this time. I told her that I was willing to pay, but it wasn't going to her. If I had to pay rent it was going to be where I wanted to live, and that certainly was not going to be with them. I also told her that I was going to check with Judge Conway Spanton, a friend and county judge, to see if that was enforceable. I believe the state of Illinois legislated for minor children: food, shelter, and clothing must be provided until they reach the age of eighteen. I'm thankful that I never felt like I fit in with my family. It gave me a deeper appreciation for the support of those whom I chose to allow to be in my life. People have a way of surprising you. Sometimes, unlike the "family" that I grew up in, I chose them to come into my life, Jerry, Bob, Carey, Pat, and Hilton. My small circle of friends became my family. They opened their hearts to me, accepted me, and showed me a love I never thought I deserved. Unfortunately, only one of the above was in the same grade as me, the others were one year ahead, so my Senior year was pretty lonely for me. All I thought about was how soon I would be able to get away from this hell hole.

My new family taught me that I had the power of choice. It's hard to be an outsider in the family you're raised in, but you can choose not to accept that life. You can choose who you spend your time with and who you let in. But I learned an important lesson: being an outsider in your own family doesn't mean you're worthless. It simply means you haven't found the right tribe. Your people are out there.

Meet the Farkles (depicted in Figure 2 - 1). I guess explaining a little bit about how I was treated in my early life and the conditions in my childhood home would be helpful. I can't seem to let go of it, such hatred and rage toward my parents. I nick-named them the Farkles, Fred, and Fanny; they had a huge negative effect on my early life, with many of the negative effects carrying over to my later life. I couldn't wait to get the hell away from them. I never felt like I belonged in their house – it was not a home. There was absolutely no love or affection available for me, only enough for Ken. I don't remember a single moment in my life when either of my parents said, "I love you."

Ken could do no wrong in their eyes. He was a master at playing the same games as my mother did. No matter what was going on, he would always go along with whatever my mother said or did. She was a devious, cunning, conniving bitch. Worst of all, she would not report all the correct and/or pertinent information to my dad about what had happened that day, which would always result in consequences for me, which were, at times, quite severe. I do not recall, not even once, that they told me they were impressed or proud of absolutely anything that I had accomplished or done. It was at this time that I first attempted suicide, I was in the second grade and was the "Crossing Guard" after school. I intentionally ran out in front of a car. However, he swerved and slammed on his brakes and just missed me. He went into the school and reported this incident, and they, in turn, called my mother and reported it to her. When I got home, she asked me if I was trying to kill myself. I thought for a moment and said, "Yes." Her response was, "Don't get smart with me; change your clothes. You have chores to do."

It was obvious that my mother never wanted me, I was a mistake and a pain in her ass; she even told me this during one of her many screaming outbursts. She was a master at advanced game playing. My dad would support her even when he was aware of her "games;" that was the case, well, at least most of the time. For example, while I was sweeping the carpets, she would go behind me and dump ashtrays on the carpet and demand that I do them again. The last time she did that, I refused to vacuum them again; I put the vacuum away and started to cook dinner for them. When dad arrived on the scene, she told him that I refused to vacuum. He stormed into the kitchen and took out the belt which was kept in the pantry. I told him this shit had to stop and explained what she was doing. He went into the living room to speak with her, and when he returned, he just put the belt away, but he didn't say a word to me. Usually, he would not confront her about what she was doing, but worse yet, he would administer what was his idea of the appropriate punishment for my so-called misdeeds. Some of these "punishments" included three broken noses, a dislocated shoulder, a broken arm, a broken wrist, or a beating with a barber's belt, the ones they used to sharpen their razors in the barbershop. I was allowed to have one Pepsi a day; one evening, I put it in a glass with ice and walked into the living room with it. The three of them had a "sip" and there was almost none left, so I put the glass down on the table and got a warm Pepsi, opened it and started drinking it. It was grabbed out of my hand and told I already had my Pepsi for the day; then I was swung around by my right arm, resulting in a dislocated shoulder. One time, my dad wanted to use the bathroom, and I didn't vacate it as soon as he thought I should. He burst through the door and took a swing at me; I ducked, and he punched a hole in the wall. Justice was served for once. I ran out of the house and stayed away for several hours. In Illinois, you get new license tags annually, not just a sticker; when it came, it was thrust into my hand, and I was told to install it. I looked at my right hand, and blood was pouring out of my middle finger. Off to the emergency room again; this time, it only took six stitches to close the wound. The good thing about this was I flashed my finger at them for two weeks. It was also at this time that I decided that I did not want to have any children; after all, how do parents learn to become parents, by how they were raised. I did not want to take any chances of repeating what they had been doing to me.

My brother left for college when I was eight, and it really went downhill after that. My parents supported him financially and emotionally until his early death in 1997. However, my "punishments" continued at an even greater rate. It seemed like I could not do anything right, every night seemed like the "Friday night at the Fights" at our house. Inflicting pain on me seemed to give them some sort of satisfaction.

The Farkles were religious for one hour a week while attending the church service. It was also around this time that my forced belief in an "all-loving God" vanished. When I was in the third grade, I attempted suicide one more time. They were out one evening so I took every prescription drug that I could find and went to bed. When I awoke the next morning, I felt just fine; I had failed again! I was never questioned about the missing drugs, go figure.

My dad didn't ever do the normal things a father usually does, like play catch with his son, go fishing, or go to a ball game. The closest thing we did (father and son) was go to Arlington Harness Racetrack in Chicago, one time. We never had a "man-to-man" talk, nor did we ever spend any time together as father and son. I had to teach myself how to tie a necktie and even how to shave. The only useful thing he told me was: "Don't look too far up the family tree, there are some branches that you really don't want to find."

During all the years I was there, we only took two vacations, one to Mt. Rushmore, the Black Hills, and the Corn Palace; the other was to Ed Gabe's Lost Lake Resort in Rhinelander, Wisconsin. On the first night in Black Hills, Dad picked up my "suitcase," which was a dress box by the center of it, of course all my clothes landed in a puddle on a wet parking lot. Dad just stood there looking at the dress box. Mom, Dad, and Ken all had hard-sided Samsonite luggage, but mine was a box. She blamed me for not getting my own clothes out of the trunk. That's how my life was, everything was my fault, at least I had a strong liquor box for the next trip.

At Lost Lake, I had my first airplane ride. A seaplane was giving rides around the lake, and a newlywed couple who were staying in the cabin next to ours, whom I had made friends with, Ed and Joann Ustch, offered to let me go along with them on the plane. Over my mother's objections, I decided that I would go with them. They even let me ride in the right front seat. Soon after takeoff, the pilot slid his seat back and actually let me "fly." He let me have control of the plane until I lined it up for landing. Wow, what a thrilling experience! This was the time I knew that I would be a pilot. The Farkles were not impressed that I loved my flight; they had never been on a plane, and my mom's comment was that if God wanted you to fly, he would have given you wings. My response to that was if he wanted your fat ass to ride in a car, he would have given you wheels. I got into a lot of trouble for that comment. My mother would have been happier if I had chosen to work for the IRS than choosing aviation as my career of choice.

One year, our Methodist Minister and family, the Pattersons, were transferred to another city. At Christmas time, Gracie (wife) sent me a Christmas gift. However, when I got home from school, there was a porcelain horse with one leg broken lying on the table. My mother said it was from the Pattersons. I questioned if it was for me and who had opened the package. She said it was addressed to "The Blackford's." Later that evening, I went to the basement and found the packaging; it was addressed to me, and it had been wrapped in Christmas paper, and the name tag was still attached, and it was to "Billy." I will never believe that it arrived with a broken leg; it had somehow been broken after it arrived and before I got home from school. The previous year Gracie had asked me what I had received for Christmas, and I told her the usual, underwear and a toothbrush. I believe she remembered and thought I should have something other than underwear under the tree for Christmas.

I was forced to join the DeMolay chapter with the idea that I would advance to being a Mason, then a Shriner, just like Fred Ferkel. I did not believe in most of their beliefs, but that didn't matter; I had no choice but to join. After one of the meetings, the mothers who were not usually in the Masonic temple after the meetings had fixed Sloppy Joes. I guess I was in a particularly melancholy mood, Mrs. Lounsbury (she was a single mother of two sons, both of which were in DeMolay) noticed this and took me aside and made the offer that if I needed someone to talk with, she could be that person. One evening when I was particularly low and things at home were really bad, I went over to her house and unloaded. It took a few hours to get that out of my system. The next day when I got home from school, Fanny informed me that Mrs. Lounsbury had called her and told her everything that I had said. So much for believing that I could trust anyone, except for Dr. Watters. After that incident, I refused to go to any more of the DeMolay meetings.

When I was thirteen, Uncle Bill purchased an ocean-going forty-foot yacht; he kept it at the Moline Yacht Club. He took it out about every summer weekend, and we were invited to cruise with him and his first wife. After a cruise, the Farkles always went into the Club for drinks and sandwiches. I had to wait outside because I wasn't twenty-one. One evening when my uncle approached the Club, he asked why I was outside, I told him, and he immediately went inside and asked the bartender if I could come inside. The bartender said, "Of course, he can come in." My Uncle usually went straight to his car and headed home. Uncle Bill gave me a handful of change for the Jukebox and bought me a Coke. I played "Patricia" over and over. Every time I hear that song, it reminds me of him and the Club. He was great that way. That was the last time I was allowed to go to the Marina with them. He sold his boat at the end of the summer; it was too far for him to go to get to the Marina, as well as it was a huge expense for him.

Before I began driving alone, the old lady backed into a power pole while she was trying to park her car downtown. She did more damage than one would normally expect. She must have been going pretty fast to do that much damage to the back end of the car. All I ever said about her 'accident" was that when I had my first one, I just remember this one.

Between the ages of thirteen and sixteen, I was involved in three auto accidents, two of which totaled cars, and one of which landed me in the hospital. For that one, I was admitted after spending hours in the emergency room. When I got to my room, I called the Farkles and told them that I had been in an accident and had been admitted to the hospital and that the car was in bad shape. They wondered where their car had been taken so that they could inspect the damage. Never once did they ask how I was or when I would be released. That pretty well explains what they thought of me, and the feeling was mutual. Remembering what I had said about her accident may have prompted their lack of concern about my situation. I wasn't the "ideal" child, but I wasn't that bad either. I was never arrested or even under suspicion for any crimes, except for driving without a license; underage driving at that time was "normal" for a small country farm town.

One afternoon after school, the Chief of Police came to the house to try to get me to tell him who was selling and who was using drugs. With my history of being a tattle-tail, I told him I would not honor his request. Strange how that, after all the years since my second-grade episode, first that he would know about that, and that I would repeat that mistake. I did know who was selling weed and cocaine, but not who was buying it.

For some strange reason, my mother thought I should have rather long hair. At that early age, I really didn't care how I looked, so a few times a year, I would get a buzzcut, crew cut, and sometimes a flat top, one time when I was told not to get all my hair cut off (only once did I get a skintight mohawk, that was a painful mistake.) I just wanted to make her angry. In my mind, there would only be one beating, but having a "non-approved" hairstyle for two to three months was worth it. I mentally called them my rebellion haircuts, that really worked. To be honest, I really enjoyed seeing that hair cascade to the floor. To this day, I still prefer to have shorter hair, sometimes almost no hair at all. I guess that is a hangover from my early childhood. Even in college, I would get a flat top or a short Ivy League haircut when long hair on guys was the style to have.

We were one of the first houses in the area to have a console color TV. It had about a fifteen-inch screen and it was a massive piece of furniture. Then there were only about three TV shows a week that broadcasted in color. The same goes for air conditioning, first in the area, not only in the house but in the cars too. She was always hot, so now she could keep the house down to sixty-five degrees, summer and winter. It was always cold in that hell hole.

Christmas 1963, there was a party at the Country Club. I don't recall who or what it was for, it must have been for a school function. But I do remember that some of my classmates and I did a massive amount of decorating for that gathering, and the cost was significant. We purchased a very large real tree, miniature lights, ornaments, table decorations, and a massive amount of garland. The miniature white twinkle lights were just becoming available in the stores and were expensive. According to our agreement with the Club, we had to have the decorations removed within 24 hours after the event. The old lady refused to take me to the Club or give me the keys to one of the cars, to remove the decorations, then I found out she oversaw decorating the Club for another event the very next weekend. She used the decorations we had paid for; she wouldn't even pay half of the cost. Then she tried to get me to take them down after her party. I refused, not sure how I pulled that off, but I did.

That's typical of how things were while I was still "under their roof." She would bring dresses home from the local women's dress shop "on approval," and in a day or two, she would demand that I return them for her. I had to take the ridicule from the staff at the store; some of them were my classmates. I told the store owner, Mrs. Beachler, what I would do if I ran the store; if a garment left the store, it had to be paid for, and if it was returned, only a store credit would be applied to the account, no cash refund; because that particular garment would not have been available for anyone else to purchase while she had it. I'm not sure if they instituted that policy because I refused to return any more clothes under my threat to inform dad of what she had been doing. I believe it was her plan was to play this game just to embarrass me, I don't believe she ever planned to keep any of those clothes. She actually purchased most of her wardrobe in Davenport, Iowa.

I wasn't allowed to take part in any "over the dinner table" discussions with them; ever since I can remember, mealtime was just a time for them to tell me how terrible I had been; I had just been a pain in their asses. I never had the opportunity to defend any of my actions, "Don't give us any of your back talk." I was not allowed to speak at the dinner table or any other time.

I was never allowed to express any emotions, opinions, or feelings in their presence while growing up. If I did, there would be consequences, sometimes severe, beatings, and/or punches which resulted in my nose being broken three times. I guess that now in the present time, that would be classified as child abuse. It was so bad that I attempted suicide three times before successfully the third time, it was 1959, they didn't ever mention anything about it to me.

As I recall it was a sweltering summer day, I had just had another bad morning dealing with my mother. That morning she told me that she did not want me, and they should never have brought me home. "You have been a pain in my ass since that day, it was your father's idea to get you." I fixed my lunch, I did not do what she had ordered me to accomplish that afternoon, probably sweep and dust downstairs or wash the windows. Anyway, I got my swimming suit and a towel, headed for the local swimming pool, on my rusty Schwinn bike, it was about a mile away. On the way to the pool the thoughts of attempting another suicide kept going through my head. I decided that my life was not worth going through many more rounds of the abuse and bullshit that I had endured.

As I arrived at the pool, I decided that this was the day. I went into the men's side of the dressing room building and put my swimsuit on and headed for the water. After jumping in, it felt quite cool and was a welcome sensation. After I swam two laps and just hung onto the side of the pool deciding just how I was going to accomplish my plan. The pool was quite crowded, one lifeguard was in his elevated chair, and his attention was to check out the girls who were out of the water working on their tans.

So here is the plan, swim to the lifeguard's side of the pool next to the edge, just where the deep end begins, thinking that he would overlook me as he occasionally scanned the water, and then I begin breathing in the water. At first there was a brief time of panic, but just as soon as my lungs filled with water, normal breathing began, but instead of air it was water. Very soon the highlights of my life flashed by, that took maybe only ten seconds, at the same time all pain, stress and anxiety vanished and was replaced with the most incredible exhilarating feeling imaginable. I really don't have the words to accurately describe that sensation. Then I was above the pool watching them take me out of the water and begin artificial respiration. My spirit then moved me to a large vacant area (maybe I was in purgatory). I was floating around (weightless) going through walls and doors, another new sensation (the fourth dimension). I really don't know how long I was there, but all of those wonderful sensations continued. I did not see the bright light that some others have described. At least I was not in Hell, as my Sunday School teacher had predicted that I would be.

Then the most horrible thing happened, I was like a shop vacuum sucking me back into my coughing and choking body. Three unsuccessful attempts, I couldn't even commit suicide. I picked up my clothes, got on my bike and took the long way home. I didn't go back to the pool all the rest of that summer. The one actual change that happened was that my eyes changed color from hazel to blue. I have been told that change occurs in a few people that have been on the other side and returned. My parents never noticed the change.

They would have been just as pissed as I was that I had survived. After that third failure, I decided that I could put up with everything that was going on around me if I just kept my mind focused on getting out of there as soon as I possibly could, and I decided that aviation was the way. But in the back of my mind, suicide was always there if once again, it got to that point.

My life in school wasn't much better than at home. I certainly was not included in the "in group," just the group that I had selected. I was one of the most unpopular members of my class, I didn't win any popularity contests. I pretty much stayed by myself and tried to stay out of trouble. I really disliked going to school every day. I did maintain a "B" average, but the Farkles couldn't understand why I didn't get straight "A's" since they told me that they had gotten straight "A's." I thought, bullshit. I was happy with my grades, but of course, they weren't. I don't remember one time when they praised me or said you did an excellent job on anything that I did; it was only, "why can't you do better." My guidance counselor Mr. Johnson met with me only one time, by my choice, and asked what I planned to do with the rest of my life. I told him I was going to be a pilot. He told me that I should probably consider a factory job, since I didn't possess the math skills or aptitude that would be required to become a pilot. That became a great lesson for me: don't always believe the advice of those around you because they are not necessarily the most brilliant people; they just happen to be in a position to offer advice. Since I had my first flight at Ed Gabe's Lost Lake Resort, I looked forward to becoming a pilot; I believed that it was my way out of the hell that I was living in. Just go ahead and follow your dreams!

Just to give a couple of examples of my home life, I was diagnosed with bleeding ulcers when I was in the 7th grade. It was determined that they were caused by the stress from my living environment. Dr. Watters gave me a prescription for Valium 10's to be taken four times a day. That did not totally relieve the stress, so the doctor suggested that I get some cigarettes and go out behind the barn and smoke a few times a day. He called the drug store, spoke with the owner, Dale Swanson, and told him to sell me two packs since I wasn't old enough to purchase them. He also gave me the

$0.50 to purchase them.

After I was diagnosed with the ulcers, Dr. Watters called to meet in the office for a discussion as to what would have caused this. The old lady would not wait in the front office but followed me into the exam room. Discussing with the doctor, he found out what my chores were. They included mowing the lawn (or shoveling the snow), dusting and vacuuming the entire house, ironing, washing the windows inside and out whenever it was above 32 degrees during the winter months, cooking for parties and an occasional dinner, and keeping the kitchen in order. That included taking everything out of the pantry and refrigerator once a month and wiping down the cans and bottles, polishing the stove and refrigerator with Jubilee. If you have ever used Jubilee, you know what a pain it is to get that stuff polished off the surfaces. Immediately after school, I had to go straight home and tend to the chores. It did not leave any time for me to be a kid or a teenager. After I left, I often wondered who did these chores. Most, if not all their friends, neighbors, and acquaintances had no idea what was really going on in our house. Dr. Watters feared that I would die if I didn't get away from the Farkles because of the stress they created for me. He would not operate on my slight bleed until the stress was under control because the bleed would just return, and I could bleed to death.

The summer before eighth grade, I had several appendix attacks, but the Farkles would not believe that I was in pain. They thought I was faking it just to get out of doing my chores. Just to get out of bed, I had to roll over on my stomach and crawl to the floor. I was doubled over with abdominal pain while mowing the yard one summer afternoon and keeled over, unable to move. My next-door neighbor, Priscilla Klemmer, picked me up, took me into the house, and told my mother that if she did not take me to the doctor immediately, she would take me. When Dr. Watters examined me, he told my mother to take me to the hospital immediately and get me checked in, and he would cancel the rest of that day's appointments and would be there shortly to perform emergency surgery. When we left the doctor's office, we had to stop in town and buy new pajamas, then go home and take a hot bath. When we finally got to the hospital, Dr. Watters was furious and asked where we had been. When I told him, he reminded her that she had been a practical nurse and knew that her actions could have easily killed me. He asked her if she was actually trying to kill me (not the first time she attempted to do this). He explained that a hot bath in my situation could have easily caused my appendix to burst, and I could have died; she missed her chance. I was in the hospital for five days, and my mother managed to come up two times. One was to take me there, and the other was to take me home; my father didn't show up once. Actually, that suited me just fine, but that demonstrated their concern for my well-being.

Not long after our discussions and the appendix fiasco, Dr. Watters asked me if I wanted to move in with his family. I said I really wanted to, but I believed the Farkles had enough political power to prevent me from making this move. My dad had been a city councilman, and the county Judge Conway Spanton was a friend, only through the church. However, he told me that if it got so bad that I could not take it anymore, I could come up to his house anytime, day or night. He would do everything possible to make that a permanent move. I was given his unlisted office number, and his answering service would pick it up when there wasn't any staff in the office. He said he would advise the service if I called that he was to be notified at any time, day or night. He also told me that he was a good friend of Judge Spanton and believed they could manage it if that became necessary. There was no child abuse laws at that time, which would have made the move more difficult.

I could not wait to leave the Farkles' house and Geneseo so I could live my own life instead of: "While you are under my roof, you will do what we say or face the consequences." The thought of being able to get as far away from the Farkles as soon as possible was the only thing that kept me going.

One day, a neighbor and friend, Jim Larimer, and I decided we should go to Florida. I think I was about fifteen at that time. I had never told my parents that I was going; we just left. On the way there, we decided we should go to Nassau since we were going to be so close. Pan Am was running flights every two hours, a shuttle so to speak for $50.00 from both Miami and Fort Lauderdale; passports were not required at that time. A gym card was good enough for the Bahamians, and any form of ID was good enough for U.S. Customs. I didn't tell Jim that I had decided not to return with him, but I planned to stay in Nassau or go even further down the island chain, believing that I would be out of the country and at last be free.

Less than an hour after arriving in Nassau, we walked to the Straw Market, the tourist trap on the island. We were walking down one of the aisles and ran right into the Riches, a couple from Geneseo. They were friends with Jim's father (his mother had passed away). They told us that I had been reported missing and the police were looking for me. We told them not to worry, that we were going to fly back to Miami later that evening. We had left Fort Lauderdale and were going to fly back to Fort Lauderdale. I thought that would confuse any law enforcement if they really were looking for me. We were pretty sure that the Riches had notified the police or the Farkles in Geneseo that we were seen in Nassau and were going to fly back to Miami. My plan didn't work; U.S. Customs detained us upon our arrival back in Fort Lauderdale. After they made several phone calls, they agreed to release us on our word that we would immediately go back to Geneseo. We did.

The recently retired minister of the Methodist Church had relocated in Seattle in 1962, the year the World's Fair was there. He called me and asked if I wanted to come to Seattle and live with them. I have no idea how he found out about my situation, but he certainly did know about it. I thanked him for his offer but declined; I didn't want to live with a minister or in rainy Seattle.

There was a canal beside the country club where a lot of my classmates bicycled to go fishing, ice skating, and water skiing. Much to my surprise, I had been invited to go ice skating but had to borrow skates because my parents would not buy a pair for me, or for that matter a softball, bat, glove, football, basketball, bicycle, or a fishing rod. I only had a long bamboo pole and Ken's old rusty Schwinn bicycle. Now back to a typical summer afternoon I was allowed to go to the club with the Siebens, (a neighbor), there were several boats towing skiers. There were two wide areas in the canal that allowed for turns for both the boats and skiers with a ski-jump between them. Late one day in my junior year of high school, one of the very few times, I was able to get away and go water skiing. I was getting fairly good at skiing, and in the turn area just below the locks, I was going at a fast rate of speed when the rudder on my right ski dug into a submerged wooden post and most of me came to a complete and sudden stop. I dislocated my shoulder (again) and pulled most of the ligaments in my right leg and was bruised from my toes to my shoulder. My companions got me into the boat and eventually to the hospital. When Dr. Watters arrived, he questioned if my parents had been notified, and they had. However, they did not show up. He proceeded to check me out from head to toe, I had no broken bones. He re-set my shoulder, and for those of you who have had that done, you will understand; for those who have not been through that it is one of the most painful procedures you could imagine. They actually get up on the examination table and use their foot to push it back into its socket. He told me I could go home and make an appointment for him to see me in a week. He helped me into a wheelchair, and we waited for my parents to pick me up. They didn't show up, so he took me home.

Canal Hennepin behind the Club

Because of my shoulder injury and torn ligaments in my leg, I was not able to use crutches. I missed about two weeks of school. When I returned, I was barely able to use crutches, so I requested "late" permits for all of my classes from the principal. He questioned where I had been, and instead of going through the whole story, I pulled up my pant leg, opened my shirt, and let him see how bruised I still was. Needless to say, I got the permits. The school itself was a three-story building without any elevators, and my locker was on the second floor, and I had classes on all three floors. It took me quite a bit of time between classes to get around on the crutches, and my shoulder wasn't pain-free either. I got one of the first backpacks to put my books, etc., into since both of my hands were on the crutches.

Also, in my junior year, I took an art class, and my teacher noticed that all of my work contained a morbid theme—death. A watercolor featured a dead tree with a buzzard on one of the branches, a sad clown, and an oil painting of five people all looking bereaved as if they were looking down at a casket. Late in the school year, he kept me after class one day and suggested that I might need to find a professional that I could see on a regular basis. He felt that my work indicated that I might be contemplating suicide. That was the first time that I realized that all my work actually reflected my true feelings and my internal strife.

Ever since I've been on my own, I have gone totally overboard during the Christmas season; still today, I carry on that tradition. I am aware that it is my subconscious trying to make up for my childhood holidays. I can truly say that I never received anything that I asked Santa to bring, such as a toy semi-trailer truck, a baseball glove, ice skates, or a fishing pole. The usual presents for me under the tree consisted of underwear, socks, and maybe a new toothbrush. Santa heard everything that my brother had requested, including a Lionel train starter set and additional pieces for birthdays and Christmas. It was always my job to put metal reflectors on each light and tinsel on the tree, but it had to be placed one strand at a time and exactly even—each side of the strand had to hang down to exactly the same length. I just learned recently that tinsel was made of lead. That was a miserable task because the pine needles stuck the hell out of my hands, and to make it worse, I already knew what would be under the tree that had my name on it. Needless to say, I have never put tinsel or reflectors on any tree that I have had since, even when it was still in style.

It was not their financial situation that explained my lack of presents; it was the fact that I did not belong in their family. There was evidence of affluence in the closet with a mink coat and jacket, dresses retailing for several hundred dollars (in the 60s), dyed-to-match shoes, and an overflowing jewelry drawer. Most of the fur and dresses came from Richter/Romberg's, where she would be treated to a luxurious shopping experience under a chandelier, offered wine or champagne, and presented with clothes one at a time.

After years of living in this situation, my frustration and disgust had evolved into intense hatred and rage towards both of them. Whenever someone showed up at the door, they would become Emmy award-winning actors, putting on an act as if everything was wonderful, even though it wasn't; this two-faced behavior made me incredibly angry.

Their favorite form of entertainment was visiting a well-known "Supper Club," Marando's, located in Milan, Illinois, just outside Moline. The club was famous for its Prime Rib and live Maine Lobster dinners, and it featured George Sontag on a baby grand piano and Marjorie Minor on a Hammond organ, providing continuous entertainment. It was a first-class nightclub that hosted celebrity entertainers like Guy Lombardo, Liberace, Sophie Tucker, and others. The swanky, semi-secret casino was also a popular feature, although not entirely legal. Many notable patrons, including Chicago Bears and Cubs players, managers, coaches, and even the Wrigleys, frequented the club. However, I was never included in these outings.

Her second favorite form of entertainment was playing bridge. She belonged to two bridge clubs and played duplicate bridge once a week in the banquet room of The Cellar. When it was her turn to host the clubs, it meant I had to set up the card tables and folding chairs, arrange bridge mix and mixed nuts, and make finger sandwiches before I left for school. She always took credit for the sandwiches, even though she had no clue about the preparation. The sandwiches were made with three slices of bread, crusts trimmed and cut lengthwise into thirds, with fillings like egg salad, pimento cheese spread, ham salad, and occasionally chicken, crab, or tuna salad. The combination varied based on my mood or what ingredients were available.

I built a mental wall around myself so that absolutely nothing could get in, except for my chosen few. I had absolutely no compassion, trust, or empathy for anyone or anything; the only real emotions I had were hate, rage, and anger.

On the rare occasion that they asked me a question, more accurately interrogated me, for example, "Where did you go last night, you put over a hundred miles on the car?" "Pat and I just rode around town; we didn't go anywhere special." "Don't lie to me, now tell me where you went." This interrogation went on for at least five minutes, then I'll tell you anything you want to hear, since I have already told you the truth. What they wanted to hear was that we went to the movies in Davenport. I didn't find out for fifty-five years that they had called Pat the next day, and she told them that we didn't leave town. That incident was never brought up again, including no apologies ever for not believing me or anything else. That was typical; I almost always told them the truth the first time, then I would tell them anything they wanted to hear just to end the interrogation.

I learned to cook at a very early age because her cooking truly was not fit to eat. I would call her a utilitarian cook, food on the table, but not necessarily flavorful food. A roast would go in the oven about noon to be eaten at 6:00. There was not enough ketchup in the world to get this down, dry and so far past well-done, similar to eating a piece of charcoal. The same with vegetables, so overcooked and overly salted, not fit to eat. The vegetables were cooked until they were the consistency of canned spinach. However, I will give her credit for being able to bake a good cake. Precise measurements and exact baking time, cakes turned out fine, although I had to make the icing. Fortunately, my cooking ability served me well until aviation became my main source of income. Speaking of her food preparation, she only cooked American farm-style meals, 80% beef, 10% pork, and 10% chicken, never seafood. Never once did we have an Italian dinner, not even spaghetti, no Chinese, no South American, or French. Only meat and potatoes were on the menu; rarely baked or fresh-fried potatoes—just mashed. We never had any game, venison, duck, goose, or even sausages. I didn't have a bagel or an English Muffin until I left home. There were four slices of Wonder Bread on a plate for every dinner; I never ate one slice. It was quite an experience, the first time I had a true Cuban dinner; I just loved it, especially the flan!

My typical morning routine was to get up around 06:30, make the bed, and straighten my room. I bathed the night before, carefully going down the stairs, making sure not to hit any of the squeaky spots on the way down. I'd fix my breakfast, usually consisting of cream of wheat and orange juice, clean up the kitchen, then out the door by 07:30. The main goal was not to wake her up; at that time, dad worked nights, so he wasn't home until I had already left. I didn't want to start the day with another round of arguments or hearing how stupid or dumb I was. Not once did I ever receive a compliment, "You did a good job," or a thank you. It was always that she was perfect as a child; in particular, she was a straight "A" student (sure she was—not), and I always screwed up everything I touched. "Why can't you be like your brother? He has never caused us any trouble." To myself, I thought I didn't want to be anything like my brother. He had the drive and ambition of a three-toed sloth. But he was good at her game playing; he would agree with everything that came out of her mouth, no matter how ridiculous it was. It was about this time that I decided aviation was going to be my way out of this hell hole. All during this time, my normal mood was rage.

Another situation happened on my twelfth birthday—nothing happened, no cake, no present, or not even a "Happy Birthday" greeting. The next day I took some of my money and bought a transistor radio. They were just coming onto the market. She caught me listening to it under a tree and demanded that I return it because I hadn't earned the right to have one. That was the first thing I purchased when I left.

On the very few occasions that I was allowed to offer my opinion on a particular topic, I could manipulate our arguments up to fifteen minutes in advance while they were in progress because their comebacks were so predictable that I would be able to steer them into saying what I wanted or needed them to say. That would come in handy from time to time, but they would really get pissed when they figured out what I was doing. But it was very entertaining while it was going on. I have been known to use that skill from time to time in my later life.

When I was about seven, I wanted a dog, I really wanted a dog – a living creature that I could love, and it would love me. But no, absolutely not, we got a dog for Ken, hoping it would help him develop some responsibility. Ken told me that he didn't want a dog and took no interest in having one. So because of that, I couldn't have one.

I was brought up to be a Methodist; I should say that I was dropped off for Sunday School. After all, that's where they went to church, and they were "good" Methodists, for one hour a week. As an aside, I was told that I could not even date a Catholic, after all I might end up marrying one, and any children would have to be raised to be Catholic. That was the only reason for this strange rule, even though many of their friends were Catholic. That was what I believed until later when I learned of the church's baby trains. Aside from that, while I was sitting in the church for the typical service, my mind would just wander all over the place. I could not have told anyone what the sermon was about, what music was performed, or anything else about the service. Back to my Sunday School teacher who came to the house and complained to them that I asked too many questions and that I would not accept her answers that were so lame. "Because that is what the Bible says," "it's God's will" or "because I said so," that was just not good enough for me, after all I had already been on the other side. I got several beatings for questioning what they were preaching. I was told that I had to at least act like I believed all the "stuff" they were preaching.

After that final beating (not a spanking), "that was it! I was at the end of my rope." That night I hid in an upstairs closet, behind the chimney; they searched the house but could not find me. They even opened that closet door three times. I packed a tote and left the next morning before anyone was awake and stayed away for two days, staying with one of my friends that the Farkles did not know anything about. I found out later that they had contacted all of my friends that they knew about and were still looking for me. I no longer had anything to do with the Farkles; no conversations, which were rare before this, but none after. I stayed out of the house as much as possible, missed almost all meals at their table, and more significantly, I refused to go to church with them. I had absolutely no interaction with them; I went into the house through the back door, adjacent to the staircase, and into my room. I was just a tenant, not part of a family, which of course I never was. While I was at school or work, they would go through my drawers and desk almost daily, like I would have been careless enough to have left anything incriminating in them. I arranged my clothes in the drawers so I could tell if they had been gone through. In my antique roll-down desk, I would put a thread or place a particular paper in an unusual position, and, of course, it would have been rearranged almost daily. I actually left a note in a desk drawer that said, "You can stop the searching because there was no way I would ever leave anything of interest to you." They didn't know that I had rented a Post Office box; that's where I received all of my mail. That included my acceptance to Southern Illinois University that I didn't tell them until one week before I left for Carbondale. I had secured a scholarship for any Illinois State School, and that was the one that was the farthest away from Geneseo.

Why the Farkles were Methodists I never understood because they violated most of the canons that the church stood for, such as drinking, gambling, and smoking. I decided at an early age that God does not even exist. An all-loving God would not allow the abuse I endured.

This brings me to a lady who I called Miss Priscilla Goodbody. She reported on anything I did at church or anywhere else that she did not approve of. The church presented each person in my Sunday School Class with a Bible in which she had placed a sticker that said the recipient of this Bible would never drink any alcoholic beverages or smoke tobacco products. I proceeded to scrape this off the inside cover while it was still damp. I was not ready to make such a life-long commitment to that, or for that matter, anything else that had to do with any religion. She saw me remove the sticker, and to her, that was an unforgivable sin, so she took the Bible back. Then there was the time that there was a party for the church's youth group in the church basement with music, and I started dancing; that was another one of my sins, even though there are passages in the Bible that talk about singing, dancing, and rejoicing. She claimed that whoever donated at the pulpit that was down there would "roll over in her grave," another sin. I guess she didn't know that there are over twenty verses in the Bible that imply "they danced in joy." She was more strict with her two kids than the preacher was with his four children. I don't know why she was allowed to act as the official monitor to report any and all sins that she witnessed. Just as a side note, the preacher at that time was caught molesting a young girl in the public swimming pool. He was forced to leave town; I wonder who she reported that to.

Just as an example of how entitled my mother believed she was, she let her driver's license expire, and the State of Illinois insisted that any driver who let their license expire had to take the written test and the eye exam. It was the examiner's decision if he would want the driving portion of the test as well. Well, since she had been driving for so long, she believed she would not have to take any of these tests. She even went to an attorney to challenge the state's policy. She was told to take the tests. It was several months before she took them, During that time, about six months, I was her chauffeur in addition to doing her housework. I went to dad and told him I was not going to take her all over the town and to Davenport any longer, so she could do her shopping. She had time enough to renew her license just like any other person had to do that let their license expire. Much to my surprise, he agreed!

My mother's half-brother, my uncle Bill, was well aware of my situation, and he would drive the 75 miles from his "ranch" to kidnap me. He would be parked in the church lot when I got dropped off for Sunday School; he would watch my dad drive off, honk his horn to get my attention, pick me up, and take me back to his home, either to the farm in Farmington, before he acquired the Mid Road Farm in Knoxville. When we got to his place, he would call and tell them that I would be staying with him. We would go shopping for clothes and toiletries on Monday morning, and I would stay for weeks until they put up such a fuss that he had to take me back. He worked with me every day, trying to teach me the fundamentals of ranching and cattle management. Unfortunately, I really was piss poor at that. That was the only "training" I had received on the fundamentals of farming. Prior to that, what I had received was getting the volunteer corn and weeds out of the fields, feed the cattle and chickens, or mow the road-sides. (Figure 2 - 2)

During my Junior and Senior years, I worked at The Cellar, an upscale restaurant in the basement of the 100-year-old "Geneseo House"; hence the name. First as a dishwasher for a few days, then as a busboy for a few more days, and soon I was cooking in the glass "front" kitchen. On our busiest days, we could serve as many as 700 guests for a "cooked to order" dinner. All orders were cooked to order except for the baked potatoes. One Thanksgiving, we prepared 27 large turkeys. We started cooking them days ahead because of a lack of oven space. All were carved the day before Thanksgiving; that was a marathon event. The recipes and procedures have served me well, right up to the present time. The skills I developed working at that job became quite valuable in the years to come, things like memory improvement. On very busy days, there was only time to read each order once. I still use some of their recipes and procedures when cooking for a large group. The only famous guests that I cooked for were Pearl Bailey and Louis Bellson. Pearl was a singer and entertainer; Louis was a drummer. He had a residence in East Moline.

It was rumored that my dad, on occasion, met with a server who worked at The Cellar. I was never able to verify that, but it would not surprise me. I know there was one time when both mom and dad were secretly seeing another married couple. For a long time, neither partner was aware of what the other was doing. It was a small town, so word eventually got out.

I don't remember what the event was that my mother oversaw the organization of, but it was the second time I met a "celebrity"; the first being Senator Dirksen, a family friend. The Senate Office building is named after him. He would have dinner with us from time to time. Jesse Owens was the second; he was a four-time Olympic Gold medal winner at the 1936 Olympic games, which were held in Germany. He came to Geneseo from Chicago to give a motivational presentation. At that event, Darlene Underwood met Jesse, and over time they became quite close. Jesse made many trips to Geneseo, and I believed they were destined to become man and wife. (I knew Darlene quite well as she had helped at our home with deep cleaning and for many parties (I did the cooking, and she would do the serving.) She told me that she turned down his proposal because she could not take her two daughters to Chicago; they were raised just outside of the Geneseo city limits, and she didn't think they would do as well in the big city.

When I was growing up, we had a neighbor who was tied to their farm. In 50 years, they only took one vacation; they drove to Key West for a week, four days of travel and three days in Key West; some vacation. They planned to travel when he retired; however, within a few months after their retirement, he was just sitting on their porch. He had a severe stroke and was no longer able to get around, so in over 50 years, they had one vacation! It was then that I made a resolution that if the opportunity ever presented itself to go somewhere or do something that I (we) wanted to do, I (we) would seize upon that opportunity.

Just before the second half of my Senior year, I made a request that I graduate early and get my diploma and get away from Geneseo and all that went with it. I had more than enough of the required credits, except for one-half in Physical Education. Drew Sieben, another classmate of mine, had gotten his diploma after his junior year, so he didn't have the PE credits either. However, my request was denied. At long last, I graduated from High School (it seemed like an eternity) at eight in the evening on June 6, 1964, and I was out of town by ten. Just a word about the actual High School Building; it had been condemned, and we were the last class not only to graduate from that building but also to witness its immediate demolition. Since I had already left town, I wish I could have seen the demolition. One example: on snow days, the snow would pile up on the inside windowsills and not melt all day. All through school, I had been rejected not only by my parents but by most of my classmates as well as the system. I stayed away for many decades (fifty years), and life instantly got much better than it had ever been. This pretty well covers my terrible life in Geneseo.

Likeness of Fred and Fanny Ferkel

Figure 2-1

Mid Road Farm, in Knoxville, Illinois

Figure 2-2

Geneseo Senior High School

Figure 2 - 3

When you get to the end of a chapter,

Put a period on it and turn the page.

CHAPTER THREE:
FREE AT LAST
1964

Up to this point in my life, my one notable talent had been resignation. I had always been prepared for defeat, had welcomed failure, and had quietly walked away from every opportunity that came to me. Now I had the opportunity to get away and start building a new life. I was beginning to learn how to let go and learn how to live. It was a very slow process, in that this was a completely new perspective for me. I have since come to believe that I should have, and everyone should grasp the opportunities as they come along, providing it is something that you are interested in or that you want to do; life is too short, don't pass those opportunities up. At the end of my senior year, I purchased a 1963 Impala convertible; dependable transportation was necessary for my new job.

Immediately after high school graduation, I was on my way to Madison, Wisconsin, then on to Yankton, South Dakota. During that summer, while in Madison, I had gotten a job with a subcontractor for Motorola, Ernie Swint, installing nurse call systems and TVs in hospitals. Ernie also owned the radio station that I did the remote broadcasters, mainly Sunday church services from several churches, one each Sunday. My time in Madison was a learning experience, very uneventful. The person that I worked with had absolutely no fear of heights. He would walk to the edge of an eight-story hospital without a safety harness and just pull the required equipment up to the roof. He also would check to see if an electrical wire was energized, just by grabbing it with his hand. He was a very interesting person, but he was very quiet and into himself. He was an easy person to work with. (Figure 3 - 1)

Three weeks later when I got to Yankton, it was a very different story; my new co-worker there, was joined by his family, which included his wife and two kids. Instead of staying in a motel, they camped along the Missouri River, just south of Yankton. I spent a lot of my free time with them, evenings and weekends, fishing and enjoying the camping life, however, I did spend my nights in a motel. Camping and living along a river was certainly a new experience for me to observe and take advantage of, on a part-time basis. Aside from when I was with Uncle Bill, this was the first time that I had the opportunity to interact with what a family should be.

The river and campgrounds at Yankton

One early evening when I got to the campsite, I was changing out of my work clothes, and my partner's wife noticed the red welts on my back. She was so upset about that, and immediately added two and two and came up with four. I was sure that when she got back to Geneseo she was going to make an issue out of this. I tried to convince her that it must have been caused by the way I had been sitting in the car, on my way out from the hospital. Although, I was sure she didn't believe my explanation. I talked to my partner the next day and I assured him that I wasn't ever going back home, and to just let it go, that it was history and couldn't be changed. There wasn't anything that could be done about the past; I just needed to look to the future. They went back to Geneseo for the weekend, and when they returned we had quite an interesting discussion, and at the conclusion they offered this: "We are very sorry about the situation that brought you here, but we want you to know that you have become family to us, all of us, we have bonded with you, and you need someone who you can come home to – and that is an open invitation that we are extending to you." For that, I was unbelievably grateful, for the first time I can remember feeling truly loved by a real family. That really got to me, I had trouble holding back the tears, and even now, while I am writing about it, my eyes are filled with tears.

The hospital in Yankton turned out to be quite an interesting place. It was a Catholic hospital and the only one for many miles. (Figure 3 – 2) They had patients from Yankton and neighboring towns, both in South Dakota and Nebraska, as well as taking care of patients from the nearby Indian reservation. It was a real "ole time" hospital. The bottom two selections in the Coke machine were stocked with Miller Long Necks. The Nun's refrigerator in their station on the first floor had a watermelon on the bottom shelf and there was an I-V bag on the top shelf. The melon had vodka dripping into it for Friday night's party. That was every Friday night.

The drinking age was 21 in South Dakota; however, the drinking age in Nebraska was 18 (until 1984). There was an extremely long and narrow bridge just south of Yankton crossing the Missouri River into Nebraska. (Figure 3 –3) It has since been replaced.

On Friday nights, and through the weekends, there were so many accidents involving teenagers on that bridge, some of them resulting in fatalities. That had a major impact on the hospital's emergency room, which was severely understaffed. That trip seemed unnecessary to me because if you just went to the Icehouse in Yankton, you could get beer and ice. I was only 17 at the time, and had no problem getting beer, and no ID was ever requested.

During the day, there was only one Registered Nurse (RN) per floor (three floors), and at night there was one RN for the entire hospital. When there was an emergency, a birth or emergency surgery, they were incredibly understaffed. That's why we were there installing a state-of-the-art nurse call system, of that time (1964).

It was also the first time that I witnessed an actual death. A local farmer, in his 20's, had raised a forklift onto a high voltage power line. He had extensive burns, internal as well as external. We held off the installation process in his room for a week, but could no longer hold off, and as fate would have it, he passed away while I was installing the nurse call hardware next to his bed. There was actually a "death rattle" at the time of his death. That made quite an impression on me, and as it turned out, over the summer, there were several more deaths, that I witnessed.

That was a great summer. I was away from the Farkles and my hometown, away from all my parents' nosey friends (small town, everybody reported anything they witnessed that was out of the ordinary), but most of all it was a completely new experience for me. It was at this time that I first discovered what a functional family should be, unconditional love and understanding. Some place where you could always go to seek refuge and understand whatever misfortune you were dealing with.

I actually thought that what I had lived with up to this time is what most of the "normal" family were like. All that I had experienced up to that time was constant put-downs and criticism. If I had gone from a "C" on my report card to a "B," what I heard was, "Why didn't you get an "A," not even a little praise for receiving a "B." I was always being compared to my brother, "he was such a perfect child and you have been such a disappointment to us." I can't recall one time when they gave me credit for any accomplishment, like "that was a good job" or "we are so proud of you."

My dream at that time was to become an airline pilot. When I was quite young, I would lay in the yard and watch or at least hear the two inbound planes going to Moline; my thoughts were "this is my way out of this hell." I spent as much time as I could at the Moline and Peoria airports. The controllers at the Moline airport invited me to come up to the tower cab, they explained how airports are designed, the runway numbering system, the taxi ways and where the corporate aircraft were housed. John Deere had a large (for that time) flight department based there. Moline only had service by Ozark Airlines – DC-3's, United Air Lines had pulled out of the Moline market several years earlier. Ozark was the first "airline" fight that I took, during my Senior year, from Moline to Marion Illinois (closest airport to Carbondale that served airline traffic) via Peoria, Springfield, and St. Louis. The few times that I could get to Peoria's airport I got to see the Super Constellations landing and taking off. It had four piston engines and seemed huge to me; I will never forget the roar of those engines on take-off.

As I mentioned earlier, Jim Johnson, my guidance counsellor in high school and everyone that I spoke with about getting a pilot's license told me that I would have to have a four-year college degree to accomplish that, and you needed advanced mathematics to qualify for an airline career. My guidance counsellor told me that I wouldn't be able to obtain a pilot's license because I didn't have the mental ability or math skills and that it required a college degree. In other words, I wasn't smart enough to become a pilot. The college requirement was absolutely incorrect. In the June 1964 issue of Flying Magazine, United Airlines ran a two-page ad that stated they would hire you if you had a private license (no mention of a college degree) and United would provide the flight training for your commercial and instrument ratings. There was a shortage of pilots at that time. By 1968, after college there was a recession in progress and with the addition of the new wide-body aircrafts that only required two crew members instead of three, their offer had been withdrawn. So much for listening to uninformed advisors instead of going directly to the source.

Methodist Hospital in Madison Wisconsin

Figure 3 - 1

"Modern" Hospital in Yankton SD

Figure 3 - 2

Dangerous Bridge from Nebraska to Yankton,

South Dakota

Figure 3- 3

No matter what your past has been,

You know what it's like to struggle.
Now, you know who you are, and where you are going.

CHAPTER FOUR:
SOUTHERN ILLINOIS UNIVERSITY AND BURNSIDE-OTT AVIATION TRAINING CENTER
1964 - 1969

Then it was off to Carbondale, Illinois, and Southern Illinois University. I had a scholarship that was valid for any Illinois State College and that was the one that was the furthest away from Geneseo. During my college years, I worked in food service in two of the state-owned dormitory snack bars. During my fresh

man year I lived at Allen Hall, one of the dorms at Thompson Point. It happened to be an end unit, four to a room. The other rooms were two to a room. Jerry Roesner lived on the third floor, I was on the first floor; Jerry was a good friend from Geneseo and was a Senior when I was a sophomore. He was a significant help to me; I'm sorry to say that I have lost touch with him and have been unable to locate him. The last time I saw him was at his wedding in Richmond, Virginia, in 1966. Walt Frazier also lived on the third floor, two rooms down from Jerry. The day after his last basketball game at SIU, I walked by his room, he had all his stuff stacked in the hall. I asked him what was going on, he replied that he would not be able to graduate, mainly because he had not been to a class in over two months. He was a fantastic player on SIU's team. If you aren't familiar with his career, Walt was a former player for the New

York Knicks in the NBA. As their floor general, he led the New York Knicks to the franchise's only two championships and was inducted into the Naismith Memorial Basketball Hall of Fame in 1987. Upon his retirement, he went into broadcasting; he is currently a color commentator for the Knicks games.

Then, five of us rented a studio apartment, off campus to save money, we all were dirt poor. We had four hammocks and a couch; the last one home got the couch. On Friday afternoons, we would pool our money to try to come up with $5.25 for a case of Miller Long Necks. There were weeks when we couldn't come up with the money. Since I was working in the snack bar, I became friends with the Hostess delivery person. He was aware of my situation and would save his "out of sale date" products and would leave them on my desk. His generosity was a lifesaver, quite literally. The snack bar at Thompson Point was just a hole in the wall and did not do much business. However, the next year a new housing area, Neely Hall opened, and it housed 1,150 students, and the huge snack bar there, according to the architects was set up to handle one transaction every ten seconds.

On Sunday evenings, the dining hall would remain closed so the snack bar was the only food service in the area that was open. It was designed like a donut, all condiments were in the center and the grills, refrigerated sandwich stations, ice cream, chips, pastries, and soda fountains were located on the outer edges. There were two or more of each of these stations placed around the edges of the bar. The grills were together on the back section, so if you just wanted a coke, you went directly to that area and then to one of the cashiers, which didn't allow for lines to form, no waiting for the person in front of you; you went to the station you needed, and proceeded to the checkout area. The designer was definitely thinking out of the box, and it worked very well. Because of my previous experience at the Cellar and working with the state at Thompson Point's snack bar, I was given the job as a shift manager at Neely Point. My supervisor was an older lady, who, for years had owned a small restaurant in town; she was a great boss and was very willing to share her recipes, many of which I still use today. The snack bar made a huge profit because of our volume, which it was not supposed to do. It was owned and run by the State of Illinois, however, we could not lower our prices because they were standardized throughout the campus. Sodas were 10 and 15 cents, hamburgers were 25 cents, hot dogs were 15 cents and ice cream was 5 cents a scoop! We also made pimento cheese, tuna salad and grilled cheese sandwiches; these were only available at our snack bar. Cigarettes were 30 cents a pack and the juke box were 5 plays for a quarter. The major downside of working in a state-owned facility was that every night after closing, we had to wash down the walls and floors before we could check out. My time was balancing the cash registers sales.

I sent a Christmas Card to Uncle Bill and enclosed a note thanking him for all he had done for me, it had my return address on the envelope, and he was able to locate me. He sent a card back to me. However, it contained a huge present, a check for $5.000.00 for my college education. A note was also enclosed, which said he was so sorry for not being able to do more for me during my rough times, he knew what I had been going through. Because my mom was his half-sister, he felt that he had done all that he was able to do under those circumstances. He said that he would send another check each year that I was in school. That was the most welcome gift that I believe I have ever received. The only item that I splurged on was that I traded in my 1963 Impala and purchased a 1967 Pontiac GTO. I continued to live the same way that I had become familiar with.

1967 GTO

Figure 4-1

Southern Illinois University grew so rapidly that the infrastructure in the town of Carbondale had not caught up with the huge influx of students. There were only three barber shops in town; the wait time for a haircut could be up to two and a half hours. I complained to the owner of the largest shop, Campus Clipper, about the extended wait time. He said if you want to learn barbering, come on weekends or whenever you have spare time and I'll teach you how to cut hair. I worked with him until I had enough hours and experience required by the state to obtain my barber's license. I became an expert at giving flat tops and Ivy League haircuts. This was a useful source of supplemental income for me; 70% of the going rate, plus any tips that I received. Granted, college students weren't great tippers, but the locals were. While I was still living in the dorms, when time permitted, I would set up shop in the hallway and cut residents hair. The money wasn't great, but whatever I received was definitely a boost to my financial status. All in all, my time at SIU was uneventful except for being dirt poor and the fact that I learned to cut hair.

In the brief time between my college and summer job, the Draft board found that I was no longer enrolled as a full-time student in

52

college, I was still in Carbondale, (it was still in the 60's) they called me over and I went to Chicago for the preliminary medical exam. The Army decided they did not want me based on my medical history, which was the only good thing that my health problems did for me.

Upon leaving Carbondale, when I got to the intersections of I-57 and I-24, I flipped a coin, heads was California and tails was Florida, Florida won! (The Mama's and Pappas song; *"Go Where You Wanna Go, Do What You Wanna Do"* and Peter, Paul and Mary's *"Leaving on a Jet Plane"* had a huge effect on my life). Making good on the promise I made to myself many years earlier, I enrolled in Burnside-Ott's Aviation Training Center in Ft. Lauderdale the following Monday. Fortunately, Bob Minter, location manager, hired me to work for the school on Tuesday. Burnside-Ott had three South Florida locations; Tamiami (South Miami), Opa-locka (North Miami) and Ft. Lauderdale. It was a very large flight school; they had 138 aircrafts and 5 simulators at that time. Opa-locka was their home base and their maintenance operations were located there. They had contracts for flight training with Miami-Dade and Broward Junior Colleges. It was fortunate that I was hired; because that was the only way, I could afford my flight training. I soloed in thirteen hours; (signed off to fly without an instructor on board) I took two or three planes to Opa-locka for 100-hour inspections. It was about a twenty-five-minute trip, engine start to shut down. I logged all that time. Opa-locka Airport was the busiest airport in the United States in 1967. They had four active runways, 9 Right, 9 Center, 9 Left and 12, when the wind was blowing in off the ocean. There were over 650,000 total operations, more than Atlanta and Chicago. The flight schools located there were responsible for the heavy flight count. Runway 9-Right even had its own radio frequency. It was the touch-and-go runway. If you were going to the flight training area northwest of the airport you would call for landing upon departing the airport area and your flight number would come up in about an hour, it was that busy.

Upon arriving in Ft. Lauderdale, I met another flight school student, Ray Higgins. He lived just a short distance from the airport and suggested I contact his apartment owner, because there was one vacancy, and it was quite reasonably priced. I rented a basic one-bedroom furnished apartment. When I was moving in, the owner stopped by to collect the rent and told me to buy my groceries at Publix, not at the Winn-Dixie that was two blocks closer. When I went to get groceries, being the stubborn person that I was, I went to Winn-Dixie. I had a full shopping cart and when I got to the meat case, when I picked up a package of ground beef, the roaches took off across the rest of the meat packages. I left my cart in the aisle and went to Publix. I have never gone into a Winn-Dixie store again.

Ray's grandmother stayed with him, and we became good friends. She would often fix dinner for me and was a great neighbor. She was a large stockholder in Anheuser Bush and was quite wealthy, which was unknown to her until after her husband's death. He had worked for Anheuser Bush for over forty years and had set up a payroll deduction plan to automatically purchase their stock. With her newfound wealth, she was paying for Ray's flight training, his new GTO, and his Bayliner ski boat. One Sunday, she convinced me to go to Mass with her. During the service, the Priest made a plea for donations to pay for a new roof for the parish. She immediately stood up and very loudly asked the Priest what in the world he did with the twenty-five thousand dollars she gave him two weeks earlier to get that damn roof fixed. I followed her as she stormed out of the church and about half of the congregation followed us.

Soon after I settled into Ft. Lauderdale there was a knock on the door late one evening. It was a person whom I had never seen before. He opened with, "You don't know me, but I am friends with Jim Larimer, and he told me that I could stay with you while I'm here on vacation." I told him that this was only a one-bedroom apartment, and he could not stay with me. But I could get him an excellent rate at Pier 66. Before he left, he told me he could not afford to stay in a motel. My response was sorry about that; I never saw him again. I had several people who I had previously become acquainted with in Carbondale request a "free" place to stay, seems like Ft. Lauderdale was quite an attraction. They all got the same response, "I can get you an excellent rate at Pier 66." The local police will not let you sleep in your vehicle on any of the city streets, including along the beach.

In 1970, the cost for flight training a Cessna 150 wet, (included fuel) was $12.50 an hour and with an instructor it was $14.50 an hour. The Twin Comanche was $45.00 an hour, wet. At that time, it was a lot of money; my furnished apartment was $150.00 a month on 15th Street in Ft. Lauderdale, just three blocks from the intra-coastal waterway across from Pier 66, that was the 17th Street Causeway. As a side note, Phillips 66 owned Pier 66. They had visions of opening several units on the Intracoastal Waterway. However, this was the only one that was built. It took 66 seconds in the elevator to get to the revolving bar and restaurant on the top floor, and it took 66 minutes to make one revolution. There was a large marina that is also part of the complex, the views from the top were incredible, it is now a Hyatt Resort.

Six months after I had moved into my first apartment, Andy McQuig, who lived in the apartment building next door, talked me into moving with him into Paradise Manor, an apartment complex located across the street from Stranahan High School, where he had attended. Those apartments were much larger and had better furnishings as well as a pool. My share of the rent was actually less than I was paying at the time. More about that later.

zIt was at this time that I met Broward County Sheriff, Ed Stack. The 1967 GTO that I had when I was still in college, when I moved to Ft. Lauderdale, was stolen shortly after I moved to Paradise Manor. The police located it, but it was stripped beyond economical repair, so the insurance covered the depreciated value of the vehicle. I bought a 1970 Chevelle 396 SS (Figure 4 – 2) from Ed Morse

Chevrolet on a Friday afternoon. My salesman actually had me do a test drive without him in the vehicle. He said if he was in the vehicle, I would not drive it the way it should be driven. They agreed to make some minor adjustments to it on Monday morning.

1970 Chevelle 396 SS

(Figure 4 – 2)

On the way back to the dealership, the actual Broward County Sheriff rear-ended me. I was stopped in a left-turn lane and the Sheriff 's vehicle pushed my back bumper about a foot into the trunk. He said he was reading an arrest warrant for a criminal that he had been trying to get for some time and didn't' realize that the car had stopped. He wanted to have the Sheriff's department do the accident report. I told him they could do a report, but I was calling the Ft. Lauderdale police to have them do their own report, because I wanted the report to say exactly what had happened. I didn't care whether the Sheriff got a ticket or not, I just wanted the report to be accurate, so that I didn't get charged with the accident. Sheriff Stack really didn't want Ft. Lauderdale police to do a report, so I mentioned to him that I was having neck pain, sometimes it was severe. That brought the resistance to an end to having Ft.

Lauderdale Police write the report. The Chevelle had less than a hundred miles on it.

One of my duties at the flight school was after the last flight of the day, to compare the actual tachometer times on the planes with the computer printout. Any extra time that was paid, but not flown, was unused time, and was mine. Being in South Florida many of our students' parents were either pilots, mechanics or stewards, and they insisted that their kids get their Commercial Pilots Licenses through the junior college programs. A few of them absolutely hated flying, for their solo cross-country flight they would go to the closest airport, for both Ft. Lauderdale and Opa-locka locations that was North Perry, they would sit on the ground for up to six hours and return, pay for six hours and would have only flown for 30 minutes. After I soloed that "pre-paid" time was mine to use. Since Opa-locka was one of the busiest general aviation airports in the country, that was a wonderful experience learning tower communications and flying in South Florida's heavy traffic environment, As I mentioned earlier, I made several trips a day. I became very familiar with operating in high traffic areas. When possible, I would request the runway at Ft. Lauderdale that the airlines used, 9-Left, again experience in operating with large heavy aircraft learning how to deal with their wake turbulence. Both airports were so busy, and I was never in the same aircraft, so the controllers didn't recognize me by the call sign, so I began using unusual reporting points on my inbound radio calls and soon I was given preferential treatment. Instead of reporting at the "Twin Drive In's downwind for 9-Left" (both airports had runways 9-Left and 9-Right) going into Opa-locka, I would report over "Gulfstream Racetrack" instead of the twin-drive ins. I would usually get a straight in instead of being number fifteen for the airport. That really pissed off the other pilots who were in the pattern. I actually logged several hundred hours of this flight time, going between Ft. Lauderdale and Opa-locka.

As I progressed with my flight training my duties increased. I went to trade shows and even landed in Broward Community College's parking lot for an aviation day presentation. Getting the plane into the lot was easy; but getting out of the parking lot was a challenge because the winds had shifted to a direct crosswind, and there were dumpsters on one end and power lines on the other end, it was close, I needed to swerve to avoid the dumpsters. I worked with our FAA designee to give the students their cross-country destinations for their flight tests. One of my obligations for the designee was to inform the applicants for their Commercial Check Ride that if they were serious about becoming a commercial pilot, they had to present the appearance of a commercial pilot. No beards or long hair and needed to wear a shirt with a collar and a pair of slacks, no jeans, shorts, or tennis shoes. Those who chose not to comply with these "suggestions," nine times out of ten would not get through the oral part of their check ride, those who did get through the oral would not pass the flight portion. For those who were very upset with my original suggestion, I had another suggestion – find another FAA flight examiner.

Bill Fulton was our FAA designee and I used him for my Private, Multi-Engine and Commercial ratings. For my Private check ride, it went as a normal ride, however on my Multi-Engine ride it was quite an experience. I got my multi rating right after my private so I could fly the twins to Opa-locka for their maintenance requirements. To obtain my multi training I would find an instructor who had a no-show or a free hour of time and get him to go with me to Opa-locka, another hour of free instruction. It required ten hours of time to qualify for the license; I only had to pay for two hours, one to get an instructor to sign me off and another for the check ride.

I had the normal engine failure on take-off and Bill (Fulton) asked if he could fly the plane right after that. He immediately drove the plane and strafed the boats in the Dania Cutoff Canal. I took the plane away from him and told him that during this ride I was the pilot in command and for him to keep his hands off the controls. As we proceeded with the ride, thirteen more engine failures and when the ride was completed, I was lined up for landing on the "airline" runway (9-Left) he asked if he could land the plane, I said that I didn't know if he could, but go ahead and try. He immediately got into a DC-8's wake turbulence so once again I took the plane away from him. We went around, and I was on short final and asked him what kind of landing he wanted, and he said just get the damn plane on the runway. It was a Twin Comanche, they are known for being difficult to land (if you fly according to the manual's instructions) but if you keep the power on until you cross the threshold then retract the flaps the plane just sinks onto the runway, almost always a perfect landing. He complained about that being a non-standard landing, and I reminded him that he said just get the damn plane on the runway. It was three hours before he wrote my temporary Multi-Engine license; and that was after I told him if he didn't give me my license, I was going to tell the FAA about his stunts in the plane. After the Designee got his pilot's license, he became a Merchant Marine then returned to become an FAA designee, he had never flown any time other than at the flight school.

For my Commercial oral test, Mr. Fulton was going through my logbook to verify my hours, and ran across my trip to Buenos Aires, it was the first time he had ever seen a four-letter designator for the airports. Actually, all airports including U.S. airports have a four-letter designation; U.S. airports have a "K" before the common designation like FLL, but for international flights it is KFLL. Nassau's four-letter designation is MYNN. After I explained that trip to him, my oral and ride were over rather quickly. His comment was that if I could get a twin-engine plane to Argentina, he thought I was qualified to be a Commercial Pilot.

Also, I was the duty pilot on nights and weekends. I flew my first charter flight before I had my Commercial License; it was a trip from Ft. Lauderdale to Jupiter Florida. It was my first time flying a Cessna 182, and my first encounter using a variable pitch prop. And

I flew it with no problem.

During the summer, the school initiated a camp for 15- and 16-year old's called The Young Eagles. I was selected to be one of the counsellors. They received a brief ground school, and each was assigned an instructor for actual flight training. Most days there were "special" activities such a trip to Miami Air Traffic Control Center, an actual hands-on flight in a DC-3 and for me the best activity was going to Pan Am's training center and actually flying their Boeing 747 simulator. When it was my turn to fly in the left seat of the simulator, my first approach to Miami International I touched down on the center line of the runway and bounced it quite high, my next touchdown was in Biscayne Bay. On my next approach I landed and kept it on the runway, that was a once in a lifetime experience.

Figure 4 – 3

Pan Am's 747 cockpit simulator

Using my "extra" flight time I would occasionally fly over to Coral Springs and land on a city street before any residential areas had been developed. There was a dinner with absolutely nothing anywhere near it where I would have a great country breakfast. All the utilities were underground, and they had a flagpole in front so I could determine the wind direction. Usually, I was not the only plane in the parking lot. Then in the afternoons, just seven miles west of the approach end of runway 9-Right at Ft. Lauderdale, there was a nudist colony. It had a lake and in the center of the lake was a small island with one tree, perfect for "turns about a point" (a required maneuver). The guests at the colony would wave at us as we flew around and around and around the island. I was certainly not the only plane in the pattern. Some evenings I would fly to Jacksonville, landing at every airport on the way up and back, a clever way to use up five and a half hours of flight time.

One cold (in the 40's, that's cold for South Florida) winter morning, a good friend of mine, also a flight school student, took a rental plane out of North Perry Airport, and I was in a school plane and we were flying formation over the shoreline at maybe fifteen feet above the water. Our minds were on the tight formation, unfortunately, he forgot to engage his carburetor heat and his engine iced up, it quit, and he went into the ocean - we were just off Dania Pier. It sank within seconds, he kicked its door open and swam out of the plane, reached the pier, and got out of the water. The plane was retrieved and was back in service in about two weeks. Carburetor ice was determined to have been the problem.

As I had previously mentioned, I lived in a "U" shaped twenty-two-unit apartment building with a pool in the center of the structure, Paradise Manor. All the tenants except for me and one other tenant were professional people, the other one was a construction worker. Almost every weekday afternoon, just after work we would all gather at the pool, have strawberry daiquiris and sometimes, meaningful discussions. The pool cleaning company was furious because each week there were strawberry seeds stuck to the tiles all around the pool. Most of my neighbors were teachers or pilots; I associated with some truly remarkable people. Three of these were Andy, my roommate, Bob and Burr. Andy was a pilot (flight engineer) for Eastern Airlines, and from time to time he would take me to Eastern's Miami Operations Center, and we would do the pre-flight inspection on the Boeing 727 that he was flying for that particular trip. Occasionally, the Captain would offer me the jump seat for their trip, usually Seattle. Among some of the interesting facts that I learned on these trips was that from the time the throttles are pushed forward, it takes seven seconds for the jets to power up. I was also selected to be on Eastern's emergency evacuation team. According to the FAA rules, the cabin had to be entirely empty within ninety seconds, even with one or two of the emergency exits blocked. Then it was across the street to the King's Inn Hotel, where water evacuations took place, (in their pool). Each member of the team received ten dollars for each land evacuation and fifteen dollars for each water evacuation. That usually added up to $60. After that, most of us went up the street to Brother's Two Bar (at the corner of 36th Street and Lejune Road. Brothers Two was owned by Billy and Bobby Ott; the same Ott as Burnside-Ott Aviation Training Center. Bobby worked at the Training Center and Billy was a National Airline pilot.

During those times around the pool, we got into some deep discussions about the Bermuda Triangle. My belief, and that of many others, including some of those around the pool, is that we are not the first people to inhabit this planet, and that it was inhabited by an enhanced race of humans who had advanced knowledge of science, space, and technology. They were here centuries before our civilization became organized. The pyramids could not have possibly been constructed by hand; the stones are so perfectly flat that they hold together not by mortar but by being so perfectly flat cut. Most people do not realize there is another pyramid under water just south of Bimini in the Bahamas. It is also made from the same perfectly cut stone and there is even an underwater road, "Bahama Road" visible from the air that goes from South Bimini out to the pyramid, and it is constructed using exactly the same method and stone as the ones in Egypt.

I believe these superhuman people were here long before our civilization and after a while, let's assume, that their computer batteries wore out, just imagine where our current society would be if we suddenly lost the use of all computers. I believe that something like this happened, and they found themselves to be back in the stone age. They also built a runway in Peru, which we didn't know about until we had satellite photos of it. There are huge rocks outlining the edges of the runway and approach markings showing the way to the approach end of the runway, they carved out the caves that the Inca Indians inhabited, the Indians didn't carve it, they just moved into them, and they carved the figures depicting man, woman and child on the cliffs in the British Isles. Skulls have been found in Peru that have had brain surgery performed on them and they survived because the bone had begun to heal over, it was done in areas of the brain that we cannot duplicate today. Also, they have found turquoise that has been so perfectly cut, again we cannot duplicate that today, because with our method, the stone will just crumble. There are many more examples, but you get the idea. There is an interesting book on this subject titled *"We Are Not the First"* by Andrew Thomas. There have been many pyramids discovered in the last few years, they are spread all around the globe.

I believe (that within the last one hundred years or so) all of the ships and planes that have disappeared in the Bermuda Triangle may have been caused by a super homing device that occasionally transmits signals from the pyramid in Bimini to assist their spacecraft in locating their base on earth. It is so advanced that we cannot even detect it, but it really raises hell with the weather and our primitive navigating devices. The most recent case that I am aware of is that of a sailboat owned by a well-known restaurant owner and his wife that were on their way to Miami from Palm Beach for a holiday party. It was recent enough that the occupants of the vessel used their cell phone to call 911; the Miami-Dade County operator received the call. In desperation, the captain of the boat was telling the operator that they were caught in a terrible unpredicted storm and they had lost the GPS and other navigational equipment on board and they needed help from the Coast Guard. The Coast Guard immediately launched a search; however, neither the boat nor its occupants were ever located, they had simply disappeared.

Sam Hamilton, the Control Tower Chief at Opa-locka when I was there, spent most of his adult life trying to figure out what happened to the fleet of navy training planes that disappeared on their training mission. There was another flight that was sent to look for the first missing flight, this second flight also didn't return. During WW-II he was the controller at the Ft. Lauderdale base that dispatched both flights on their missions. I had many conversations with Sam about this phenomenon.

Back to reality, just sitting around the pool we came up with the idea that we should put sand from the beach in a small glass vessel and make it into a necklace. Then sell it in beachfront stores, "You can have your own piece of the Bermuda Triangle." That's as far as this idea went, just a discussion about it. Then it was time for another Daiquiri.

Andy was the grossest person I have ever met, however, his method of delivery was incredibly smooth and extremely funny, for everyone except the person he was picking on. He was also a brilliant person, with a photographic memory. When he read a book, he could recite the text word-for-word. He was his high school teacher's biggest nightmare, except for his English teacher, who was his afternoon delight; she was just one of many of his afternoon delights, which were usually stewardesses. He was so bored with school that he would cut-up in most of his classes, and the teachers would call on him with a question about whatever she was discussing at that time. He could recite the text perfectly, what could she do? One day the principal even caught him sniffing the girl's bicycle seats; that was Andy. He had re-titled many of the current songs, such *as "Chitty Chitty Bang Bang"* became *"Nitty Gritty*

Gang Bang," "Spanish Eyes" was *"Spanish Thighs," "Girl I Got News for You"* became *"Girl I Got Nude for You"* and "Love Is A Many Splendid Thing" became *"Love Is A Long And Slender Thing."* There were many more, but you get the idea.

Going out to dinner with Andy was always an experience, I never knew what to expect. One time we were in line selecting our food items at Piccadilly Cafeteria and a rather large lady was in line in front of us and her dress was, how shall I say this, following the contours of her body very closely, especially the rear portion of it. So, Andy did her a favor and pulled it out of the crack, she threw such a fit, that he tried to put it back. We were asked to leave the premises. Another time we were in line at Arby's, it was during Spring Break and the place was packed; he ordered two of their famous roast horse-meat sandwiches. The manager was very upset with his order, so Andy explained that his father owned four Arby's franchises, and the last time they had beef in the place was for the grand openings. Again, we were not so politely asked to leave and to never return. (Andy's dad did not own any Arby's franchises.) When we walked out, about half of the people in line left with us.

Andy's father was an airline pilot for many years, and he had a perfect flying career; not even one incident. Because of this, he was chosen to be the pilot for a multitude of political candidates. One of the walls in his home office was covered floor to ceiling with framed invitations and letters from many notable people who he had flown. After seeing these, I began keeping those that I have received over my career. I currently have over 50 framed autographed photos and documents in my home office. There are only a few that I failed to keep; one of those was a personal note from President Nixon that was included with a box of dishes from Air Force One. The note said that he would rather see me have those dishes than have the press steal them, which they did on every flight. By the way, I still have the complete set of them. When I set the table with them, my guests are usually freaked out, because they are so afraid, they may break one of them, so I rarely use them. But in over fifty years not one of them has been broken or chipped.

Bob's father was the owner of Air Convoy, a company that ferried planes to all parts of Canada, Central and South America, Europe and Africa. Most of the aircraft were new ones from Piper. They would pick them up from Lakeland or Vero Beach in Florida or from Lock Haven in Pennsylvania and bring them to Ft. Lauderdale to install ferry tanks, and in some cases an HF radio. From time to time there would be a Brittan Norman Islander to be delivered from the Isle of Wright, Ireland to somewhere in the U.S. These aircraft were dreadfully slow, about 100 mph. During the hay days of the late 60s and early 70s there would be planes stacked up at their hangar awaiting a pilot to return from a previous trip to take the next one to its destination. Bob was a full-time pilot for his dad and Burr would take an occasional plane for them when they were in a bind.

Burr, on the other hand was a corporate pilot flying a Beechcraft D-18 with a Dumod nose gear conversion, (they came from the factory as tail wheel aircraft). (Figure 4 – 10) It was based at Miami Aviation Corporation, where I was employed right after my flight training at Burnside Ott. His primary duty was photo mapping most of South Florida for various government agencies. That consisted of flying a preset course, back and forth – back and forth for hours. The first time I rode with him, I was in the right seat just following along with everything he was doing. When we were cleared for takeoff, he taxied onto the runway, applied full power, slid his seat back and said you've got it! It was the first time I had flown a D-18 or anything that complex or that heavy. That is how Burr operated. I flew with him on countless trips. He is the only person whom I have met that had almost identical beliefs as I have. He would let me use his Hobie Cat sailboat whenever I wanted to use it. We spent many hours making a recording (in his apartment) of an actual Eastern Air Line's scheduled flight, all the radio calls, cabin announcements and center handoffs. It was set to music and turned out to be a very good and a very authentic tape. It ran for about 35 minutes. Several flight schools, including Broward Community and Dade Community Colleges aviation training departments used this tape for training purposes. I had several holiday meals with Burr and his parents, who lived in Dania; we were good friends and still stay in touch. On one of the afternoon pool conversations, Burr arrived with an employee of Burnside-Ott's Opa-locka branch. Her name was Lynne Merritt. That was the only time she came with him, but it was the first time Lynne and I actually had a meaningful conversation. The rest is history,

There were very few restaurants in Ft. Lauderdale that served dinners that any of us could afford, but one of these was The Reef. Every evening there were lines that went almost all the way around the building, most of which were older retired people. We soon learned that in one of their dining rooms they had Violet Joy on the Hammond, she performed nightly and would play requested songs. She thought Lynne and I were married, and Lynne told her we were married in Hawaii. Every time we walked in, she would stop whatever she was playing and play the *Hawaiian Wedding Song*, just for us. She was not very good, but you could almost always be seated immediately if you requested that dining room. Almost every night the EMT's were called for somebody that was waiting in line, you know it was Ft. Lauderdale – hot and very humid outside for those standing in line.

One evening Burr and five others, including myself and Lynne, decided we could afford to go to the Reef. There was a huge line outside, so Burr went to the hostess and told her that we were a few minutes early, but he wanted to confirm our reservations that he had made the day before, that the request for a birthday cake and to be seated in Violet Joy's room had been noted. Of course, he had not made a reservation, but the hostess asked us to wait bedside her pedestal and she would check. We were seated within five minutes and a cake was delivered to our table at the completion of our meal. The cake was very cold, just out of the freezer, but it was delivered.

One evening, after our time at the pool, we gathered to watch the Moon Landing, the first visual was inverted "upside" down. We were all looking at the TV with our heads held below our knees to see Neil Armstrong's first steps. So proud to be an American!

Burr and I were at the pool one Sunday morning when a representative from The Seventh Day Adventist church appeared with her pamphlets. She positioned herself between the lounges and the pool, when she got into her scripted speech, on the count of three, we immediately jumped up and she took one step back and found herself in the pool with her pamphlets floating across the surface. She never came back.

Another time, another lady from the church and her young daughter knocked on Burr's door and asked a minute of his time. He was in the shower when they knocked, and he arrived at the door with just a towel wrapped around himself. She asked for a minute of his time, and he told them that they had 60 seconds and then he was going to drop the towel. He did - they went past their 60 seconds! She and her daughter promptly left. That was life at Paradise Manor.

Up until this point in my life, I did not have a need for a passport, I was the only person at the pool that didn't have one, and it was suggested that I get one, after all I lived on the coast and the Bahamas were just a few miles away. My roommate at the time was Bob Iba, Jr. He offered to take me to the Passport Office in downtown Miami, because he needed to renew his. It took me quite a while to obtain my Birth Certificate, I was finally able to get a certified copy of mine, from the Court House in Henry County, Illinois. I just hoped it would be approved and come before the planes had to leave for Argentina, that trip was one that had been approved in advance, so that I could go as a passenger. The passport was delivered via mail, the next day! Much to my amazement good things were beginning to happen in my life.

Air Convoy was backed up with planes to deliver and they needed to get two Aztecs to Buenos Aires, Argentina. Bob Jr. took one and Burr took the other, I went along as a passenger and to learn about international flying. Burr got called back to Miami soon after we departed and out of desperation, Air Convoy allowed me to take the other one the rest of the way. I used that trip for my solo Commercial Cross-Country flight. It was on this trip that I had my first experience with flying outside the United States.

That was quite a learning experience; I learned that not all towers have English speaking controllers, that is a requirement that at least one controller must speak English during the time the tower is in operation, when you clear customs you also need to report to public health and immigration, which are usually in three separate locations on the airport. The only way you can get to all three is that you need to take a cab that can take the interior airport perimeter roads. The customs inspector's brother-in-law usually operates that cab. Also, when flying over the water, looking for a particular island, you need to be careful not to land on a cloud shadow, they actually closely resemble islands from your altitude, you usually don't realize it is a cloud shadow until it is too late.

The route we planned and took was:

Fort Lauderdale to

Nassau for fuel to

South Cacaos for fuel to

San Juan for fuel and overnight to

Piarco, Trinidad for fuel to

Paramaribo, Surinam for fuel*

Belem, Brazil for fuel and unfortunately overnight to

IT AIN'T JUST ABOUT PLANES

Brasilia, Brazil for fuel and overnight to

Florianopolis, Brazil for fuel to

Buenos Aires, Argentina

to home via Lima, Peru and Quito, Columbia, to Miami.

In Paramaribo there was a "snack bar" next to the FBO's shack, so I ordered a ham sandwich for lunch. It consisted of two slices of two- or three-day old dry bread and one slice of ham that was so thin it only had one side to it. That was lunch.

For your overnight stops in a third world country, you always want to tell the cab driver to take you to a four-star hotel, even then it's not what we are used to in the U.S. You also take a ten-dollar bill (in 1969) and tear it in half and tell the cabbie that he will get the other half when he picks you up at six o'clock in the morning. One particular "four star" hotel in Belem, Brazil had a piece of ¾ inch plywood for springs on the bed with a mattress that was about four inches thick. When I got to that room, I was so frustrated and tired that I just flopped onto the bed, that's when I discovered the mattress situation. When I went into the bathroom to take a shower, I decided not to trust their water heater. It was a burner from an electric stove placed in a rusted coffee can with holes punched in the bottom of it. There was an outlet in the ceiling above the shower to plug the heating element into. In order to get hot water, you had to reach up and plug it in. You could regulate how hot the water would become by the amount of water you ran through the can. A four-star hotel!

I took a bottle of apple juice to drink en-route, and I would re-fill it a bit later. The lady customs agent in Belem confiscated the bottle because I could not bring "food" into their country. I truly hope she took a big swig of the "apple juice" before she discovered what the bottle really contained. Also, in Belem while checking in with customs, immigration and public health, the customs agent

70

confiscated the planes because he decided that our U.S. insurance was not acceptable to him. The inspector's brother-in-law just happened to sell insurance that was valid in Brazil for only $1,000.00, imagine my surprise. They had glued newspapers over the aircraft's door and baggage compartment door and had armed guards (teenagers) positioned around the plane. Basically, we were under house arrest until we purchased their insurance policy. When we got back to the planes, we even had to pay for the guards that were watching them, twenty-four hours a day, they were there just in case we tried to leave before purchasing their insurance.

The rest of the trip was normal except the further south we got the less English the controllers could speak. On approach to Florianopolis in Southern Brazil, I requested the wind direction and speed and was told "Cleared to land runway 17," once again I requested the wind direction and speed, and received the same message; never did find out the wind direction and speed. From Florianopolis to our destination, it was normal except for the controllers only speaking Spanish, at that time my Spanish was poor at best, and still is. Bob's plane was in front of me, and he would call as a flight of two in Spanish and would relay the landing instructions to me in English. Bob's mother was Spanish, he was truly bilingual. Because of the International flight rules that I mentioned earlier that there must always be at least one English-speaking controller on duty when the tower is open, that does not happen, also I wish France would follow that same rule, they only speak to all aircraft in French. They usually will not acknowledge any foreign registered aircraft.

We finally got to our destination in Argentina, delivered the two planes and checked into a hotel. When departing the hotel in Buenos Aries, we took a cab to get to the international airport. The cabbie said he knew of a short cut, and soon we were speeding through stop lights and alleys. When we got into the alley it had cars parked on both sides, and he tried to squeeze through, bad idea, we got jammed between two of those vehicles. We couldn't open the doors to get out, that was the horrible feeling of being trapped. The driver put his car in reverse and gunned it and we scraped our way out and finally made it to the airport in time to catch our flight. We were booked on Aero Lineas Argentina to Lima Peru, then we transferred planes and boarded APSA Airlines along with the chickens and goats and so many passengers that some had to sit on the floor. The stewardess could not get down the aisles, they just stayed in the nearest galley. We landed in Quito Equator where we got a Pan Am flight to Miami. That blue Pan Am globe on the tail sure is a welcome sight when you are traveling through most of the third world countries. The trip home was almost as exciting as the trip to Buenos Aires.

Ferry flights are a real departure from normal flight procedures. The biggest change is to run the fuel tanks, both the ferry tanks and the regular wing tanks completely dry. When the engine stops, turn on the fuel pump and change the tank selector to one that still has fuel in it. The engine will usually restart immediately. A few gallons left in each tank will not do you any good when you are about five miles from the end of the destination runway and both engines quit. This procedure usually happens at the most inopportune times; when you are transmitting your position report to flight service, they freak out when you tell them that your engine just quit and for them to hold on for a minute. The other time it happens is when you are refilling your apple juice bottle. You also needed to take a tape player to hopefully keep you awake on those twelve-hour legs. Flying over the equator where the two hemispheres meet is quite challenging. On a warm summer day, the clouds build up and you cannot fly a straight route, you need to swerve around the rain clouds, it's warm, the sun is bright, sleep is fast approaching. The tape player blasting your favorite music will help keep you awake. Fortunately, just as you are falling off to sleep, your hearing shuts down first, silence, did the engines both shut down, wake up! Also, you place your life raft and life vest as close as possible to your exit, so if needed you can just grab the life vest and attach the raft to yourself on your way out.

Soon after the Buenos Aires trip, the opportunity came along to take a Navajo to Nairobi, Kenya. Let me tell you, that was another learning experience. For a trip of that length, you will need about 100 copies of your General Declarations, thank God for Xerox machines. For the Argentina trip, we only needed 50 copies for each plane. The more paper you can give the inspectors, the better they like it. Depending on the radios that are installed on the plane you are taking, you may need to take a "portable" HF radio for communication. A hole would usually be drilled in the belly of the plane for a trailing antenna that you could adjust how much was trailing to tune into a particular frequency. In addition to the radio, you would have a life raft, a life vest, and your bag to take back to the states. You will also need a paper grocery bag full of cash, small bills preferably because most foreign operations do not take American credit cards and cannot make change for their charges. And again, the more paper you can give the locals, the easier it is to get the proper stamps in your passport. First, you need to plan your trip, day to day in advance, so you can request visas for each country where you are going to land. Unfortunately, the visas are usually only valid for one day. It can take up to two weeks to obtain these visas.

The first leg of the trip was from Ft. Lauderdale to Boston to test the ferry fuel system since you would not be out of gliding distance from land if it failed. Then on to Gander, Newfoundland overnight. The weather station there was the best of anywhere in the world. They had weather charts prepared for your next leg and went into the details of its contents. On take-off from there, the plane was 2,000 pounds over gross weight because of full fuel in the ferry system and the regular fuel tanks are topped off also. It would take about three hours of flight time to get it to the max gross weight for the plane. As you depart the runway the land drops off at the end of the runway and there are dozens of crosses below you are indicating where other planes have not made it, chilling. The next stop is Shannon, Ireland. On the way, there were two ocean stations, Charlie and Juliette, (ships anchored in the middle of the ocean.) This was before GPS, they only had ADF (Automatic Direction Finder) radios for navigation, they would make sure you were on course and send you on your way. The best time to fly over the North Atlantic is at night, because the airlines fly the same route that you are using. They are all going to the Shannon VOR, then on to various destinations in Europe. Their position lights show you the way. Also, who wants to see all of that ice and water for twelve hours, and you are only looking at the surface. It is very difficult to stay awake during these many hours of nothing but darkness and water.

In Shannon, they have excellent controllers, we needed help for a night landing because the runways were fogged in, as well as all alternate airports. They got us in, and I was very grateful. The next stop was Malta, in the Mediterranean Sea. The only problem on that leg was that we were flying a U.S. registered aircraft, and the French controllers would not answer our calls to give them a position report. Finally, a British Airways plane heard us and relayed our position to London. No problems in Malta, another overnight so I took the opportunity to walk the beach and stick my hand in the Mediterranean, when I pulled my hand out it was covered with oil. The Mediterranean has no outlet. That is probably the reason I was the only person on the beach. The next leg was Khartoum in Sudan, flying around Egypt and that's when the trip became eventful.

If you are delayed en-route only by one day, your visas are no longer valid. And you will have to convince the local authorities that it was their error in dating that document not ours, cash would help them decide it was their fault. In addition to paying for fuel, you will also be charged for the use of navigation aids and airport lights, even if they are not turned on. They were simply not turned on for the approach, because hey did not want Israel to use them. They will tell you that they will turn them on for your departure, but you don't need navigational aids outbound, you are not looking for the airport, you are departing.

At that time when flying near Egypt, it was best to schedule your trip to go around the country at night, instead of overflying it. You needed to fly with all your lights off, including interior lights, the exception being your instrument lights. This is to make it more difficult for the local air force to find you and use you for target practice. The glare from those instrument lights reflecting off the curve of the windshield creates the perfect situation for vertigo to set in. It is really hard to believe your instruments instead of what your body is telling you, which is that you are in a continuous turn. Particularly when flying in Mid-East and Africa, it is wise to file fictitious flight plans so the local "air forces" will not be able to find you for their target practice.

There was no current weather available for this area, Malta just had a report that was over a month old, it was not helpful at all. Khartoum and Egypt had all their navigational aids turned off so that Israel could not use them should they be planning an attack. We could not find our destination and finally climbed as high as the plane could go and were able to make out a glow in the distance, fortunately, it turned out to be the airport we were looking for. We had drifted about 100 miles off course. When landing in Khartoum we were met with armed military surrounding the plane. By the way, it is a violation to take a camera into the airport because it's a joint Russian military and civilian base. You can't take pictures of the MiG's on the other side of the field. It was night when we arrived and had a few hours to kill before 03:00 for departure, the coolest time of the day, to help the aircraft gain flying speed because of the density altitude. So, with that in mind we first needed to pay the fees and find the restroom. When I found them, I could not read Arabic (Farcie) for Men's and Women's, so I waited until someone came out, still couldn't tell which was which. When I finally went in, it had two kneeling pads with a hole in the floor. Next, I ordered a beef steak, and I am sure it was camel, so tough you literally couldn't chew it, no matter how thin you sliced it. As a side fact, at that time if you were traveling in that part of the world, you needed two passports; if you landed in Israel, you could not use the same one if you landed or had to land in Egypt or the other way around.

It was common knowledge not to fly over central Africa because of the probability that you would be forced to land or would be shot down. If forced to land you would be held as a spy or a smuggler of munitions. They have been known to hold ferry pilots for months, even years. The next stop was Nairobi. On the takeoff roll from Khartoum, it took every inch of the 12,000-foot runway. It was so hot, and the air was so thin, that when full power was applied the plane just shook before it even started to move forward. Near the end of the runway, you needed to lower the flaps to create an additional lift to urge it off the ground, then retract the gear and slowly retract the flaps to gain speed. It was very nerve wracking, again the plane was very over gross weight so that another landing wouldn't be necessary before getting to the destination in Kenya.

Upon arriving late in the afternoon, the Piper dealer took delivery of the plane. When I returned to the terminal it was dusk and there were literally hundreds of natives standing along the fences and on the roof of the terminal. The planes landing and taking off was their entertainment. Inside the terminal, I went to the Pan Am counter and was told the next flight would not happen for two days. They only had Pan Am service twice a week. I ended up flying on East African Airways, what an experience. My flight was diverted to Cypress for an unknown reason. All passengers with a US or Israeli passport were not allowed to enter the country, we were held in the Customs facility until our flight continued. After a few hours in Customs, it was on to London, I was fortunate enough to get booked on Pan Am's Flight #1, a new 747 – Heavy. Upon entering a 747, it felt like you're walking into a vast cathedral of modern engineering – it was huge, but when boarding one of these incredible machines, you never felt like you were in a metal tube, so I can confidently say that the 747 felt very different. I showed one of the flight attendants my pilot's license and asked if I could visit the cockpit. She called the captain, he said sure, bring him up.

Going to the upper deck the first thing that hits you for the first time is it really does resemble a lounge, with couches and large comfortable chairs, it had the largest bowl I had ever seen, full of ice with hundreds of shrimp, just waiting for me to have some. In the cockpit the windows were covered with navigational charts to block out the sun, but all three crew members were awake when I went in. I told them that I had flown their simulator, they acted like they were impressed. Then it was back to the "cheap" seats.

The pilot disengaged the autopilot to "hand fly" this behemoth of a plane. The slightest movement of the yoke caused the plane to really sway back and forth, most noticeable in the rear section. One of the stewardesses was trying to serve coffee and the movement in the cabin caused her to do a real "dance" just to keep the coffee in the pot. Another stewardess called the cockpit and advised the pilots of what was going on in the aft cabin. As soon as the autopilot was engaged the flight smoothed out. There was one passenger who was apparently very uncomfortable about flying because about every thirty minutes or so, he got up and went to the lavatory, he had to climb over two other passengers to get to the aisle and repeated this process to get back to his seat. This continued for the entire eight-hour flight. Then Northeast (Yellow Bird for those who remember them) to Ft. Lauderdale. It was a red-eye flight, and I requested a blanket and a pillow and not to be awakened until we landed. As luck would have it, I was the only passenger in the row of three seats. The Stewardess came by and asked what I wanted for dinner, then would I like a beverage, at that point I was finally able to make her understand that I wanted to sleep for two hours, not eat or drink.

At this time in my life that I felt that I was coming out of my shell, it was a slow process lasting over many years. It was the first time that I needed a passport with visas and a yellow health card, which indicated the vaccinations you had received, (smallpox, cholera, and yellow fever), I had been to several countries and was making my own decisions. At long last, I was making new friends, some of which I'm still in contact with. So, I decided to start going out and generally begin to have some fun. I began to believe that if you say no to adventure, you say no to life. I began to believe that remarkable things can happen when you step outside your comfort zone.

Three members of the house band at the Newport Seven Seas Lounge (it was on Collins Avenue in North Miami Beach, across from where The Castaways was located) were in flight school with me. It was a very popular club in North Miami Beach. I (we) often went there, and during the time that the band was not playing they would join us at our table. After a few trips to the club, the Matre'd recognized us, we would get a table next to the stage. The house band could absolutely duplicate the songs that Jay and the Americans made popular, to refresh your mind, their biggest hit was Cara Mia. You can only imagine how impressive a date was when half the band came off the front of the stage to your table and pulled up the chairs and joined you. Unfortunately, after several months at the Newport, the band got a booking and went on to Las Vegas, before they got their pilot's licenses, that's the last I heard from them.

A few of the performers at the Seven Seas Lounge were: Wayne Cochran, the CC Riders, The Platters, the Drifters, Frankie Avalon, Paul Revere & the Raiders, Ike and Tina Turner also Frankie Valley & the Four Seasons, just to name a few.

When Wayne Cochran was performing, he would come out into the audience, he always went to the bar first and picked up as many liquor bottles as he could carry and pass them out to the crowd. As a poor kid from the corn fields, this was an almost unbelievable experience being in the same room as these famous performers. We (me, Lynne, Andy, and his date) were frequent customers at the club. One evening Andy actually had a short conversation with the members of The Platters while they were on stage, something about what their mink cuff links reminded Andy of, he got the whole group laughing till they had to pause and re-group. The only live show I saw when I was in Illinois was The Smothers Brothers, and that was in Davenport. Not only did I get to meet these famous people, but also I actually got to have discussions with many of them.

At the Seven Seas, there was a three-drink minimum per show, three shows per night. When the band joined us, other customers would send bottles over. Oh my God, you could get very drunk, and I had to get back to Ft. Lauderdale. While living is South Florida, I only got pulled over two times. The first offense, the officer asked me why I was trying to drive, and I told him I was too drunk to walk; he laughed and took me home (just a few blocks) and had the other patrolman in the police car drive my car home and made me promise not to drive until I sobered up. The other time I was pulled over by a Ft. Lauderdale officer for speeding. His first statement was "you went flying past me; let me see your pilot's license." When I produced it, he cracked up laughing and said in all the years he had used this line I was the first one to produce a pilot's license, he told me to slow down and let me go.

A depressing sight at that time was Miami's South Beach, so many older people just sitting on the porches of the run-down deco hotels, waiting for God. This was before *Miami Vice*, which started the turn-around for the area.

The HMS Queen Elizabeth came into Port Everglades, and it was open for tours. The ship was magnificent, with the huge stained-glass ceiling over the Grand Plaza, the carved woodwork, the artwork. The tour of the ship even took us to Elizabeth Taylor's cabin(s), she had an adjoining cabin just for her dogs. The QE-2 was under construction and Cunard put this ship up for sale. A group of us, including some investors (a Venezuelan group of business executives), submitted a bid for her. Our plan was to anchor her just outside U.S. territorial waters and open a casino, a hotel, and restaurants as well as various forms of Vegas type shows. There were already several bars, several working kitchens and even a theatre on the ship. It should have been an easy transition from a cruise ship to a resort. We would have launches take guests from Port Everglades to the ship on a scheduled basis. Guests could come out for the afternoon, all day, remain overnight or on vacation for as long as they wanted to. There would have been restaurants to cater to all tastes from snack bars, a buffet and first-class dining room. At this time, only Vegas had legalized gambling, so there was a demand for this type of entertainment on the East Coast. The mafia thought so too. They informed us that they would be our partners, but they didn't know we had already lined up our partners. Fortunately, Cunard took the ship off the market and donated her to a college in the Far East, I believe it was Singapore. Anyway, she sank as she entered her new home port. That took care of our great idea.

While I was in flight training, I made friends with some of the employees at Eastern Aviation Service, (it was owned by Eastern Airlines through a purchase of Mackey Airlines by Eastern, they made this purchase to get Mackey's Cuban routes) it was considered to be a world leader in FBO Customer Service; one of the first in the nation to concentrate on truly serving the customer. This is where I learned what Customer Service really was, and where I met Marty Sinker who was to become my best friend. At that time in the industry, there were usually a couple of vending machines in a small area, one of which was a coffee vendor. The other operations were turnpike gas stations for airplanes where you could get fuel and a Coke and that was about it. Eastern Aviation Service had complimentary coffee in the lobby with real cream on ice, a private customer lounge with leather top tables and actual wood paneling on the walls. There was even a swimming pool for the pilots to use, however, only the staff used the pool after cleaning it every day (jet fuel exhaust scum on the water's surface and on the surrounding tiles). The airline's jets used the runway closest to Eastern Aviation, causing most of the jet exhaust, there were relatively few turbine aircraft at that time. At this time, turboprops and corporate jets were just coming into service.

One of those customers was Arthur Godfrey, at that time he had Gulfstream I. It was the forerunner of the G-II, only it was a turboprop plane instead of a pure jet. The cabin size was exactly the same as the G-II. During the winter months Arthur would come to Ft. Lauderdale on a regular basis, in fact he did many of his winter shows from Bal Harbor, a high-end neighborhood that's just north of Miami. At his peak in the 50's, he had two 90-minute CBS Television shows a week and a daily 90-minute radio show. He was truly the most popular entertainer of that era. He would come back to the airport at closing time with a case of beer, just to meet with the staff and get their opinions and just have conversations with them. By the time I was hanging around he would arrive in his Baron, a twin-engine Beechcraft. When I first met him, I was so "Star Struck," I could barely speak. I guess he felt sorry for me, and finally got me to relax and made me believe that he was just another person who put his pants on just like me, one leg at a time. It was from this experience that I became comfortable having discussions with "famous people," even Presidents, Vice Presidents, Cabinet Members, Governors, CEOs of Fortune 500 Companies who were the owners of corporate aircraft.

At Eastern Aviation, whatever a customer "guest" asked for, it was provided. Everything from having new deck shoes for them when they arrived, to opening a local restaurant to have their special cold tenderloin lunches ready for their arrival and a quick turn. During this time, I was fortunate enough to meet Len Povey, manager of Eastern Aviation Service. It was Len's vision that made Eastern Aviation Service a leader in the corporate aviation service. Len was a wealth of stories about his early flying experiences. This FBO only had Jet fuel, they had no fuel for piston planes. Len had taken the FBO to a level that was so far ahead of the industry standards that it would not be challenged for decades.

Long after Len retired, I did some research on his aviation background; it was so impressive that I have included it as part of this story. Here is a brief recap of his accomplishments: His career in aviation spanned several decades and included, but was not limited to, serving in the U.S. Army Air Service, barnstorming, creating the Cuban Air Force for Fulgencio Batista, and as executive vice-president of Mackey Airlines which was based in Fort Lauderdale. I didn't know much about his aviation career until many years later. Imagine a poor guy from the corn fields actually knowing somebody who had associated with the true pioneers in aviation. The stories he shared with us were incredibly interesting and for the most part amusing. This was the first time I actually became friends with notable people and found out they were just normal folks.

Near the end of my flight training, Southeast Banks was running a TV ad that said "in your lifetime you will earn $250,000.00 and we would like to help you manage your funds. At that time that seemed like an absolute fortune. I didn't have any long-term prospects for gainful employment, and I was barely living paycheck to paycheck. We were in the middle of a recession and the airlines were laying off pilots, not hiring them, and their pilots that had been furloughed would be called back before any hiring would take place. One of my flight instructors was "hired by Piedmont Air Lines" to be included in their next class; he never got that call. For the first time in a long time, I was really feeling depressed. Being a bit of a nomad with no roots, I contacted the Australian Embassy and requested a work visa. Several weeks later I received their response, request denied because Australia had no immediate need for additional pilots. I couldn't even get a job in Australia.

Soon after arriving in Ft. Lauderdale, I learned about the waterways within the city limits. Three hundred miles of navigable waterways plus the intra costal waterway. There were water taxis operating in the canals, yes, they were yellow. The county courthouse, drug stores, the Los Olas Blvd. shops, a lot of the restaurants on the waterway, and the post office all had docks. Some of the restaurants even had valet parking for the customer's yachts. It was a wonderful place to live and work, and of course, Spring Break.

Eastern Aviation Service
Figure 4 – 4

Burnside-Ott Home Facility
Figure 4 – 5

Piper Aztec
Figure 4 – 6

Piper Navajo
Figure 4 – 7

Brittan Norman Islander
Figure 4 - 8

Cesena 182
Figure 4 – 9

Beech D-18
Figure 4 – 10

Ft. Lauderdale International Airport 1968
Figure 4 – 11

Ft. Lauderdale International Airport 2018
Figure 4 – 12

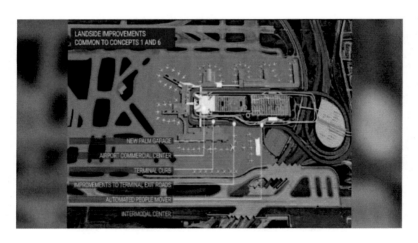

The Most Beautiful Sight in a Foreign Country
Figure 4 - 13

The minute you settle for less than you deserve,
You get even less than you settled for.

CHAPTER FIVE
MIAMI AVIATION CORPORATION
1970 - 1975

When I left Burnside-Ott, I went to Opa-locka to work for Miami Aviation Corporation (MAC), which was next door to Burnside-Ott's home office. The sole owner was Frank Hart, known among most of the employees as Rank Fart. It was the largest FBO at Opa-locka Airport, BATC (Burnside-Ott Aviation Training Center) was the largest tenant at that time. Our only competitor was Hangar One, a chain which had five operations in the southeast. Frank Hulse, who was also the owner of, Southern Airways, owned it. FBO actually stands for Fixed Base Operation, makes no sense; a closer name would be ASO, Aircraft Service Organization. A major chain of FBOs tried to change this, however that idea never caught on. FBO dates back to the early days of aviation, barnstormers would fly from field to field with no base. If they needed fuel or bailing wire for repairs, they would send a kid into town to get whatever they needed. As the aircraft became more complex, they needed a base from which to operate, hence Fixed Base Operation.

Shortly before I was hired, Miami Aviation Corporation had purchased their next-door competitor, Butler Aviation, which included among other buildings and ramps plus Hangar 101. (MAC already had a matching Hangar 102) Along with that hangar came a tenant that scared most people – a ghost. This hangar was the closest to the main turnoff for runway 9-Left, (the longest runway) so our

Customer Service Department moved into that hangar. All of our employees were familiar with the ghost, and some would not even go into the building, they found other employment. Fortunately, he was a fun loving being and just loved to pull pranks that would annoy us. We called him "Casper" for lack of a better name, and would let him know that his actions were disturbing to the operation. At night, he would open the front door, walk through the lobby area, and go through the door into the hangar. The hangar doors were rolling steel doors and were secured with chains. There were ten doors on each of the two sides of the hangar, and he would go down one side and rattle the chains on his way to the back door of the hangar. During the day, he would turn off the public-address amplifier, this was before handheld radios, it was the method of contacting Line Service, and the PA system was the only way of contacting them. This amplifier was located in a closet on the second level, in a locked closet. We would have to go upstairs, unlock the doors (2 of them) and turn it back on, yet it would still be warm when we got there. He would turn off the bell on the phone system, we would realize that we had not received any calls for a period of time and look at the switchboard and all six lines would be lit up, like a Christmas tree, but were not ringing.

My first job at MAC was in the parts department, it was in a separate building on the leasehold. The most exciting part of that job was being challenged by rats about the size of large cats, when we opened the building each morning. Ultimately, we contacted Dade County's Public Health Department, it took them about six weeks to rid the building of the rats. After a few months, I transferred to the Customer Service Department. I learned Line Service and working at the front desk as a Customer Service Representative. In a few months, I was appointed to the position of Customer Service Manager because the previous manager resigned. My first morning as Customer Service Manager all of my Front Desk Customer Service employees staged a protest that I had been appointed to that position, each one of them thought they deserved the position, and they were all going to walk out. Lynne, who later became my wife, was one of those employees. The first was Michael who said, "I quit." My response was, "don't let the door hit you on the ass on your way out." My next statement was: "who's next?" Nobody else stepped forward, and I requested their help and that I would rely on their knowledge to make this work. By the way, Michael came back later that afternoon and apologized and asked if he could have his job back. I gave in and let him come back but took away his seniority and put him on ninety-day probation. I inherited quite a group of outside employees, commonly known as Line Men. One was Ralph Deshon, he told me that he won the first Sebring Auto Race. Two years later a group of friends, including me, went to Sebring for the race. I opened the program, and sure enough, Ralph had won the first race – in a Crosley. Most of the Linemen were only there for a paycheck, they had no other interest in airplanes. They just didn't show their interest in the customer's plane other than to ask how much fuel they needed. That was something that the customers noticed. Every applicant that I hired displayed an interest in the aircraft, many from the flight school next door.

Within a few weeks, I learned that the company was in serious financial trouble. A previous Vice President had run off most of the based customers to make room for large corporate aircrafts such as Convair 440s, Boeing 727s and DC-9s, which had been converted from airline configuration to corporate configuration, which could accommodate up to 24 passengers, have a dining area, a lounging area and in many cases a bedroom with a full bathroom. However, these aircrafts never arrived.

The closest we came to handling a large aircraft was a Navy DC-6 (a four engine propeller aircraft) that came in twice a month to pick up members of the Naval Reserves and take them to Jacksonville and two days later bring them back. They only used us for our front ramp, air stairs, Hobart power cart, parking lot and lobby. They didn't ever purchase fuel. However, they did drop off a jet air-start unit, which we used one time for Warner Brothers' G-II.

The President, Frank Hart gave up the Aero Commander dealership (a very successful plane) in order to take on a British made plane, the Beagle. I think he sold one Beagle - it was a good aircraft, but not for the South Florida market. There was so much glass in the cockpit that the sun coming into the cockpit was very uncomfortable for pilots. In addition to the Beagle, he became a dealer for de Havilland of Canada's DHC-6, commonly known as the Twin Otter. That plane was very successful in the commuter market, however, very few were sold by Miami Aviation. On the other hand, the Twin Otters did become good and dependable maintenance customers.

We were on COD with almost every supplier that we used (and needed) including our fuel supplier, Esso, which later became Exxon. There were times when a supplier would get a judgement against the company and have the sheriff deliver a copy of the judgement, and somehow, we could come up with the money to cover it, so that they did not chain the doors. Within about six months, the Customer Service Department was making enough profit, and through negotiations we were able to settle almost all the outstanding obligations that we were responsible for, the most important supplier was Esso, but they kept us on COD. No more visits from the Dade County Sheriff's department except as a customer; we fueled their helicopter, a Bell 47. The Sheriff's flight department was located within our leasehold.

All of the buildings at Opa-locka were World War II leftovers. We had two large hangars and three "out" buildings, an unoccupied restaurant, the parts department, and Burnside-Ott's home base. Dade County was the property owner; the only thing they did was to put some paint on them. One of the original hangars, known as "Hangar 102" is still in use today, after undergoing extensive renovations. Our next-door neighbor was the Miami Coast Guard Aviation Unit, one of the busiest bases in the United States. When any transient military aircraft came in, they sent them to us, because they said they were too busy to handle them; and that did not happen very often. However, one of them was Air Force One. The Coast Guard let them park on their ramp, but we fueled them. That was the first time I was able to get onboard the Presidential Aircraft.

Late one evening, Lt Colonel Peppoli asked Lynne and I if we would like to go on board. The Secret Service for the plane were at the bottom of the air stairs and I heard the rifles being readied, but the Lt. Colonel said they would not take a shot at us as long as he was with us. When we got to the President's office the "red" phone was on the desk. For those of you who don't know, it was during the Cold War and that phone was a direct line to the Kremlin, to prevent an accidental war. Well, I couldn't pass up the urge to pick up the receiver, and I was connected to Moscow immediately. I asked their operator in Moscow to disregard the call, that I had knocked the receiver off of its cradle. As we toured the plane, when we got to the galley area, the Lt. Colonel offered us the dishes with the Presidential seal emblazoned on them. I told him I couldn't accept such a large gift. Maybe a pack of cigarettes or a book of matches would be fine, at that time all had the Presidential seal on them. When we deplaned, Lt. Colonel Peppoli had the Secret Service fill out the paperwork to get security clearances for both Lynne and myself. It was about nine o'clock in the evening, and by ten o'clock the next morning we had our security clearances. The next morning when I got to my office there was a box of dishes on my desk from Air Force One, with a note from President Nixon stating that he would rather that Lynne and I have them than the press that travels with him. The press would steal anything that is put in front of them that had the Presidential seal on it. More about my experiences on Air Force One and Air Force Two later. Actually, I can't reveal much about this since my security clearance will not permit me divulge anything about these trips.

From time to time, I would receive a request to "offer my assistance." Not only for the Presidential aircraft, but for many civilian aircrafts. The military pilots were not "checked out" in those planes. Many of those trips were into South American countries. Usually, the request would be to wear civilian clothes, take a flight to Dallas, you will be met and your aircraft (that was usually located at a nearby airport and had the plane had been confiscated and the interior would have been modified by installing a bulkhead between the crew and passenger areas. Also, electronic equipment would have been installed in the passenger compartment) only then would the flight plan be given to you. Most of the time, the route would take you to airways that are not published for civilian use. Often, upon landing on a private strip there would be one hangar with the doors open. According to the plan, you would taxi into the hangar, shut down while the doors were being closed, get off the plane and be driven off the airport in a black vehicle with blacked out windows. Then the passengers would deplane and do whatever they were there to do. On departure, the same procedure, only in reverse would happen. The crew and passengers would never come into contact with each other.

Another time we went over to the Coast Guard Ramp was to fuel a C-130, a rather large four engine (turboprop) aircraft. When Line Service connected the single point fuel nozzle to the aircraft, turned on the trucks pump, the fuel gushed out of the lower level of the fuel filter, 3,000 gallons of fuel was on their ramp. The seal on the lowest part of the fuel system had blown out. The emergency shut off valve was inoperative. Exxon's quality control employee had inspected that vehicle the week before this incident and had written the report that the truck was in perfect condition. I had our truck mechanic go inside the fuel tank and inspect the shut off system. He found that the cable which engages the system was wrapped around one of the steel support beams inside the tank. That system had never been operational. Exxon's inspector was more concerned about a burned-out position light on the roof of the cab, than checking the safety systems.

When I took over the Customer Service Department, we had about fifteen hangar tenants in 80,000 feet of hangar space, and about fifteen ramp customers on seven acres of paved ramp. Many days we did not have a single corporate jet come onto our ramp. I started a direct mail campaign that targeted Hangar One (our only competitor at Opa-locka) and Miami International's executive customers. Much to my surprise, we got about a 10% response to our letters each time we did a mailing, about four times a year. In addition, we instituted a real customer service attitude, much like what Eastern Aviation Service was doing in Ft. Lauderdale. Our only limitations were financial; we could not afford to give away polo shirts or Green Stamps. However, our willingness to provide service was the most vital component; we gave service and provided hospitality. Most FBO's at that time thought their job was to be a turnpike gas station for airplanes. Soon we started to serve more and more jets, turbo props, and large piston aircrafts.

One of the first transient jets to come in after I took over the Customer Service Department was Elvis's Jetstar. The door didn't open as quickly as I thought it should, and when it did a crew member had a dog standing beside him. As it turned out the dog was flown in to go to his veterinarian in North Miami, no other passengers were on board.

After months, we still did not have a single Gulfstream customer, the Rolls Royce of corporate aircraft. I had targeted them with my mailings, the Miami International customers, because Hangar One didn't have any of them either. Then out of the blue one day we had three G-II's on the ramp at the same time. One of them was McDonalds, another was a Gulfstream on a demonstration flight and RCA's brand-new G-II, worth a gazillion dollars, their pilots had picked it up in Savannah, flew to White Plains, New York and picked up General Sarnoff, CEO of RCA and flew him to Opa-locka. (Prior to that trip, RCA had a Lockheed Jetstar, which was a regular customer.) They ordered fuel and when the truck pulled up to the aircraft and the lineman got out of the cab, General Sarnoff said that our lineman could not fuel his new aircraft. I asked if I could fuel it, he thought a minute and he said, "well OK." Later that evening I asked the Chief Pilot, Pat Kernan, why the General was so particular about who serviced his plane, he said that the General's son had hair down to his ass and he could not do anything about it, but he could insist on only allowing well-groomed people (All American boys) to work on his plane. The next day I got my hair cut much shorter, almost a crew cut; the only barber in Opa-locka refused to cut my long hair, he said he only cut men's hair. He refused to listen to me and find out what I wanted. So, I went to another barber in Hialeah, it was quite an experience watching my hair cascade to the floor as it did many years before, my rebellion haircuts. Then I called a meeting with all Line and male Customer Service personnel and relayed the situation to them, according to Captain Kernan, most corporate heads wanted to see well groomed "All American" looking people service their multi-million-dollar aircraft. With that in mind, we instituted grooming standards for all Customer Service employees, similar to the ones Disneyland had in place. Two resigned, the rest shaved and got their haircut. I have kept those standards in place for the rest of my career and have had remarkable success with my policies, including this one.

About this time, I started a campaign with the President of MAC to get our starting pay up to $3.20 an hour, so my employees would take home at least $100.00 dollars a week. After all, they were working with aircrafts worth millions of dollars and not even taking home a reasonable wage. It took months, but he finally gave in and authorized the pay increase.

With the purchase of Butler's leasehold, a fuel farm that was designed for Texaco's dealers was included, it was above ground, and it consisted of four 20,000-gallon tanks. The Exxon fuel farm was much smaller and was an inoperable underground facility. Exxon demanded we use their farm. They said they would send their maintenance person to check it out, the same one who pronounced our fuel truck was in "perfect" condition. He came and immediately called another company to rebuild the farm. When their maintenance person said it was in working condition, I requested our Exxon Representative, their maintenance person, be on site when they delivered the fuel to test the farm. After they put fuel in both tanks (100LL and Jet), we pulled the 100LL truck up to the farm, and found that the connection adaptor was the wrong size. Hence, it could not connect the farm to the truck. When they pressurized the system, it looked like a sprinkler hose, fuel spraying out of the pipes and all connections. Same for the Jet side of the farm. I asked if they replaced all the underground plumbing, and received no answer. We continued to use the Texaco farm. So much for their maintenance person, we never saw him again.

Not long after I began working at MAC, Brian Grothe, who worked in the maintenance department, got into a motorcycle accident. He was a passenger on the motorcycle, and a car ran a stop light and plowed into them, pushing most of Brian's lower body through the frame of the bike. Brian and Pete Bolins were hospitalized in the same room for a long time. They put Brian back together with titanium rods, strips and screws. It was the Seventh Day of Adventist hospital; no meat was served. Lynne and I made many trips to see them and smuggled pizzas, Big Mac's, or fried chicken to them. While hospitalized, Brian and Pete made plans for a bar to be built somewhere on or near the beach in Ft. Lauderdale. They made the drawings and plans with such detail that they even knew where the liquor would be placed behind the bar.

About this time, Lynne and I took our third cruise, the first two were on Cunard, while this one was on Royal Caribbean Cruise Lines. It departed from San Juan, Puerto Rico. We were on an early flight and they provided transportation that took us to the ship. Unfortunately, we got there at noon, but we couldn't board the ship until 2:00. It was summertime and we were in a rather lengthy line waiting to board. It was hot, no clouds in the sky, I mean really hot. I noticed a street vendor about a block from where we were waiting, selling slushies. I bought two of them and headed back to the ship. I tasted one of them when I got back in line, it was Bacardi 151 and ice! I knew we couldn't drink two of them, so I turned around and offered one of them to the couple behind us. They were more than pleased; so we struck up a conversation. They introduced themselves as Eddy and Dorothy White from Riverside, California, and said that were traveling with another couple. Our friendship with the Whites lasted for many years, until Eddy got confined to an assisted living facility.

The trip included going through the Panama Canal, ending in Long Beach. Their travel agent had arranged for Champaign and appetizers to be in White's cabin when they arrived. We got a phone call a few minutes after we found our cabin; Eddy invited us to join them with their traveling companions. That trip was during the Falkland's war. About half of the entertainment staff from the HMS Queen Elizabeth that was on war duty, had been assigned to our ship. Their lecturer was on our ship; he gave a three-day lecture as to what we were going to see going through the canal. Myself along with a couple of other people attended the first one, however, by the third one they had to broadcast his comments throughout the ship, because there were not enough seats in the theater to hold the crowd. He was that interesting and informative. As we sailed through the canal, he pointed out the items that he had mentioned that we would see.

That was an excellent trip except for a couple of items. The portable water that we picked up in Panama was not pure, virtually every passenger and crew member had the "Hershey Squirts." That hung on for a few days until the ship passed out liquid morphine on the pool deck. It worked immediately; however, Lynne would not take it because of what it was. One week after we got home, she went to her doctor and requested the liquid, but he could not prescribe it. Her situation went on for another week.

Then when the ship was off the coast of Central America, we got into a furious storm. It was so violent the propellers would come out of the water shaking the ship. I found out why there are handrails along both sides of the hallways. Just a few of us assembled in the center of the ship. When the ship's captain's wife joined us, her comment was when the waves came over her windows, it's time to get to the center lounge. The kitchen sent a cart of food up to us;

there were not enough cooks available to fix what was on the menu or enough servers to deliver the food, if it would have been available. That day we had dolphins playing in front of the ship; they would dive under the bow and come up on the other side. There were two whales beside us also. Very few passengers believed us when we told them about what we had seen.

We had also struck up a professional relationship with our cabin steward, coffee delivered at 6:00 left outside the door, who didn't bother to make the beds into two couches unless we left a note for him, and if a bottle of wine was on the desk, we would have it iced. One year later, we booked a cruise on the same ship, it was sailing on a new itinerary. As we were making our way to our cabin, he recognized us and called us by name. He asked what cabin we had, as luck would have it, it was in his section. He repeated my requests from the year before. He invited us to the crew's area and bar (that was not permitted), where drinks were about 1/4 the cost in the other bars. It was like *Dirty Dancing* in there; we joined in and learned a few new moves. We had a wonderful time. In addition, many of the ship's staff recognized us as frequent cruisers and we got special attention throughout the trip. That's the Royal Caribbean style of service.

In the early 70's Maida Heater (Gabriel Heater's daughter, he was a very famous radio news personality) was writing one of her several dessert cookbooks. Her husband had a beautiful yellow Cessna 195 based with us, and every morning he would arrive at the FBO with a banana box full of the most delicious desserts that she had made the day before. We would all have one bite out of them, a small price to pay for the best desserts we had ever tasted. Her husband said that they ordered butter and eggs by the case; and sugar and flour in fifty-pound bags. We all put on weight while she was writing that book, but it was worth it. Maida gave Lynne and me an autographed copy of her *Great Chocolate Desserts* Cookbook.

Cessna 195

In December of 1972 Saturn V (one of many Saturn V flights,) it was the first night launch taking three astronauts to the moon and back, many of our based customers flew to Merritt Island to see that impressive event. Lynne and I also flew there to view the shot. The earth actually shook, and the roar of the rocket was absolutely deafening. As soon as it was out of sight, we rushed back to Opa-locka to help the night shift manage all the customers who had also flown to the Cape. That was the most impressive event I had witnessed up to that point in my life.

A local doctor had a Beech Travelair, a twin engine, four-seat plane, based with us. He rarely flew it, but allowed any employee of MAC to use it, while the user just had to refuel it. That was a great deal, because I sold our employees any products, we had for cost plus 10%, this included fuel. The disadvantage of using the plane was that it did not have any brakes; so, when landing you had to use aerodynamic braking – hold the nose off the runway until it was slowed down enough that it was no longer flying. To make any turns you had to use asymmetric power (just apply power to one engine).

To come to a complete stop, you just let it roll until it stopped on its own. I used that plane a lot. Later on, the doctor had several malpractice cases filed against him, which resulted in the Florida Medical Board of Examiners threatening to pull his license unless he agreed to move to Arizona and provide medical service for an Indian tribe. And so, he moved to Arizona.

In 1972, the Secret Service demanded that both National Political Conventions be held on Miami Beach, this was a result of the violence in Chicago for the 1968 Democratic convention. I received a call from R. H. Haldeman (President Nixon's Chief of Staff) at 04:00 in the morning, demanding that I come to the airport and unlock several vacant offices that they wanted to use for the Secret Service. It was on the second floor in Hangar 101, where the former avionics department had been located. When I told him that I would see him at 08:30 he proceeded to ask me if I knew who he was, and I told him that I knew, and I would see him and unlock the offices that he wanted at 08:30. They had previously inspected the area, but never confirmed that they wanted to rent the space. They just showed up in the middle of the night and gave my midnight crew a ration of shit about not having the keys ready for their arrival.

After they settled in, it was quite an operation, twenty UH-1 (Huey) helicopters arrived (they were equipped with single point re-fueling, I had never seen this on a helicopter), security cameras were secretly installed everywhere, even in the bathrooms. The helicopter crews were on duty 24 hours a day during the actual conventions. The conventions were scheduled two weeks apart. They had catering set up 24 hours a day. Every time the helicopters landed, we would immediately refuel them. Between the conventions, I learned why Miami Beach was chosen. There were several planned demonstrations, so they would let the leaders cross the intra-coastal waterway bridges, from Miami to Miami Beach, then they would open the bridge and keep the rest of the demonstrators on the Miami side. They also sanded all the major streets in the area of the

Convention Center, this is where the helicopters came in, they would fly very low and blow the sand on any demonstrators that made it that far. That definitely put an end to the demonstrations.

In addition to the air traffic that was associated with this operation, especially the Republican convention, we were getting very busy with the traffic, other than that which the conventions generated. One of the convention arrivals was Burt Bacharach, we had advance notice that he was going to arrive, one of my counter girls stayed on until he arrived. When she greeted him, and said, "You're more handsome than your music is beautiful." They went off together. Barry Goldwater was the Keynote Speaker for the Republican convention; he arrived very inebriated in a Sabreliner, tripped on the threshold of the plane, and literally fell down the aircraft stairs. I met him at the plane and caught him on the way down. He was feeling no pain, they put him into a limo and two hours later, he gave his speech, perfectly. I don't know how they got him sober enough, but they did. It turned out to be a very busy month for us, as we got all of the traffic for the conventions.

We had one causality, one of my employees quit as soon as he found out that there had been cameras installed in the men's room. I often wondered what he had been doing in there. They removed them during regular business hours after the conventions, that's when we first learned about them.

Eastern Air Lines Flight 401 was a Lockheed L-1011 Tristar that crashed into the Florida Everglades on the night of December 29, 1972, causing 101 fatalities. All three pilots, two of 10 flight attendants, and 96 of 163 passengers died, while 75 passengers and 8 members of the cabin crew survived. The crash occurred while the entire flight crew was preoccupied with a burnt-out landing gear indicator light. They failed to notice that the autopilot had inadvertently been disconnected and, as a result, the aircraft gradually lost altitude and actually flew into the ground. It was the first crash of an L-1011 wide body aircraft up to that time, the second-deadliest single-aircraft disaster in the United States. At the time of this crash, the Air National Guard was based with us, operated Bell UH-1's (Huey) helicopters; they immediately mobilized and initially brought the survivors from the crash site to various hospitals.

The next day they started to bring bodies back and unloaded them into our Hangar 101. All were in rubber body bags; we unloaded them with a forklift and placed them on large metal drip pans. The "handlers" were my employees, volunteers only. It was almost 24 hours before refrigerated trucks arrived, and they had to be moved once again. By this time, the bags were ripping open, and snakes and swamp type matter covered the hangar floor. The base commander was reprimanded for not obtaining prior authorization for this operation. Go figure, rescuing survivors from the Everglades, and not waiting for prior authorization!

During this time, I was still living in an apartment complex just east of the airport in Opa-locka, which was not the best neighborhood. I hosted a birthday party for one of my employees, an older lady who ran the switchboard. During the party, she had what appeared to be having a heart attack, we called 911 and both an ambulance and squad car arrived, they were running under lights and their sirens were blasting. I was outside to direct them to my unit and noticed an unusual number of toilets being flushed. One could only guess what was being disposed of. That gives a pretty accurate idea of the area in which I was living. It was time for me to find a better place to live.

Shortly after our G-II success, I got a call from Mobil Oil, asking if we could keep their two G-II's in a hangar for a week, out of sight. They arrived, and we immediately put them into the hangar, they had a large red "O," part of their logo, painted on the tail. This was the beginning of the artificial fuel shortage in 1973, and they did not want the public (shareholders) to see how their executives traveled. When the tenants of the hangar and offices located in the same building, which we had put their planes in, they wanted to know who owned them, to which our response was "would you believe Lifesavers has two Gulfstreams." It worked; they believed our story. When Mobil's planes departed, they had ordered catering for both planes, one and one-half meals and wine for each passenger plus four crew meals. Up to that point, almost all catering orders were under one hundred dollars, but their bill was over three thousand dollars. I was almost ashamed to tell them what the cost was, but I had no choice, their response was that if they had gotten the catering in New York, it would have been twice as much, what a relief! About a month earlier Texaco took off from White Plains, New York in their G-II, their corporate office received a call that there was a bomb on the plane, and it would detonate when the plane descended through 5,000 feet. Fortunately, the plane had enough fuel to make it to Denver, and it landed without incident. The bomb squad removed the bomb, and it was detonated. It was a disgruntled shareholder that had placed the bomb on board. That prompted most corporate planes to have their company logos removed from the exterior surfaces of their aircraft. CBS had their plane painted pure white, no need for a logo, everybody knew who owned that plane. Heinz had their planes painted "sweet pickle green and ketchup red" same for the ownership.

Jeno's Pizza had a Falcon 20 as a corporate plane that came in a few times during the "season," and then it started arriving on a regular basis. Jeno's mother had a condo in North Miami, and they brought her down for the winter. When she got home sick for her friends back in Minneapolis, she would take the airline back home to see her friends. So, Jeno arranged to bring her bridge club to Florida every other week. In addition to those trips, they flew her favorite rocking chair down for her on one trip and a case of tomato sauce came on another trip, just to keep her from going back to Minneapolis in the winter.

Soon, I moved to the "Executive Club" in Miami Lakes. It was a group of quadraplex units around a small lake. Miami Lakes was adjacent to the west side of the airport. There were several break-ins in this complex, I always had music playing in my unit even when I wasn't there. One day the three other units in my building were burglarized, but mine was untouched. My roommate at this time was Lynne who later became my wife. Back to "Casper." One night we were working late and when Lynne went to her car, she said Casper had followed her. She heard his footsteps following her in the gravel lot, she drove to the front of the FBO, and came running in and was terrified. "Casper followed me to my car!" I said he must want to go home with you. I said, "I didn't mind if he moved in with us, do you care if he does?" She thought for a moment and decided that it was all right with her, so we decided to invite him into our home, he accepted the invitation. Soon we noticed that he was up to his old tricks. Quadraphonic Stereo was all the rage, and he would go around the room and shut off one speaker at a time, it was things like this that he would be doing, he would reset the alarm clocks and get us up in the middle of the night, annoying but not causing any damage. It was an interesting experience.

As we moved from place to place, he moved with us, and he would go back to the airport daily. He stayed with us after we left Miami. The only time he actually appeared was in Gatlinburg, Tennessee. We had rented a cabin for Christmas week; it was a few miles from town on the side of a steep mountain. Another couple went with us, they had gone to bed upstairs and I had fallen asleep on the couch while I was watching a movie. Lynne was asleep in the downstairs bedroom. I woke up in the middle of the night and saw a figure in a military uniform walking past the kitchen window. The next morning, I looked out the window and it was about a twenty-five-foot drop to the ground. The back of the cabin was on stilts, only the front porch was touching the ground. So, it would have been impossible for any person to have walked past the window.

For the first few years Lynne and I were together, it was difficult for her to understand how anyone could grow up and not have the ability to deal with such a lack of emotional feelings, a lack of trust in people and most of all not understanding what most people's home life was actually like. In my house, it was a constant battle, arguments would go on for weeks and it was absolutely the last place I ever wanted to go. Each time one of these situations came up, Lynne would explain how most people would feel or react to a particular situation. It was very hard for me to tear that wall down; it was one brick at a time. I learned later, as a result of this, I had not learned or possessed the normal emotions and feelings that most people have, all that I had was hate and rage. That mental wall was impenetrable, with the exception of a very few people who I allowed to come in.

We moved across the street to apartments located on a lighted golf course. It was much larger and very comfortable, until a golf ball came through the window in the shower while I was using it, and the golfer requested his ball back. Then one evening. I heard a rifle shot just outside our back-sliding glass door. I saw a person running away from where I was standing on my deck. The next day, we learned that the shooter had picked the wrong apartment, he was two units off, we were two units the other way. Screw the lease, we moved out within a week.

Then we moved to an even larger apartment adjacent to Loch Lomond, the very exclusive neighborhood in Miami Lakes. Our immediate neighbors were George Roberts (Miami Dolphins kicker) Mike Kozlowski (defensive back), across the street in Lock Lomond were State Senator, Florida Governor, and U.S. Senator Robert Graham, Harry Casey – KC and the Sunshine Band, Jimmy Conners, and Don Shula just to name a few. Many of the '72 undefeated Dolphins were scattered throughout that neighborhood. We got to know many of them at a Miami night club in Miami Springs, it was about a thirty-minute drive from Miami Lakes, and Manero's restaurant in Hallandale is where they all seemed to congregate.

As a side note, one of the Christmas trees that my wife and I started was on our first vacation together; it was our "Travel Tree." Every time we went on a trip, Lynne would get an ornament from our destination. To this day, I have continued that tradition, it is my "Memories on Branches" tree. It has grown to become a 6 ½ foot tree and there is not a single branch that does not have an ornament on it. I currently put that tree in my office, that's where I spend most of my time. I also have four other trees that go up each year, a "Lodge Tree," an "Antler Tree," an "Airplane Tree," and an outside tree that is done with typical ornaments.

By this time (early 1973), Exxon had replaced Esso, and Exxon had us on a ration of 60% of what we had purchased the year before, that was not acceptable, for our business was growing quite rapidly, but Exxon would not budge. I explained we were not like the corner gas station that could just close when they ran out of fuel, we were open 24 hours a day and were serving more and more aircraft than we did in the previous year. So, I was forced to go outside and purchase fuel wherever I could find it. As it happens, I made a deal with Delta Airlines in Palm Beach that I would purchase all the fuel they had been allocated for flights that were cancelled. When that reached 7,500 gallons, I would send a truck to pick it up and pay them a premium for their product and send a nice tip to their dispatcher.

As it would happen, the Exxon rep showed up at the end of the month while a delivery truck was unloading, and another was waiting to unload. He went ballistic for us to be putting unbranded fuel through their trucks. I was putting it into the Texaco fuel farm that came with Hangar 101 that Mr. Hart had purchased. We had long since used up our monthly fuel quota from Exxon. He demanded to know where we got the fuel and I refused to tell him, but it just happened to be an Exxon product. He told me that Exxon was going to take us to court, and I told him to get in line. I'm sure the judge would be pleased to hear how giant Exxon was refusing to sell product that was in Port Everglades, giant Exxon not servicing a contracted small business customer. Furthermore, there was nothing in our contract that covered this situation. Their refusal to sell their product and the customer going on the black market to purchase it elsewhere. Actually, this was an artificial shortage; the tanks in Port Everglades (just east of runway 9L at Ft. Lauderdale International Airport) were filled to capacity. Those tanks had floating tops and when you flew over the port you could see they were all full and there were several tankers offshore waiting to unload. However, our next contract with Exxon did contain clauses that product purchased from sources other than Exxon Corporation could not be dispensed through their fuel farms or their branded leased trucks.

At the beginning of this shortage, many FBO's would limit the quantity that each type of aircraft could purchase. I heard that Warner Brothers' Gulfstream was limited to 500 gallons in Miami, which wouldn't even get them to Jacksonville. I placed a call to their flight department and offered to provide them with as much jet fuel as they needed, but it would be at retail and if we found out that they were using any airport from Palm Beach to Miami, then the deal would be terminated. Their Chief Pilot said he would have to get in touch with their corporate office and would get back to me either way. He called back in about two hours and gave us their arrival time. They would take as much as 10,000 gallons in a 24-hour period. That amount of fuel was challenging for me since we were still COD with Exxon when they would sell it to us. That year the Warner Brothers jet set was going to Barbados, so they would come from Burbank, on to Barbados, back to us and on to Burbank; virtually nonstop, they had two crews to maintain this pace. They were tremendous customers, we even set up a bedroom just for them upstairs in the terminal because they did not want to waste twenty minutes getting to the Mimi Lakes Inn and checking in. The catering we did for them was fun too, they would tell us how many passengers they had and the time of their departure, the menu was up to us. They were tired of sandwich and vegetable platters. We would get them pizzas, fried chicken, rib roast dinners, cold seafood platters, anything we could think of that would be different, since the cost was no object. Speaking of catering, McDonalds' G-II came in one evening for a morning departure and they ordered 25 egg McMuffins for their breakfast catering.

Not long after the fuel shortage was over, we got a call from Minneapolis asking if we could hangar a BAC 1-11 mentioning that they would be requiring office and shop space as well. A BAC 1-11 is a full-size airliner similar to a DC-9. We asked how long they would need the space for and they said they wanted to base with us, providing we could accommodate them; and since we had the only hangars in the South Florida area that could handle their aircraft, we told them sure, no problem. They asked what the costs would be, we told them we would get back to them, as it required us to know what their estimated monthly fuel usage would be in order to give them a firm quote. Then we set out to find out what the size of the aircraft was, it's dimensions, and fuel capacity, and it turned out that we could handle it. About a week later, they showed up on our ramp.

The owner of MAC went crazy because we had to terminate our relationship with a piston twin that flew once a month to make room for the BAC 1-11. He told me that no company in Miami could afford a plane like that, and it wouldn't be here more than a few months. My response was it will generate more income in one month than the piston twin had been generating in a year. The BAC 1-11 stayed for over five years. Their typical trip was to go to New York every Monday morning and return from southern California every Friday evening. We rented their space out all week to transient aircraft for additional income. On their weekly return, they would have enough "extra" catering for all of our employees that were on duty, and a bottle of Champaign to go with the catering for the crew, Lynne and myself. We would have "dinner" on board the plane as it was being put into the hangar.

Shortly after the BAC 1-11 moved in, we got a call from a Hangar One customer who had a Falcon 20 and a MU-2 asking if we had room for them plus two BAC 1-11's. That took some real hangar management, but we couldn't pass up that opportunity. So then, we had three BAC 1-11s in one half of our south hangar. Ralph Morales was my Line Manager and was a master at stacking the hangars. That took some real skill to get them all in at the same time. The owner of the two BAC 1-11's was Roy Carver, a billionaire. Roy was originally from Muscatine, Iowa, not far from where I was from, and because of that connection, we easily became friends. He owned the Carver Pump Company, which was the pump that sat atop the Hughes drill bit that was used for drilling oil wells. In addition, he owned the Bandag Tire Company, a cold recap process for tires, which are used on trucks. He also had a major interest in two banks, and he underwrote the Miss America Pageant for several years. In addition to his aircraft, he had two yachts (one foot longer that Aristotle Onassis's) and two penthouses, one on Miami Beach and the other in Cannes France, and that is where his second yacht was docked. Not to mention his mansion that was in Muscatine, Iowa.

Roy was quite a character. He always had a slide-rule in his top shirt pocket, sometimes it was in his top pajama pocket, and he flew the Falcon solo many times. That aircraft required a two-person crew. On one particular trip returning from Muscatine, Opa-locka was fogged in and he made several missed approaches before landing, we were still below minimums. When he taxied to our terminal the two FAA inspectors were waiting for him in the lobby. When he came in, he asked them to wait a few minutes, he needed to make a phone call. He asked if he could use the phone in my office, I said of course you can; he asked me to please stay in the office. He proceeded to dial a number from memory and requested to speak with Dick. He told him that two of his FAA inspectors were about to give him a tough time and to please handle it. Within five minutes, another FAA inspector came into the lobby and advised the first two inspectors that this investigation was over. It turned out that the "Dick" he had called was actually President Nixon. I asked him how he was able to get that response, and he told me he had donated $50,000.00 to the Republican Party. I asked what would have happened if Humphry had won, and he responded that he also donated $50,000.00 to the Democrat Party. We would have Roy over for dinner occasionally and just chat. One evening he told us that he believed we were his only loyal friends, he believed that the other "friends" were just trying to get their hands into his pockets. That really meant a lot to us. Roy passed away while on a fishing trip in Belize, what a way to go!

Three years later, my front desk employee, Michael was hired by Air Jamaica as a pilot; just before he left, we flew to Clearwater. The only time he was on course or at our assigned altitude was when we were passing through them. Then he was lining up for landing for Tampa International, not Clearwater where he had filed and was talking to. I let him get within about five miles of Tampa when I told him that he was lined up for the wrong airport.... Just to think that Air Jamaica had hired him as a pilot!

By mid-1973, we had the hangars packed and the front ramp area was full. There was a Boeing 720 (a version of the 707) based with us on the front ramp, it was Cavanaugh Communities plane that was used every weekend to fly potential land and home buyers to Florida's west coast. Also, we hangered Context Communities Gulfstream 1 which also flew every weekend, for their potential land customers. Our lobby was really full-on Saturday mornings. There were also four Convair 990's (same size as a DC-8) on the back ramp. By this time, Customer Service was actually becoming a very profitable part of the FBO, we were actually supporting the whole company. Fuel sales had grown from about 350,000 gallons a year when I became the Manager to 1,200,000 gallons in annual fuel sales. Gallons sold, is the measurement used to determine the strength of an FBO.

Another Hangar 1 customer came in to try our service; he was based in Venezuela and had a Falcon 20. He needed some maintenance and requested hangar storage. When he was departing for the first time, he put his brief case on the counter, which was full of $20's and I happened to be working the counter at that time. He said that he did not understand US dollars only Venezuelan B's, just take what I needed. As I recall his bill was just under $30,000.00 so I took out as close to the total as I could, he said thank you and I said wait a minute, you have change coming. His son told me much later that had been a test, and he did understand dollars. As time went on, we became good friends with Gustavo and his entire family. We were living in Miami Lakes at that time and their entire family purchased a cull-da-sac in the Country Club of Miami, adjacent to Miami Lakes. Both my wife and I would run into the family members at the Chevron station or Publix quite often. They were always very pleasant to us. As it turned out Gustavo was the Godfather of Venezuela. I mentioned to him that my wife and I were going to be in Caracas in the coming week, and we would be in there on Tuesday. He gave me his card and asked if we were arriving on the cruise ship, I told him that we were, and he said we must have lunch with him, to just give him a call when we arrived, to which I said we would do that.

When the ship arrived and was cleared by customs, an announcement was made that all passengers could go ashore, Mr. Blackford please report to the Purser's office, all I could imagine was something bad had happened at work. When we got to the office, where we were told that our transportation was waiting shipside, and we should depart via the aft gangway instead of the forward one. The rest of the passengers had to walk about a block uphill to get to their buses and cabs. At the aft gangway, waiting for us was the longest Mercedes limo I have ever seen, and our driver/guide spoke very good English and asked where we wanted to go, while relaying that the only stop we had to make was to be at the Tomanico Hotel at noon. I told him that this was our first time in Caracas, and that we would rely on his judgement.

He took us through the government buildings and into the congress building, where we were escorted to the balcony, in the center of which lay a glass enclosed box – that was built for Gustavo. Then we went on to the racetrack and toured the center of the city. When we arrived at the hotel, we were greeted by the hotel's general manager, who guided us into a private dining room. Gustavo had his entire family there: wife, three grown children, his mother, his brother, and his entire family. It was quite a gathering! And the highlight of the gathering was the chef rolling in an entire roast pig for lunch. Some Lunch! After lunch, we were taken to a glass factory, followed by more touring of the city. When we got back to the ship, we were driven onto the pier with direct access to the aft gangway. My! How the other passengers were impressed! For the next few days as we walked around the ship, we could hear them whispering among themselves as to who we were and how did we get to have a limo pick us up shipside. We really ate all that attention up!

Several members of the Royal Air Force came into the FBO to rent a car. Through the rental process they indicated that they were off an aircraft carrier that was anchored about two miles offshore. In jest, I asked if I could fly out to the carrier and make a landing, they said sure, they would inform the ship's controllers that I would be making an approach and landing in a Cessna 150. I took off, located the ship, and lined up for landing; the ship was gently rolling at anchor, but I had the lights and clearance to land. The closer I got the shorter the runway looked, and I didn't have a hook to catch the retaining cable. I chickened out, and went around and returned to the airport. In hindsight, it's a good thing I did, I don't know how I could have taken off from that short of a runway. They would not have been able to launch me, there was no connection point on a C-150.

That didn't even occur to me because I was so excited about landing on an aircraft carrier. It was a thrilling experience anyway. Many years later, when I was actually on three aircraft carriers, I noted how slick the runways were from the jet fuel residue. As it turned out, it was a good thing that I chickened out.

A Jetstream (a medium sized turbo prop aircraft) arrived one evening, and when the cabin door opened the marijuana smoke just poured out and so did Loggins and Massena. They were probably going to Criteria Recording Studios (more about Criteria later). I asked the crew how they could fly under those conditions; they told me they were on oxygen for the entire flight. We began to have more and more famous people fly in to use the Criteria recording studio, it was located in North Miami. We also got some traffic for Ivan Tors Productions in North Miami Beach. They produced Flipper, Sea Hunt, Gentle Ben, and Science Fiction Theatre.

For the first few years at Miami Aviation, Lynne and I were working so many hours that we ate out almost every evening. One of our favorite restaurants was Manero's, we ate there at least once a week. It was located on the intra-coastal waterway in Hallandale. They were famous for their steaks; the meal came with a shrimp cocktail, garlic rolls, a gorgonzola dinner salad, and an entrée; a potato and a Crème-de-Minth parfait. The cocktail sauce on the shrimp was fifty percent cocktail sauce and fifty percent horseradish. It was a light pink in color and would clean your sinuses for about a week. That sauce was addictive, after about a week you would start craving another one of their shrimp cocktails. It was quite amusing to watch people who had not eaten there previously, take their first bite. Their expression was priceless, and they would gulp down vast amounts of water that would do nothing to lessen the bite of the sauce, but the garlic rolls would do the trick.

Manero's was also the "winter office" for the Godfather of Quebec. He would hold "court" from the back corner round booth located in the bar. It was always very interesting to meet the rest of your party in the bar and spend some time in there, watching the procession of people walk up to him, and have a quick conversation, then depart. Manero's was always very busy and a wonderful place to see who was in town. The Evinrude family and Frances Langford were frequent guests, as was Howard Cosell, who would pour ketchup on his filet. One night, he was seated at the table next to us, and I actually witnessed that tragedy.

There were many other regular customers, including the Dolphins. Manero's took a storeroom and remodeled it into a dining room just for them; they could get, shall I say, rather rowdy. It had large Leroy Neiman type oil paintings on all the walls depicting the 1972 undefeated team, synthetic turf instead of carpeting, and French doors, which they kept closed to keep the noise down in the main dining room. On very busy nights, we would be seated with the Dolphins in their private dining room. We ate there so often, all year-in and out of season, we got to know the entire staff and started receiving special treatment, where we took advantage of not having to wait in a line that would stretch around the building on busy nights, including one New Year's Eve. As we were walking in, we passed our next-door neighbors, however, we were in a rush and did not notice them. We just wanted to get to Bill the Mature d' to get our name on the list. Our neighbors noticed that we did not come back out and get in line, because we had been seated immediately; it pays to be a year around regular customer. I even got a tour of the kitchen and was given the recipe for their famous cocktail sauce. Unfortunately, they are no longer in business and the building is gone, a tall condo exists in its place now. By the way, I still make their cocktail sauce.

One evening, while driving back to Miami Lakes after having dinner at Manero's, we stopped at the airport, just to see what was happening. As we rounded the corner and could see what was parked in front of the terminal, to our amazement it was a United Air Lines

727 and over a hundred passengers were standing in front of the

building and in the lobby. TV crews were on site with their live reporters. They were scheduled to land at Miami International and they were talking to Miami's tower but were lined up for landing at Opa-locka. Miami Tower cleared them to land, thinking they were lined up at MIA, but they landed at Opa-locka.

The passengers were quickly taken to Miami and the plane was flown out the next day. There were several times when an airliner would be lined up to land at Opa-locka instead of Miami, but they always figured it out in time to correct their error. In their defense, Ft. Lauderdale, Opa-locka, and Miami International all had the same runway configuration. During the day, it was easy to tell the difference, however, at night, with just the runways lit, and the bright lights on Miami Aviation, the Coast Guard and Hangar One's hangars, it was more difficult to tell which one you were lined up on, especially if you had cancelled IFR flight following so the controllers were not watching you very closely.

After a particularly rough flight through South Florida's summer thunderstorms, a regular customer in a Jet Commander landed; Mr. Vandorn, who must have been in his 80s by then. He was the only passenger, and when a crew member opened the door, Mr. Vandorn emerged amongst the mess inside, soda and beer cans rolled out onto the ramp, trash from the catering, etc. was strewn throughout the cabin, and his only words were "ride 'em cowboy." The crew was very relieved that he had his seat belt fastened securely and was fine, and in especially good spirits. That was one of the lighter moments at the airport.

Much to our surprise, J. Edgar Hoover arrived with Mackle Brothers on return of their kidnapped daughter, Barbara Jane Mackle on a Gulfstream II, on loan from Gulfstream Corporation (another Gulfstream on our ramp). Deltona had a Jetstar-8, two King Air 90's and a Cessna 182 that were based with us in the same hangar that housed the three BAC 1-11s. Mackles founded the Deltona Corporation. Their site planner, Ralph Gleason was an office tenant in the other hangar (more on him later). They were major planned community developers in Florida. Among others, they developed the city of Deltona, Marco Island and twelve other communities. Barbara Jane was a kidnap victim and buried alive. The kidnappers took Barbara, buried her alive in a box on an isolated hillside in Georgia and demanded a half-million-dollar ransom from her father, Robert Mackle. For 83 hours, the 20-year-old Emory University student remained underground, until the ransom was paid and she was located - dirty, hungry, and cold, but unharmed. Her kidnappers were later on apprehended.

Ralph Gleason had rented a large office on the balcony level in our main hangar, he was the site planner for Deltona's communities. The first night he was working there, he came downstairs and asked what in the hell was going on. I said what are you talking about, and he said that he would put his pencil down and turn around to get a cigarette and when he went back to the computer his pencil would be gone; when he went back to get another cigarette his pack would be gone. I told him that he had just met Casper. He questioned that, and I told him about the ghost we had in the hangar. His response was that must be the Lieutenant that flew into the hangar doors. Ralph was assigned to Opa-locka during World War II and only two soldiers were killed here. One had hung himself in the upstairs bathroom three doors down from Ralph's office and the other was a happy-go-lucky pilot who would fly his plane through all three hangars on Friday afternoons. One Friday, he lined up for his weekly flight and somebody was closing the steel hangar doors on the northern most hangar (Hangar 101). He was committed and could not pull up in time to avoid the crash. Ralph had the duty to inform his wife of the tragedy. Casper was still doing his "thing," nothing serious, just annoying. However, that was the last time Ralph had a problem with items disappearing and then re-appearing.

When Howard Hughes was thrown out of the Bahamas, he didn't have any place to go. For two days, they could not find a country that would allow him to enter. He could not go through U. S. Customs because of all the subpoenas that had been issued against him. His entourage had chartered a corporate Jetstar from Eastern Air Lines to take him from the Bahamas to the country that would accept him. I have no idea how they avoided Customs, but they landed at Opa-locka several times for crew changes and to take on fuel and catering. When he got off to stretch his legs, his entourage surrounded him, and I didn't get to see him, except for the top of his head. They had also chartered a DC-3 to haul his personal effects from the Bahamas to an unknown location. That crew had also come in to take on fuel and catering, after they had been flying for twenty-four hours. They were so exhausted when they came in, that they just asked for a place to park the aircraft, and if we had any lockable storage space available so they could unload the plane and take it back to the charter company. We did have some space and while we were putting his stuff in storage, they opened his desk and pulled out an eighteen-inch metal ruler and said, "Howard would want you to have this." I still have that ruler today. Howard was finally allowed admittance into Mexico.

Two doctors and their wives took off one evening in their Bellanca (it is the only commercially produced plane that had mahogany wings) heading for Chalet Suzanne for dinner. It was located in central Florida and had a private landing strip. Pilots were to circle overhead, and someone would come out and remove the barrier that was installed across the middle of the runway. They didn't circle and with night approaching did not see the barrier until it was too late, they crashed into it on landing; all four passengers were killed.

One of our neighbors at that time were the McBrides. He owned McBride Construction Company, and had just gotten his pilot's license with a Multi-Engine rating. He bought a Cessna 310 (a twin-engine plane) and had a mechanic friend do some work on it, what we would call a shade tree mechanic. After the work was completed, he loaded up his wife, mother and father-in-law and the family dog. I was outside and watched them as they took off, and they barely gained altitude and almost immediately made a steep left turn and crashed into a residential area of Miami Gardens. I could see the flames from our ramp, NTSB discovered that the mechanic had cross-controlled the cables. When you pulled back on the yoke, the plane went down instead of up and when they tried to turn right it went left. He was a very low-time pilot, with that being said, I am not sure any pilot would have figured out what the problem was in time to prevent a crash. One of the most disturbing things about this accident was that they had parked their car in the first space in the parking lot and every morning and evening we had to walk past it to get to our vehicles. It was there for over six months, as there were no immediate relatives left to take care of their personal items. That was the first crash I witnessed, but it was not the last one.

The Amana Corporation had a Sabreliner, Figure 5 – 11 and were regular customers every winter season. George Foerstner was their CEO and our staff, including myself and Lynne, became friends with him and his crew. As time went on, we always had a large bag of Key Limes for him to take home. He would repay the favor with a gift from the Amana Colonies General Store, smoked cheddar cheese, fresh baked sweet rolls, steaks from the meat market, or hams and sausages from the smoke house. Amana is actually a town, Homestead, it is in Iowa near Cedar Rapids; it is a 25,000-acre farm and is a communal society and is made up of various villages. There is a General Store, which is a prominent historic landmark in the village. It served the community with all their material needs that the communal society did not provide, and now has a bit of everything, mainly food products, such as smoked cheddar cheese, bacon, and hams, homemade pickled everything. There is a handmade furniture store – for example if you need a dresser, you choose how it is configured, how many drawers, how many shelves, what wood is used, what color stain, everything. The day when we were there, a young couple was ordering one and they said just like the one on the showroom floor, and the store manager would not accept that, instead they wanted to know what they planned to keep in it and would build it accordingly. The clock shop is also located in the same building, a 19th century handcrafted woolen mill, and of course an appliance factory (Amana Radar ranges, washers and dryers, refrigerators, and freezers, etc.).

After a few seasons, George asked if there was anything special that I would like him to bring and I somewhat jokingly said a Radar Range. On their next trip down, he brought me a certificate to take to their Miami warehouse for a Radar Range. I was quite happy but felt somewhat guilty for asking for such a valuable item. One of the employees of the warehouse said, "Boy you must know some important person in Iowa" and I replied that I was a friend of Mr. Foerstner, the CEO. They didn't believe me, but he had a good laugh at my reply.

Lynne and I were on one of our road trips and we were in the area and stopped by to say hello to George, and he had his secretary give us a guided tour of the villages. At lunch time, we were taken to the "residents" dining room. There were long tables with white tablecloths, and a society member asked what we would like for lunch. We had a choice of three entrees; I chose Swiss steak, and my wife chose a ham steak. It was family style service; all the side items were what was in season and in very large bowls set out along the center of the tables. When our entrees were brought to us, my wife's ham was an entire one-inch-thick center slice, and the Swiss steak was the whole chuck steak. I asked if I could cut off what I could eat, and they could serve the rest to someone else. They said don't worry about it, we'll feed whatever is left to the hogs. One of the older residents worked in the bakery and had made concord grape pies for dessert. It was so good, although I have never had another one, but that alone was worth the trip.

Early one evening, a twin-engine Piper Aztec had just landed and was taxiing to the front of the terminal. We had previously parked a Gulfstream II in front also, but there was plenty of room for both planes (and a lot more) when the pilot of the Aztec applied his brakes – he had none. To keep from running into the G-II he applied differential power (powered up only one engine) and the plane swung around rather violently, and his right wing hit the back of a 1,000-gallon 100LL (octane) fuel truck, ripping much of the plumbing off. His plane came to a sudden stop upon impact. Fuel from the truck ran down the wing, and when it got to the hot engine, it immediately burst into flames. The pilot escaped from the plane with very minor burns, however, the plane and truck were really blazing; they were burning right next to the tower. We parked the fuel trucks in a line under the tower, which was attached to the front corner of the terminal. The controllers, seeing the flames, bailed out of the tower on the emergency ropes, rather than using the elevator or the stairs. The airport fire department arrived quickly and proceeded to dump flame retardant foam on the truck and plane. While all of this was going on, the line employees raced to move the other four fuel trucks from the area. The fuel continued to drain from the broken plumbing and the 3,000 gallons of foam they sprayed on the truck had no effect on extinguishing the fire. One of the fire fighters actually climbed on top of the burning truck and sprayed more foam down the back of the truck where the flames were coming from. (He was later given special recognition for his heroism.) I thought he was crazy, climbing on top of a burning truck!

Then, along came Lieutenant Commander Pell from the Coast Guard hangar located next door. He was holding a coffee can and asked me if I wanted him to put the fire out. I said sure, since the fire department wasn't having any luck. He took a hand full of blue crystals from the can and spread them over the top of the accumulated foam, the fire went out within seconds. I have no idea what those blue crystals were made of, I just know they worked. Fortunately, the truck had just been topped off for the evening so there were no fumes in the tank, only fuel, otherwise, it probably would have exploded instead of the steady burn that actually happened.

Hangar One - Miami Aviation Corp. U.S. Coast Guard

After five years, my employment with Miami Aviation Corporation was cut short by their CFO, who set me up by accusing me of embezzlement. Frank Hart, President of Miami Aviation Corporation, was well known for letting employees go for supposedly misappropriating company funds. On my way out, I told Frank that he was letting the wrong person go, that he should keep looking for the guilty party. I was hired by our competitor on the field, Hangar One. Six months later the CFO at Miami Aviation Corporation was fired for embezzlement! I'm sure you made the correct assumption.

Miami Aviation Corporation 1972 (Notice Full Ramp – Hangars Were Full Also) – Figure 5 – 3

Opa-locka Airport in the early 70's, in 1967 the busiest airport in U.S. – 650,000 total operations; four active runways; 9-Left, 9-Right, 9-Center and 12.

Sabreliner Figure 5 – 11

Convair 990

Figure 5 - 4

Cavanaugh Communities Boeing 720

Figure 5 = 5

BAC 1-11

Figure 5 = 6

Gulfstream II

Figure 5 – 7

Typical Interior of a Gulfstream

Figure 5-8

Jetstar Dash 8

Figure 5 – 9

Leroy Neiman Style Artwork at Manero's Steak House –
Dolphin's Room

Figure 5 - 10

Every day is a second chance.

CHAPTER SIX:
HANGAR ONE
1975 – 1980

Shortly after my departure from Miami Aviation, Marty Sinker hired me to be Customer Service Manager for Hangar One, Opa-locka (Miami Aviation's only competition). Marty, was mentioned earlier, he worked for Eastern Aviation Service as Manager after Len Povey retired. Eastern Airlines sold their only FBO to Hangar One, a small chain of FBOs in the southern states. Marty was then transferred to the Opa-locka location, a much busier base and it had very large maintenance and parts departments that required a strong General Manager. By the way, that deal was negotiated at a Super Bowl game, so those who say that going to the game cannot be a business expense, think again. The previous General Manager was a General in the Army. One day he was just reminiscing and told me that the only way he became a General was that he was always ready to re-locate. It wasn't his talents or training; but he would go to any location where his talents could be put to effective use. That piece of advice stayed with me for the rest of my career.

Hangar One was a much smaller facility than Miami Aviation, it was an all in one building, housing Customer Service, maintenance, a parts department, an aircraft sales area, the Civil Air Patrol, a large parking garage and a paint shop. The hangar was only 40,000 square feet, half of which was taken up by maintenance and the paint shop. There were 45 aviation mechanics plus their back up staff, a really busy shop. The sales department gave hangar space to their customers; I did institute charging the going hangar rate to the sales department for the space they gave away. I didn't have any available hangar storage space. The space that was left was already rented. I couldn't handle the large aircraft anyway; the door clearances were only 100 feet. The backside of the hangar could only be accessed by going down a rough road between the hangar and the fuel storage area, then out onto a street. Those of you familiar with Beechcraft tow pins; well we went through a lot of them. We stored the least active planes back there. The ramp was crowded also, only two rows of tie-down spaces and limited overnight parking for larger planes. For special events, Super Bowls, and Boeing type aircrafts, we were granted permission by Dade County's Aviation Department to use an adjacent inactive taxiway for short term storage.

One night, Line Service was towing a Beechcraft Duke down the road to get into the back of the hangar for storage and a Miami Dade Sheriff's Department vehicle was running without any lights on and it ran right into the wing root and fuselage of a Beechcraft Duke, which is a very expensive twin-engine plane – a pilot's dream aircraft. The Deputy Sheriff ended up issuing four tickets to the driver of the tug who was towing the aircraft. I went with the tug driver to the traffic court and explained the entire event to the judge. The officer failed to mention that he was traveling without any lights on. The judge ended up voiding all the citations and requested a private conference with the Deputy Sheriff after the court was out of session. The patrol car, driving without having any lights turned on, that too on an unlit street, was the turning point in the case. I requested voiding these tickets instead of a not guilty verdict so there would not be any record of this incident on my employee's driving record, he agreed. The county also paid for the repairs and the diminished value of the Duke, due to the extensive repairs that were required.

We were a Citgo dealer when I arrived, I think the only Citgo FBO in the nation and their service was poor to say the least. Our largest jet truck was a reconditioned home heating oil truck. The first time we used it, the single point hose blew out. I had made a deal with them that when we reached a volume of 100,000 gallons a month, they would replace all our trucks. When that time came, they said that they had no recollection of agreeing to that. Soon thereafter, we became a Phillips 66 aviation dealer, widely known as the best in the industry. Marty was a Phillips dealer in Ft. Lauderdale and had served their aircraft on a regular basis. So, that was a no-brainer.

Shortly after I went to Hangar One, Marty arranged for Murray Smith, the founder, owner, and publisher of *Pro Pilot* magazine to tour our facility. Pro Pilot serves the corporate and regional aviation industry, including pilots, managers, and dispatchers. Marty's only comment to me prior to his visit was that all he wanted to see from line service was asses and elbows. Murry and I got along immediately, as if we had been friends for years, it was then that he gave me the nickname of Blackie Bilford; hence, my email address is bbilford @___.___. Murray is responsible for many FBOs going from turnpike gas stations for airplanes to being in the hospitality business. He started a nationwide annual survey of FBOs. Ranking them by combining several categories; facilities, line service, customer service, etc. and having professional pilots do the voting. This put a sense of competition into the mix, who is number one, who are the FBOs in the top twenty. As the survey has evolved over the years, more categories have been added, thereby, creating more number ones, and so on. The entire general aviation community looks forward to the annual survey results.

There were two flight school tenants at Hangar One in addition to our own. One was Tursair, owned and managed by Don Chalmers, they catered to a more personal approach in their teaching techniques, the other catered to Spanish students. The county installed some security fencing and a rolling gate located at the vehicle entrance to the ramp area. The leading edge of the gate had a jagged bar instead of the normal smooth round pole. Timing on the gate was such that it allowed only one vehicle at a time to enter the ramp. This was noted by a large sign, posted on the gate, however, shortly after the gate was installed, Mr. Chalmers tried to enter immediately behind another vehicle. The gate began to close while his Mercedes was in the path of the gate, resulting in his vehicle having the shit beat out of it, a few holes, and a lot of deep scrapes. He was rather angry and while screaming at me about the damage and telling me that Hangar One was going to pay for the repairs, he was actually jumping up and down. He was known to have quite a temper, and while this scene was going on in his lobby, his artificial leg flew across the room, and he landed on his ass. Everyone in the immediate area was trying to contain their laughter, but not all were successful – including me. The outcome was that his insurance paid for the repairs, not Hangar One.

A few years after the Bellanca crashed at Chalet Suzanne's restaurant, an Eastern Airlines Pilot, George Sullivan who was a Hangar One tenant, with over 30,000 hours flew his twin engine sea plane (Figure 6-2) up there, and extended the landing gear down; he attempted a water landing and didn't return either. (You don't extend your gear for water landings.) Chalet Suzanne has been closed for some time now.

During the 1970's artificial fuel shortage, President Carter had issued an Executive Order stating that any facility selling fuel could not discriminate on who they sold fuel to, providing they had proof of an acceptable method of payment. They could limit the amount of fuel they sold to customers if it was uniform and based on vehicle or aircraft type. There was only one time that I called the Sherriff's Department, we had a free-lance flight instructor, Ted Robbins conducting a flight ground school in our lobby one evening. We had our own flight training operation as well as two tenants who paid a considerable amount of rent to conduct flight training on our leasehold. I requested that he leave the property and he refused and told me he was a fuel customer and since we were open to the public, he had every right to be there. I explained that the public was welcome until they were asked to leave, then they were no longer welcome; so, consider yourself asked.

Fortunately, the officer who came was also a pilot and understood what was going on; it was not like Ted described the situation, just a de-briefing after a flight. This instructor had all his training props strewn all over the tables in the lobby. De-briefing, no way according to the Sheriff; he is running a ground school. Ultimately, he was arrested and taken to the lock-up. After depositions, we went to court and the judge found him guilty of trespassing and sentenced him to fourteen days in jail. He argued with the judge about his guilt, not a smart thing to do. The judge explained that it was just like someone going to McDonald's and selling ham sandwiches in McDonald's' dining room. The sentence was revised to six months in jail, and the judge asked the defendant if he now realized that he was guilty, and he could not conduct his flight school in Hangar One's or any other FBO's lobby when he was released, to which he did not respond.

One summer afternoon with an approaching thunderstorm, a bad one, Ted tied his plane down on the unused taxiway that we had used for special events. During the storm, one of the tie-down rings came out of the pavement and Ted's plane was damaged. He threatened to bring a lawsuit against Hangar One for the cost of the repairs of his plane, since it was on an area that we had used from time to time. He tied it down, not a Hangar One employee, on county property – not in our leasehold, he believed we should be held responsible. That is what it was like dealing with him. Oh, the joys of being the Customer Service Manager.

A long-time friend of Marty's was Upjohn's Chief Pilot, Virgil Williams, they were based in Kalamazoo, Michigan. He arranged to bring his flight crews and planes to Florida for an annual re-current training week, every February. This was done in Ft. Lauderdale until Marty transferred to Opa-locka. The first year it was scheduled for Opa-locka he brought Marty a case of wine matching what President Ford had served at a State Dinner in the White House. It was my turn to host the "monthly" supper club, which consisted of four Hangar One's employees and their wives, and Marty brought that case of wine. Eight of us polished off the case of wine, it was all from a Michigan winery, and very good! It was during the disco era, and after dinner the dancing began, even the grandfather clock found a partner. Oh, What a Night! Our neighbor called the police to complain about the noise coming from the next building. However, the noise they heard was actually bouncing off the next building, so the police went there, not to my townhouse. Lucked out again!

About this time, a Dade County Aviation Department employee, Alvey, assigned to Opa-locka became comfortable enough to have private discussions with me in my office. He never felt "at home" when I was at Miami Aviation, he just went about his business at MAC, but never opened up about his psychic abilities. He claimed he was only a healer, not a medium to contact people on the other side. There are so many examples of his abilities that made him believable; I will just mention a few of them here. At that time, my wife's parents were both quite ill and in the hospital in upstate New York. He would give Lynne almost a daily report of what was happening to their health. He was correct 100% of the time, both passed away within days of his prediction.

We had a new line service employee that happened to walk past my office, Alvey immediately got chills and asked me if he could speak with him, privately. I gave him my permission, provided that the employee wanted to speak with him. To make this as short as possible he gave him a phone number in California and said his sister was anxious to get in touch with him. He replied that he was an only child. When he went home after his shift, he relayed this to his parents. They told him for the first time that he was adopted, and that he very well may have a sister. He called the number that Alvey had given him and found out for the first time that he did in fact have a sister. Also, he predicted that he would soon be diagnosed as a diabetic, and his body was still producing insulin, but the delivery system had a kink in it, and surgery could correct the problem. A month later his prediction came true, and his doctor put him on twice daily insulin injections. I don't know if he went ahead with the surgery because he found another job.

Alvey and his wife came over to our home for dinner one evening. After dinner, we were having coffee and I asked if I could take a picture of them. They were seated on the couch, I had a Polaroid camera, so we had the print in sixty seconds. On the wall over Alvey's head there appeared to be a ghost image similar to an Egyptian dog's head coming out of the wall behind him. He couldn't give us an explanation of the appearance of that surreal image. That gave me more confidence in his physic abilities. He could make headaches disappear by holding his hand close to, but not touching, your forehead for about thirty seconds. He had me feel his hand after he did that procedure on me, it was incredibly hot.

My personal interaction with Alvey was when he came into my office one evening and was not acting in his usual laid-back manner. I asked him what was wrong, and he said that one of the few times he had a message from the other side, and it was for me. I was sure what it was going to be about, and I was correct. He said my mother had contacted him and wanted him to relay a message on her behalf. She wanted me to know how deeply sorry she was for the way I had been treated by herself and my father and would I please forgive them for what they had done. I told Alvey that if he was ever in contact with her again to please relay this reply to her; that apology was not accepted, and I would never accept an apology from them. They had abused me for so many years and that an apology wouldn't even begin to make up for the way I had been treated. As time went on, Alvey remained silent on that subject and I didn't press for an answer as to whether he had been in contact with her again. The most amazing thing about this is that I had never told him about my early home life.

Hangar One's sales department received an $80,000.00 cash deposit for a new King Air 200, late on a Friday afternoon. He had the cash in a large paper grocery bag. We immediately called our bank and asked them to stay open until we could get there with the cash, they said NO. We then hired off duty Sheriffs to sit in the accounting department behind locked doors, where our safe was located, until Monday morning when the bank opened. Too many people found out about the cash that we had taken in and that the bank would not stay open for us. At the end of this story, the purchaser never returned to pick up his aircraft. We waited for several months before we used that deposit money to do an extensive refurbishment of the facility. The results of the refurbishment were astounding, even though corporate stepped in about halfway through the project, and ultimately, we got used to some of the colors and designs that were forced upon us in the final stages of the project. It was still such an improvement in the facility that our regular customers and employees were very pleased with the results.

Some of our notable transient customers arrived to go to Criteria Studios, which became very famous in the recording industry; Criteria's clients amassed over 250 Gold and Platinum recordings. Their operation was based in North Miami and Opa-locka Airport was the closest airport to their operation. Chad Hunt (worked for Dumor Avionics, which was based with us) was the actual inventor of the first 32-trac recording equipment for Criteria, they were the only studio in the world to have such sophisticated equipment. They made recordings for Atlantic Records along with many other labels; Bee Gees and 87 other famous artists such as: Fleetwood Mac, ABBA, AC/DC, The Allman Brothers, Aerosmith, Beach Boys, Billy Joel, Bob Dylan, Chicago, and the Eagles. Many of these performers used the airport; it was usually just in and out, for a day or two.

Back to Chad, one of his most remarkable aviation related feats involved a new Super King Air 200. Hangar One delivered the new twin engine turbo-prop aircraft, (not the one that was never picked up) and occasionally during a flight, when the autopilot was engaged, the plane would go into radical climbs, dives and turns. Our maintenance department and Dumor Avionics could not locate or duplicate the problem, so the plane was sent back to the factory, and they could not find the cause for this erratic behavior. The auto pilot equipment checked out perfectly when it was removed and tested in the lab. They sent it back and once again, the problem occurred shortly after the factory indicated the plane was fine. Late one evening, Chad was still on duty (not unusual for him), he came into my office and asked for the keys to this King Air. He told me he was going to go out and have a discussion with the plane. I looked at him with a curious expression on my face but understanding Chad, I gave him the key without hesitation, and out he went, to have his discussion with the plane. The next morning, he requested that our maintenance department remove one of the folding tables that was attached to the side panel. Sure enough, when one of the folding tables had been installed by the interior department at the factory, they had put a screw through a bundle of cables. When the vibration in the aircraft was just right, it would short out the autopilot. Problem discovered and solved.

We got word that Bob Hope was on inbound as a passenger on Mrs. Paul's (fish sticks) Learjet and he was coming to town to do a charity show at Miami Beach. On landing, the crew said it was the hardest flight they had ever had. All the way from New York, Bob kept them in stiches; they could barely stop laughing long enough to talk with the various center controllers. Bob stopped on our porch and asked the linemen if they would be at the show, and they told him that they would be working, that I wouldn't give them the night off. He said that's not right, and he proceeded to do his complete show for them, from our porch. His handler tried to get him into the limo because he was already late for a news conference, and his reply to him was, "I'm Bob Hope, and they will wait till I get there." By the time he finished the impromptu performance, almost all Hangar One employees were in attendance as well as many others from around the airport and folks that arrived on inbound flights. It was quite an event to be sure, our own private performance by Bob Hope!

Southeast Banks had purchased two King Air 200s from Hangar One, but they were purchased at the Atlanta location, however they were hangered at our facility. Their Chief Pilot, Bob Mulligan was a pain in the ass to all the employees at Opa-locka, always demanding special treatment. One afternoon he came into my office and told me that the next day he was going to have a "very special passenger" on board their plane and he wanted the entire Line staff that was on duty to meet the plane when it arrived. As it would happen, I was the only one available to meet the plane. When he opened the cabin door, he questioned me as to why I was the only one to meet him since he had requested that I was to have the entire staff there to help. I told him that since he had not given us any advanced notice of his arrival time, not even a radio call when he was in range, the Line Staff was busy with other duties. By this time his "special passenger" came to the door, it was Don Shula on board, for those who don't know he was the head coach of the Miami Dolphins And... He was my neighbor and called me by name, sorry Mr. Chief Pilot, Don, and I were friends. Southeast Banks had a large financial interest in the Dolphin franchise and on Joe Robbie Stadium; anyway, I asked Don if I could help him with his bag. This is a quote from Don, "Bill, when I can't carry my own bag, you have my permission to kick me in the ass." At least that made me feel good, and for the first time Mr. Chief Pilot was speechless.

The first Boeing 707 that I handled at Hangar One, was the Los Angeles Dodger's aircraft. They came in for a pre-season game. The entire team and coaching staff were the passengers. I got to meet Tom Lasorda; that sure was a good day. Figure 6 - 7

One afternoon, I got a call from the captain on a Boeing 707 whom we had already been communicating with, that they were in the process of filming a movie, *The Pilot,* and would be arriving quite late with just the crew on board. We had the necessary equipment in position (on the outer taxiway) to handle his plane. It arrived after ten, and much to our surprise the "crew" consisted of the entire movie production staff, about fifty people. It took about two hours to get enough transportation on site to get them to their hotels. The next morning Cliff Robertson arrived in his Baron; he was staying in his Palm Beach residence. The other major cast members included: Frank Converse, Diane Baker, Gordon MacRae, Dane Andrews and Milo O'Shea, really a lot of stars of that time. The movie was based on the novel *The* Pilot, it's an enjoyable read. It was about an alcoholic pilot who seeks help in controlling his drinking, not stopping it!

The "stars" trailers (dressing rooms) also arrived that morning and we positioned them in a vacant grass area across the street from the FBO. There were several scenes to be shot in an aircraft lavatory, two of those units were set up in the garage area. It took two mockups to provide the various camera positions that were required.

A catering service had been set up in a small portion of the hangar. Food was provided from dawn to dusk for the movie crew and all our employees. It was truly a "Hollywood" production. We set up in the classroom behind the Maintenance Department, so they could preview the "rushes" that were shot the day before. Lynne and I were requested to be in attendance because of our familiarity with aviation. Lynne and I did make several suggestions to Mr. Earls about the previous day's rushes. The movie was given praise as being the most authentic aviation movie that had been made up to that time. Lynne and I were responsible for a lot of the authenticity. I was also listed in the credits when the movie was completed. The producer, C. Greg Earls, told me that I was qualified to become a member of The Screen Actors Guild (SAG), and I regret having declined the offer.

One of the scenes depicted a crash sequence and there were about one hundred extras (passengers) for that scene in very believable "crash" makeup. After the shoot, many of the extras walked down to 135th street and Lejune Road to catch a bus; those of you who may be familiar with that intersection know it is a busy one. To that point, they were all still in makeup and many passing motorists called 911 to report that there had been an airplane crash at Opa-locka, and the passengers were just walking through the grass to get help. Guess the makeup was very believable.

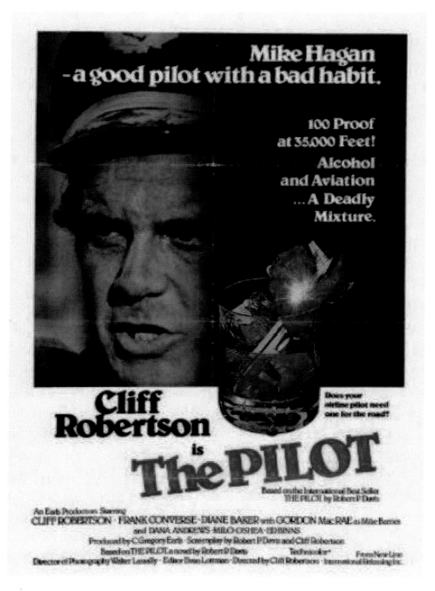

The movie, *"The Pilot"* was actually filmed in 1979. It was kept out of U.S. distribution by the pilot's union, it went directly to Europe and then to HBO. There were two other movies shot at Opa-locka, the *Equestrians* and *Limbo*. The *Equestrians* was shot before I arrived at the airport, and *Limbo* was about the trials and tribulations that the wives of POWs were going through during the

Viet Nam war. They just put fake fronts on two of the vacant buildings and did a few shots on location, not many of those productions were shot at the airport. Miami Vice also used the airport as a backdrop for many shots, especially the area in and around the old Goodyear Blimp Hangar.

About this time, I began to get offers for many management positions; the first one was with Alsage Management, a company that had several Holiday Inn franchises. I was serving them on their Jet Commander. They wanted me to manage one of their hotels; I believe they had the Holiday Inn on 103rd street (Hialeah, FL) in mind. Our discussions never progressed far enough for me to be sure, but my answer was "Thank You for your confidence in me, but No Thanks."

Then the AVITAT, a Premier Exxon dealer in Teterboro New Jersey, flew Lynne and me to see their operation. These facilities have gone away, but they were the first to have several amenities, services, and hours in order to have this designation. The main problem I had with their facility was that it was totally unionized, they had to have designated fuelers, linemen who could only tow aircrafts, baggage handlers, lavatory handlers who could only dump honey buckets, you get the picture; the airport was only 15 minutes from Midtown Manhattan. Each time I declined their offer, they raised their offer, still I could see so many problems with the operation and location that I couldn't accept. I could not imagine living in or near New York City. At that time White Plains was the home base for most of the corporate jets that were based in the New York area. One good thing that came out of this trip was one afternoon we drove to White Plains, New York to call on many of their tenants, some of which were already our customers including RCA, their receptionist made calls to several of the other tenants and asked them to take the time to speak with me. On our drive up to White Plains, Lynne had a map, and was giving me directions. For some reason, I soon disregarded her input, cut through a mall's parking lot, and took numerous side streets. Then a "Welcome to Connecticut" sign appeared on the side of a two-lane road. She said "well you found Connecticut, not White Plains," I replied to her that the airport would appear just over the next hill. That is where it was. I had absolutely no idea how I knew how to get there!

I also got an offer to manage a new facility at Stewart Air Force Base in Newburgh, New York. It was in the process of transitioning from a military base to a civilian airport. It was too far from the city to attract much based or transient business and the town itself was not the most desirable place to take up residence. To this day, there are very few corporate operators located there.

Page Airways (later to become half of Signature, Butler Aviation was the other half, both had horrible reputations within the aviation community) had their home base in Rochester, New York. Their plan was for me to manage two of their many locations; they were going to provide me with a Bonanza to go back and forth. The wage offered was not much better than what I was making in Florida. I didn't believe that I could successfully do the job that needed to be done by only spending half of my time at each location. Both of these bases needed a full-time manager on site.

Signature's corporate office was in Orlando, we were having discussions about employment, but a particular location was not specified, even when I told them that my decision to accept an offer was dependent on my need to know where I would be based. Not only that, but the pay scale was subject to the location that they would decide at a later date, No Thanks!

Disney World had plans for their own airport, they even had architectural drawings of the facility. However, insurance problems arose, the insurance underwriters refused to deal with private planes overflying the Magic Kingdom, so there was no airport for Walt Disney World.

The governing authority requested bids for the operation at the

Aspen FBO and related services, they were not pleased with the operator that was currently in place and a change was going to happen. A bidder was talking to Marty and myself about managing it for him. However, they did not get the contract. I was really looking forward to that one. Marty was becoming well known within the corporate aviation industry, and I was being noticed.

After I had been at Hangar One for about two years, the President of Miami Aviation (the one who had accused me of embezzlement) sent Brian Grothe, the director of his maintenance department, over to Hangar One to see me. Brian and I had been good friends for some time, and the purpose of the visit was to see if I would consider going back to MAC (go figure). At that time, I had taken about 90% of their transient jet business. The replacement for me at MAC was one of their line men, and it wasn't working out very well. For the Super Bowl, at Hangar One we had had 74 jets and MAC had 6. I took immense pleasure in telling Brian not only no, but hell no!

For Super Bowl week, I had reserved every room at Calder Holiday Inn. The down side of the reservation was the thousands of dollars that Hangar One had to pay when we made the deal with them. The good thing was that the deposit was returned in full when all the rooms were rented out. I was very lucky; that we had made reservations for every room. The last room was rented the day before the game. The next closest available room was in Naples. Billy Hulse, who was the President of Hangar One, Inc. came to Opa-locka to see how we were going to handle the anticipated influx of planes. He had doubts that we could handle the number of reservations that we had for the game. We even had several arrivals that had made reservations with Miami Aviation Corporation, the pilots said they believed that they had made the wrong choice based on the number of planes we had 76 versus the 6 at MAC. Some had even ordered catering through MAC. Fortunately, they did bring the catering over before the game ended.

A G-II pulled onto the ramp. As the steps lowered, the CEO of a major corporation was coming down. Mike Wallace. One of the original reporters on "60 Minutes" was waiting for him with mike in hand and the cameras rolling, Mike got the surprise of his career. The CEO had a drink in his hand and tossed it into Mike's face. Mike asked him why he did that, and he responded, "You looked like you needed a drink," and he went on to his waiting limo.

Billy was impressed, as every plane taxied up to the terminal and discharged their passengers at the lobby door, got into their rental cars or Limos, the plane was immediately towed to the remote parking area which I had reserved for the event. For departures, we took the crews and passengers in vans to the remote parking area. The vans were stocked with bags of ice and huge containers of coffee as well as any catering they had ordered. It would have been impossible to tow all the planes back up to the terminal, since 80% of them left right after the game, the remaining planes departed the next morning, and we towed them to the main ramp. That plan worked out really well. I used that plan for several other events that came my way, such as the Olympics and future Super Bowls. A few years after (Brian and Pete) were released from the hospital, Pete and his partner Lenny Boyer opened Pete & Lenny's - it was a large club with a stage, dance floor and even a balcony on three sides. It was located on Commercial Boulevard, just a few blocks from the beach. Pete & Lenny's became the location for several disco TV shows, such as: Disco 77-78-79 and Disco Magic. Their house band was Ecstasy, a terrific band. Some of the many performers were: The Village People, Odyssey, Vicky Sue Robinson, Tavares, Donna Summer, Alicia Bridges, Al Green, KC & the Sunshine Band, just to name a few.

Pete contacted Brian to see if he knew how to get in touch with me, he wondered if Lynne and I would be interested in attending any of the recording sessions, so Brian told him that he could reach me through Hangar One's switchboard. He called and invited us to one of the taping sessions, it was a long evening, but very entertaining. We went to several of those sessions and got to meet many of the disco stars, even a neighbor, Harry Casey (KC and the Sunshine Band), my neighbor. Strange how things work out.

Hangar One was the first facility where I tried out a new idea, we had a girl on the ramp who worked closely with Line Service. Maritza's duties were to direct all transient traffic on and off the main ramp, do a quick clean on all cabin-class planes, this included dumping the ice container(s) dumping and cleaning the coffee jugs and if required do a quick interior pick up. For departure, she was to make sure their coffee and ice were on board and assist with baggage when necessary. Being in South Florida it was especially important that she was bilingual. Over thirty percent of our business was from Latin and Central America. This gave the guys more time to dispense fuel, position planes either into the hangar or park them in the tie down area on the ramp or position them for departure. She was an especially big hit with our Latin American customers. The line guys affectionately referred to her as the "Ramp Tramp," a title well deserved. The biggest problem I had with this idea was the matter of tips. The crew would give the tip to her, she was the first Hangar One representative they saw and the last one they saw. She thought it was meant for her and not to be equally divided among all who were on duty. Line Service thought otherwise.

Late one very windy afternoon, our company pilot taxied in and discharged his passengers, as he was walking into the lobby a gust of wind blew his toupee off his head. He started to chase it as it was rolling across the ramp, I told him to let that ugly thing go. He said, "then I'll be bald," and I said, "Dexter, you are bald, that thing you have been wearing on your head looked awful." That was the last time he wore a hairpiece. Quite honestly, he looked much better without it.

Julian Carroll, Governor of Kentucky was a regular seasonal customer, he flew in the state plane which was an F-27, a very large twin-engine turbo-prop plane, Figure 6 – 6. We became friends due to his regular visits, and on his last trip, when his term expired; he honored me by making me a Kentucky Colonel. I was speechless, which for anybody who has been around me will find very hard to believe, but it's true. That document hangs proudly in my office to this day.

One afternoon when Warner Brothers (my largest former transient customer from Miami Aviation and now a Hangar One Customer) came in for a morning departure, their steward, Tim said he had something to show me. It was his private pilot's license, which was limited to "Twin Engine Jet, Center Line Thrust. The story behind this is that Tim had no previous interest in aviation before Warner Brothers hired him, but after many months of flying with them, he mentioned to the Chief Pilot that he would like to get his pilot's license. The Chief Pilot and his Co-Pilot were both certified flight instructors as were both members of the second crew. So, his flight training began on deadhead (no passengers) flights in the G-II. When Tim had enough flight time and his skills were good enough to take his flight examination, he was ready for his flight test. He had passed the written test, and went to the FAA to take his flight test. After his oral examination, he and his FAA designee walked out of the office and the examiner looked around the ramp and asked where his plane was parked. He responded that it was that G-II parked in front of the FAA building. After the FAA examiner regained his composure, Tim got into the left seat, the Chief Pilot was in the right seat and the examiner sat in the jump seat between them. Tim passed the test and got his license, but he was only legal to fly Gulfstream II's. He did not have one flight hour in any other type of plane. Tim soon went on to fly for the airlines.

Ralph Levitz (Levitz Furniture Stores) had two planes based with us, a King Air 90, which was his personal plane, and a Learjet that was the corporate aircraft. He was planning an extended vacation in Europe, if my memory serves me correctly. Anyway, he kept his Rolls Royce in our garage and requested that I park my car and use the Rolls while he was gone. I responded that I would drive it once a week, and take it around the airport and return it to the garage. I told him that the first weekend that he would be on his trip, Lynne and I had plans to go to Key West, and I could not afford to take his car down there. He asked why, and I told him that I could not afford to pay the hotel rate that I would be charged if I pulled up in a Rolls; he was quite surprised that would happen. My refusal to take his car did not suit him, so he asked me to get in the Rolls and he drove it around for a while. Then he said I bet you have never been in a Rolls before and I replied, "well not in the front seat." He got a good laugh over that and then agreed that my once-a-week exercise of his vehicle would have to do.

At about the same time, State Senator Robert Graham was running for Governor of Florida and he was using his plane daily. It was a Beechcraft Duke, and was based with us. Many afternoons, on his return, he would ask me to go to the owner's lounge with him. What happened that day was that some reporter had asked him a particular question, to which he did not have a previously prepared answer, so he used my debate skills and the fact that our political beliefs were totally opposite, and we would go back and forth until I ran out of responses as to why his beliefs were incorrect and he had crafted an answer for that question. This happened on a regular basis.

He was running against Jack Eckerd (drug stores). On several occasions, they would both be at our facility holding press conferences. Two of the Miami TV stations kept their remote broadcast vehicles in our parking lot.

On Election Day, Senator Graham flew back into our facility and requested that Lynne and I attend his victory celebration at the Miami Lakes Inn and Country Club. I questioned the invitation in that we were Republicans, and he was a Democrat, and I was sure that Lynne and I would be the only Republicans at his celebration.

He replied that this was a command performance, and we would be there. So, we went, and when his victory was called, he took the stage and thanked all those who worked so hard to get him elected, and sure enough he introduced me as the only Republican in attendance, but then he explained what I had done for him, and he was very grateful for my assistance. My only two requests of him as Governor were to keep Florida on daylight time all year and to allow casino gambling in Dade and Broward counties. We all know that didn't happen. By the way, he was also one of my neighbors. His family developed Miami Lakes on a small portion of the farmland they owned. As Miami Lakes grew, there were fewer cattle in the disappearing pastures.

After three years at Hangar One, at the annual company banquet I was quite surprised for the honor to be awarded the Location Manager of the Year for the Opa-locka facility. Then I was called back up on stage, and I received another award, Hanger One Man of the Year for 1977. It just so happened that I was sick that day, I did go to work but I was going to pass on the banquet. Billy Hulse, Hangar One's President was in town for the banquet and had a fit that I was not going to attend the event, he actually ordered me to show up. Later that night I found out why.

After five years, my employment was terminated for not properly handling the cash transactions. Then, it was on to more experiences at Miami International Airport, with a brief stop at Air LaCarte. They were a premier first-class caterer for almost all the international airlines serving Miami, as well as doing the catering for Hangar One and through us, for Air Force One. I was the manager of Lufthansa Airline's account. It was a wonderful experience, but my heart was still with corporate aviation.

One afternoon the owner of Aero Facilities, Nick Silverio (one of two FBOs at Miami International, the other was Butler Aviation, but Aero Facilities was the busiest by far) gave me a call and asked if I would be interested in working for him. The rest is history, back to the corporate aircraft world.

Hangar One 1974
Figure 6 – 1

Hangar One Front Ramp
Figure 6 – 2

Ralph Levitz Airport Car

Figure 6 – 4

Goodyear Blimp Hangar = Used often for Miami Vice Productions

Figure 6 – 5

State of Kentucky's F-27

Figure 6 – 6

Los Angeles Dodgers Boeing 707 at Hangar One's Opa Locka
Location

Figure 6 - 7

To those I may have wronged, I ask forgiveness.
To those I may have helped, I wish I had done more.
To those I neglected to help, I ask for understanding.
To those who helped me, I sincerely Thank You so much.

CHAPTER SEVEN:
AERO FACILITIES, PAGE AERO FACILITIES, SIGNATURE FLIGHT SUPPORT
1980

After I received the call, I had a meeting with Nick Silverio, the owner of Aero Facilities, as it turned out his current Customer Service Manager, Ed Hayes, had made an ultimatum; and Nick had no intention of giving in to his demands. So, he hired me to give him more leverage in his negotiations and he had a ready-made replacement for Ed if it came to that. Instead of becoming the department manager, I became manager of the second shift. Well at least I was back in my world, and I did meet many very interesting people. I was not exactly a welcomed new employee, especially by the Customer Service Manager and his first shift's staff who were very loyal to him. Since I was the only one who was there, who could immediately replace him; he lost all of his advantage against Nick.

One other situation with Ed's employment was that his wife, Bonnie, also worked in customer service as the manager of the front desk. If Ed would have left willingly or not, Bonnie probably would have left also. In the early days, the only thing that did attract business for Aero Facilities aside from being at Miami International was the front desk team of "Bonnie and Maxine." Their reputations stretched well beyond the airport; it seemed to have something to do with the King's Inn, a motel relatively close to their facility on 36th street. One time they even called Lynne to see if she could help them out because they had more crews than they could handle. At that time, Lynne worked for me at the front desk at Miami Aviation. Lynne asked Maxine what kind of help she was looking for and she told her "Just entertain the crews." Lynne passed on the invitation.

Several months after my arrival, the union's local staff were courting the line employees, and they had a vote scheduled to unionize. By then the second shift's attitude toward me had changed dramatically and they confided in me about the upcoming vote. I immediately informed Nick about this. When he confronted Ed about this, he claimed to have no knowledge of these impending actions. Bull shit! Nick and I both believed that was Ed's way to get back at him because of his move of bringing me into the picture. Nick headed off the vote by giving pay raises to all employees that were just a bit higher than the union had promised – and there would be no union dues or meetings that they would have to attend.

One afternoon, I struck up a conversation with a customer who I didn't know (not unusual) and found out he was handling the flights to Cuba for "Cuban Nationals" which departed from Miami. I mentioned to him that going to Cuba was one of the items on my bucket list. He asked for Lynne and my passport numbers. About two months later, he came in again and had the visas necessary for our entry into Cuba. He indicated that my previous association with the State Department, had a lot to do with getting them for us. We went as "Cuban Nationals" on a Boeing 737, it was painted white with a blue stripe, with no logo or indication as to who was operating it; It was registered in the Netherlands. On arrival in Havana, an airplane from the Soviet Union arrived just behind us. There are no jet ways, so all the passengers use air stairs to deplane, those from the Soviet plane were men and were all dressed exactly the same, in all black. They lined up to pick up their luggage from the ramp and carried it into the terminal, all were completely silent and expressionless. Our group went through customs first; and they collected our passports to be returned on our departure. We were assigned to a group of West Germans and were directed to a Mercedes bus.

There was a host who spoke excellent English and of course Spanish and hostess who spoke Spanish and German, both of whom were serving rum and something that resembled Coke. We were on a preplanned tour of the city, we made stops at some gift shops (that didn't have anything except designer items), and a liquor store only Russian Vodka and Cuban Rum were available. I purchased three bottles of Havana Club Rum. While in the business district I looked into a grocery store, a clothing store, both were completely empty and near the end of the tour, Lynne told the host that we wanted to go to the Havana Libre Hotel (formerly the Hilton) and to the "black market" area. He informed us that that was not on our tour, and we couldn't do that.

He lost the argument; we first went to the hotel. The rest of the passengers were held on the bus by very young armed guards that were on the street corner and summoned by the host. We were told that we couldn't purchase anything there, it was just for West Germans. Our Cuban friends in Miami told us that we needed to go to this hotel; as it afforded excellent views of the city. There was no carpeting on the bare cement floors, and of course, Lynne needed the bathroom. There were no toilet seats, an attendant tore off three sections of toilet paper and handed it to her upon her entry. We then went to the top floor (for the views) and entered the bar. An older bartender had tears running down his cheeks, I asked what the matter was. He told us that we were the first Americans to enter since 1953. He asked what we wanted to drink, and I requested Cuban Coffee, he directed us to the restaurant. There were a few "customers" in there; however, none of them had any food in front of them. I asked our host what was going on, and he explained that when actual customers came in, it would appear that they would not be the only ones dining there. When we got back to the bus, the tour passengers that remained on the bus told us, through the hostess, that they believed that we would not be returning.

Our next stop was the "black market" area where we purchased a few locally made items. Then, onto the Tropicana Night Club for dinner and a show. We entered into a rather large lobby area, while looking around, I recognized about ten folks that I knew from Miami, not sure how they got there but we were introduced to the Chief of the US Interests Section, Wayne Smith. During our discussion, he told us that if there were any problems to go the airport, not to the former Embassy building and they would try to get us out. Then to a large open-air dining room, the walls were royal palm trees and we looked up to the sky. After a dinner of fish (not roast pork), we were served a thimble size cup of Cuban Coffee, I requested more, and they brought a regular size cup, and I asked if I could have even more, and they brought me a small pot full of coffee. The servers were laughing, saying among themselves that I would not be able to sleep for a week. They set the table with regular plates, and had torn paper napkins in half and they needed to wash the tableware between courses. As they were hot from the dishwasher after an unusually long wait, we were served the next courses. We were seated next to the center of the stage, which came up out of the floor. As I previously mentioned, the dining area and stage are located outside under the stars. Chandeliers came on overhead cables and there were three stages; one above, the other backed up with the royal palm trees with the orchestra on the upper level. The show was excellent, Las Vegas style, however, we were seated close enough to see that the costumes were truly thread bare.

Then back to the airport for the flight home. We entered the terminal and were ushered into a small room without any windows. They checked our identity and returned our passports. Then into another small room, but this one had a window, and we could see our aircraft about one hundred yards from the terminal; there was a

Jeep type vehicle about halfway between the terminal and the plane with a bank of flood lights and six-armed young military men between us. They let us out of the holding room, one at a time after checking our passports. Then back to Miami. I went to sleep on the flight back, so much for Cuban coffee. We were not sure how Miami Customs would handle our Havana trip since our passports restricted us from traveling to: Cuba. China, North Korea, and North Viet Nam. We followed the aircraft crew into Customs; however, they walked directly through an unmarked door into another room, and then we were the first in line, the first thing the Customs agent asked was how did we like our trip to Havana? Apparently, traveling to Cuba as Cuban Nationals waived the "do not travel" rules. The agent told us that since we were not out of the U.S. for 72 hours, we would have to pay duty for our purchases. I responded that if the duty on our purchases was worth more than I valued them, I would leave them in Customs. The duty was $5.00, which I paid to another agent whose counter was adjacent to the outside door on the arrival level, not wasting any time, we went out to the cab area.

The Aero Facilities terminal building was quite old and run down, it hadn't been updated in over 20 years. Like Opa-locka, it was a left-over WW-II building, the facility was kept clean, but old. The plumbing was in poor condition, a real downer for the people who were using it. Dade county would only grant five-year leases with an option for five more. That was not enough time for a tenant to make any substantial improvements to the property, and Nick certainly didn't. Not only that, but the employees' attitude was not very far removed from being that of a turnpike gas station for airplanes; with virtually no creature comforts for the crews or passengers; there wasn't even coffee available for customers. There was a coffee maker in the line shack where Line Service would make coffee for the planes, and they charged for that and even charged for ice. Their only competitor was Butler Aviation, located adjacent to them. Aero Facilities' situation was just a little better than Butler's small cement block building and tiny ramp, but not by much. Both operations shared a common taxiway into their facilities, so location was no factor in attracting business.

One morning, a corporate Boeing 727 came in and was going to remain overnight, that was unusual, it was parked in an area of the ramp that was rarely used for overnight storage. Sometime during the night, the left main gear broke through the blacktop ramp. It took air bags borrowed from the airlines to lift it up, and place steel plates under the gear and tow it to a stronger area on the ramp.

Another time, one chief pilot of a Gulfstream III requested to have his main tire changed, so line service towed it from the normal parking area to the maintenance area. The job was completed the next morning and there was an area available in which to park it, just where it had been the day before; between two other Gulfstreams. However, this time, one of the planes had departed and another one parked in that area of the ramp. So when the line man with no wing walkers, was towing the plane from maintenance and going for the opening, it was not wide enough, and he ran into the wing tips of the two that were parked on each side of the opening with the wing tips of the one he was moving. Three damaged and grounded Gulfstreams in one accident. Aero Facilities insurance not only had to pay for the wing tip repairs, but for three charter Gulfstream aircrafts until the repairs were completed.

On another evening, a BAC 1-11 was doing a quick turn, no fuel, just dropping off some passengers. He landed rather fast and really had to apply a lot of pressure on his brakes to make the turn-off adjacent to the FBO's taxiway. The brakes were smoking when he came onto the ramp. The pilot went into the terminal, and paid their landing fees and went back to the plane for departure. When he applied normal power the plane wouldn't budge, so he applied 100% power before the plane would move because the brake pads had become so hot that they had actually welded to the wheels. It took several seconds at that power setting before the welds broke loose. The jet blast from this amount of power blew out the large plastic fronts from a four-sided Arthur Treacher's sign across 36th street and blew a motorcyclist off his bike, he was on the perimeter road next to the ramp. Oh, just some more of the joys of working on the ramp.

Mel Fisher is the world leader in historic shipwreck recovery and the source for authentic shipwreck treasure. Mel was a frequent customer (guest) at Aero Facilities; we were more than acquaintances, but not quite what I would consider a friend. One evening when he came in, he slipped a coin in my jacket pocket. I have no idea what it was or what shipwreck it came from, but I'm sure it had some value associated with it. I keep it locked up in my safe.

The owner of Moctezuma Brewery in Mexico City, the producer of XX plus many other beers and Kahlua flew in quite often, as his personal dentist was in Miami. On arrivals in his Gulfstream, the tips for the Line guys were a case each of XX Beer or a quart of Kahlua. I still have several bottles of Kahlua behind my bar. Paco was his captain, and his English was so poor that we even had to file his flight plans for him.

Speaking of unusual tips, on Brach's aircraft it was a five-pound bag of Gummy Bears, when they are fresh, they are so much better. Hershey's would give out large bags of miniatures. Upjohn's tips were a year's supply of One-a-Day multi-vitamins. Of course, left-over catering was usually enough to cover meals. But cash was the most appreciated tip, in fact during the season Line Service would put their paychecks into a savings account and live on their tips. That was rent/ mortgage, utilities, groceries, and entertainment. The tips often exceeded the amount of their paycheck, but that was just in season, during the summer, it was living on their paychecks. The season in South Florida is from Thanksgiving to Easter. Late afternoon, on Easter Sunday, there would not be a single jet on Aero Facilities or Butler's ramps. There were no based aircraft at either FBO. That is one of the advantages of being in business at Opa-locka or Ft. Lauderdale; i.e. the number of based aircrafts that were based there, which could support the operations year-round.

Within a few months, Nick sold out to Page Airways out of Rochester, New York, so the name was changed to Page-Aero Facilities. A few months later Page Airways and Butler Aviation merged to become Signature Flight Support. Now it has become part of the chain of FBOs with the worst reputations in the nation. Signature soon acquired several U.S. and international locations; creating the largest chain of FBO's in the world. Their backer was BBA Aviation, a British held company, with Signature's corporate offices located in Orlando.

Aero Facilities had never sold fuel, they contracted that service to another company, Tursair. When Page purchased the company, that all changed, and for the first time they had their own fuel trucks, and the maintenance problems that came along with them. Page sent five old Jet trucks and one 100LL truck to their newly purchased facility. The trucks were in poor condition, very hard to start, sometimes the PTO (power take off) would not engage, so it could not pump. That was a tough situation for a busy ramp. Line Service would sometimes have to go through all five trucks to find one that would start and pump. The jet fuel farm was located halfway around the airline terminal side of the airport, and the route to the farm required using the interior perimeter road, not a smooth ride. One of the "junk" trucks broke in half, right behind the cab as it was returning from the farm with five thousand gallons of fuel on board. That was an additional thirty-nine thousand pounds; the truck's frame could not handle the extra weight while traveling over the "washboard" interior road. Fortunately, no fuel leaked out of the tank. Another time the line person drove back from the fuel farm with his hand brake engaged, when he got to the ramp, his tires had gotten so hot they started burning. Had to call the Fire Department for that one, flames just under a full tank of jet fuel.

Miami International did not have any storage facilities for 100LL fuel, so they leased a tank mounted on a trailer and parked it on the exterior perimeter road about a half a mile from the ramp. When we needed to fill the 100LL truck, it was a trip down the road and hook up hoses to transfer fuel, thereby, blocking one lane on the interior perimeter road, which was only a two-lane road. To make matters worse, this usually occurred after dark. The line guy, using just a flashlight as there was no overhead lighting, had to connect the two tanks and not over fill the truck. It was quite a tough situation especially since the truck had to park for the transfer directly on the road.

The line personnel were very good at towing aircraft, with a few exceptions, but if they had only worked at Aero Facilities, they didn't know anything about fueling them. Some planes require the fueling to be in a specific sequence to prevent an airlock, others of the same model are over-the-wing fueling, while some require single point fueling. Most planes have four or more fuel tanks; some inboard fuel tanks are considered to be the "mains" while on other planes they are the "auxiliary" tanks. Some pilots will request fuel in the mains only, which tank is that. Older Learjets and MU 2s have a differential limit on how many gallons you can put in only one tip tank before you put fuel in the other one, to keep the plane from actually tipping over. This was a difficult learning experience for these guys.

A regular customer was The Edward J. DeBartolo Corporation's Lear. Eddy was the undisputed leader in the shopping mall industry from the birth of the industry until Edward's death, owning almost one-tenth of all mall space in the United States. He had a great apprehension that he would be kidnapped. Something about his Italian heritage. When his Lear would arrive, we would have two identical limos waiting, they had to have blacked-out windows, and he would choose which one he would ride in. When they were underway, a chartered helicopter would fly over the limos until he reached his destination, usually it was a high-end shopping plaza in Coral Gables. If he had additional destinations on his schedule, the same convoy would be in place.

Another time, a Venezuelan Westwind jet, Polar Beer's plane was in position to depart. As soon as he started to move his left main gear started to retract. The crew was not paying any attention to the line man who was giving the signal for an emergency stop. He then actually pounded on the side of the plane to get the crews attention to get them to stop the plane and get the people off. After an inspection of their hydraulic system, it was discovered that there were some Venezuelan coins that had been placed in the hydraulic reservoir, which in turn had blocked fluid from flowing into the lines that apply the pressure to hold the gear down. It was never determined where the aircraft was located - in Caracas or Miami, when someone put the coins in the reservoir. The plane would have fallen onto its wing tip, if the line man had not noticed this and got them to stop, or the gear may not have extended on the next landing if it made it into the air. There was no damage done to the plane, the coins were removed, the plane was jacked up and the gear was swung, and the plane departed.

After the merger with Signature was completed, things really went downhill in Miami. I was sent on weekends to Orlando International Airport to assist with their "Off Route" charters, for Disney World. Signature had a terminal just for these non-scheduled airline flights on the west side of Orlando International Airport. It was set up just like a regular terminal, complete with ticket counters, a duty-free store, restaurant, and baggage handling capability.

The Signature Operation at this "Off Route" terminal was really difficult to handle; it was only a weekend operation. There would be up to nine airline planes on the ramp at a time, usually they would arrive two or three at a time. For departure, of course, all had different destinations, most were international flights. Signature had hired part-time people, usually off a street corner, very few could actually speak and read English, and they handled the checked baggage. If someone like me wasn't right there as the bags came down the conveyor belt, the bags went on the closest baggage cart. They did not pay any attention to the four-letter abbreviations for the various cities that the planes were returning to. Each baggage cart was tagged with the destination city, but it would not necessarily be loaded with those bags or be loaded on the correct plane.

There were six of their poorly maintained fuel trucks dedicated to serving these aircraft, and the fuel farm was quite a distance from this ramp. You can begin to imagine all of the problems that would have been associated with this operation. One of the managers figured that each truck could deliver 300 gallons per minute, so he figured we only needed 3 ½ trucks to deliver the correct number of gallons on any given day. Therefore, we should send two of the trucks back. He had no concept of what the line was really like, inoperable vehicles, time spent at the fuel farm, three departures within ten minutes, takes more than one truck per plane. So much for the brilliance in the corporate headquarters, for they selected the key people to manage each location.

The one thing that was very helpful to me was that while I was trying to straighten out this mess at MCO (Orlando International Airport) was that Bill Harger, owner of Prestige Jet had been quietly observing me and offered me a job to manage his facility at ORL (Orlando Executive Airport).

IT AIN'T JUST ABOUT PLANES

Habana Aeroporto

Figure 7 – 1

4444444
44

Cuba 1980

Figure 7 - 2

Cuba 1980

Figure 7 – 3

Cuba 1980

Figure 7 – 4

Cuba Tropicana

Figures 7 – 5 & 6

American Embassy Building

Just go ahead and chase your dreams!

And -

Don't wait for Holidays.

To celebrate life!

CHAPTER EIGHT:
PRESTIGE JET
1981 - 1986

Prestige Jet was one of three FBOs at Orlando Executive Airport, and it was the smallest in size and in gallons pumped. There were very few based aircraft, a relatively small hangar and very limited ramp area. They did have one Learjet on a management contract for a customer located in Miami, and a small flight school.

About this time, Lynne and I bought our first house together, a three-bedroom, two bath home in the newly planned community of Bryn Mar. It was in an old orange grove between the two airports, we had the small end lot on a tear drop section in a zero-lot line development. We had twelve orange trees in our back yard. When they ripened, we sold them to Tropicana. That covered our cost for maintaining them all year plus quite a bit extra. We staged several rather large parties under the trees. When they were in bloom that was an extra treat. Round tables with pergola umbrellas, it was quite an elegant setting.

Our ghost, Casper, also made the move with us. After several delays during the construction process, such as having to rebuild the fireplace three times before the brick mason got it right, and the kitchen cabinets along the outside wall had to be replaced the day before closing, just to mention two of the problems. We moved in just days before Christmas (the original move in date was the week before Thanksgiving). We didn't have any of our pictures hung yet, and I had leaned a rather large picture that I had taken of a hot air balloon on the brick mantle above the fireplace. On Christmas morning, during the opening of the presents, Lynne handed me an envelope, there were tickets for a hot-air balloon ride in it. Just as I was opening the envelope, the picture of the balloon literally came flying off the mantle, hit the floor, and the glass shattered. We interrupted the opening session, cleaned up the broken glass, and finished opening the rest of the presents. But the envelope was gone. For some reason, we believed it would turn up, it wasn't in the trash, so we went on with the day. Several months later, a balloon caught fire and crashed killing all three passengers. When we got home from work that evening, the missing envelope was on the coffee table, it contained tickets for the balloon that had crashed that morning.

Some months later, we had a couple over for dinner. When we were sitting down at the table, the lady said that she hadn't seen any evidence of the ghost that we had told them about. At that exact moment one of the French doors directly behind her opened and slammed shut. I told them that they had just met Casper. That was enough evidence for them, they left immediately after dinner, before dessert.

After we lived there for about a year, I ran for president of the homeowner's association. I won the election, barely beating the incumbent. The reason I ran was that the previous board used the HOA fees for such things as having live bands perform at the pool on weekends and they would have a beer dispensing truck in the parking lot; and allowed people who did not live in Bryn Mar to use the facilities, including the pool and tennis courts. My administration immediately did away with all of that. One spring weekend a local nursery agreed to bring a truck load of trees and shrubs to the community center, and we allowed the residents to pick the ones they wanted. The association paid for one tree to be planted between the sidewalk and the street, and any other plants they wanted were priced very competitively; in addition, we had a tractor on site that would drill the holes for all the plants. Our agreement with the nursery was that the association would buy any plants that were not sold. We would have planted them in the common areas; however, all were sold. Also, we were able to lower the annual fees, give a discount if you paid annually, and worked out payment plans with the residents that were struggling to pay their fees. We put new floors in the club house and rented it out to other neighborhoods in the area for their meetings. We had a pool/tennis court monitor to only allow residents that were in good standing and their accompanied guests use them.

Bryn Mar was divided into two sections with a lake in between, there were 176 homes in the development. In a way to get the neighbors to work together, we arranged for Corn on the Curb and block parties. For Corn on the Curb, we would get a field case or two of sweet corn, have a big pot of water boiling and melt a few pounds of butter on a side burner and slice a case of tomatoes and have it ready as the neighbors were coming home from work. Hot corn slathered with butter and fresh tomatoes, what could be better, unless it was the conversations and friendships that were created. That helped to establish true neighborhoods. The next election I won with only one dissenting vote.

Chad (From Dumor Avionics in Opa Locka) was a man of many talents. In the late 70's, he came to Orlando to do contract work for all of the sound design and installation at Church Street Station, which was another one of Orlando's major tourist attractions. The sound systems were outstanding! Church Street Station included Rosie O'Grady's Speakeasy (Rosie would make her grand entrance by sliding down the banister while belting out a honky-tonk tune) the Cheyenne Saloon and Opera House and Kittenger's Grill as well as many other businesses. During its heyday, it drew over 1.7 million visitors a year. Joe Kittenger is a retired colonel in the United

States Air Force and a USAF Command Pilot. He was well known for his record setting accomplishments, following his initial operational assignment in fighter aircraft. He participated in Project Manhigh and Project Excelsior in 1960, setting a world record for the highest skydive from a height greater than 102,800 feet (19 miles). He was also the first man to make a solo crossing of the Atlantic Ocean in a hot-air balloon. As a side note, when the balloon landed just outside of Paris, he broke his ankle getting out of the basket. President Regan hosted him at the White House after he completed his balloon flight; he was still on crutches when the President welcomed him.

Later, Joe became the manager of the Church Street Flight Department. They flew very powerful single engine planes out of Orlando Executive Airport and the neighbors complained about the noise these aircrafts created. To soothe the neighbor's tempers, Joe would take the complainers on a short flight to "calm them down". I believe some of the complainers just wanted a ride in one of his planes. The aircraft flew over Orlando and around Disney World with banners advertising Church Street Station, in other words they were what is commonly known as "rag draggers". They took off and made a steep dive to pick up the banner and apply full power to gain altitude. Most evenings Joe would be at the restaurant and was always happy to speak about his past experiences with the guests. There was a cover charge for the Church Street Complex, however, if you presented your pilot's license, they would waive the cover charge. When I was working in Orlando, I sent a lot of pilots to Church Street Station. It was a pleasure to meet with Joe and it became more than just an acquaintance relationship.

Shortly after I began working at Prestige Jet, the government DOD (Department of Defense) contract came up for bid and we did secure that contract. Orlando Naval Training Facility was located just a few blocks from the airport, and we did have quite a bit of traffic for their operation. Their military flights were handled like any other customer, and they were so impressed with the service that they would direct all the traffic that they could move to our facility. Once a week, on Tuesdays (our slowest fuel sales day), we would have a cook-out for them. As a thank you for the service we provided to the Naval Base, the Base Commander invited my wife and myself to many of their private functions. I would receive a hand carried engraved invitation to attend, as the Commander's guests, for their Sunset Serenades, which was a monthly event on the base. Patriotic music and appetizers were part of the ceremony, which took place on the base at their training lake. The lowering of the flag at sunset as the orchestra played The National Anthem really brought our patriotism to the forefront of our lives. Also, with the DOD contract we served all the government aircrafts including Air Force II. It came in for a fundraiser, but first they had a small gathering in our lobby. That was the first time I met with and had a conversation with Vice President George H. W. Bush and Barbara Bush. Barbara had a smile that could light up a room, the Secret Service's call sign for her was "Tranquility". What wonderful, kind people they were!

The Secret Service did a thorough investigation of the employees who indicated that they would be present for the public part of the visit and did a careful inspection of the facility. This included taking the ceiling tiles down and opening every locker to inspect for explosives. They even had snipers on all the roof tops. One of my Line Personnel indicated that he would not be attending the event, and he was not given clearance identification, which was a silver bar to be worn on your collar. Well, he showed up during the public appearance portion of the visit and the Secret Service had him on the ground, in hand cuffs within seconds, then they hauled him away. He was not returned until after Air Force II had departed. The Secret Service had designated a room in the terminal that had no windows and only one door, a "safe room". My wife and I were actually speaking to the Vice President and Barbara in the reception line, when we were basically thrown into the safe room, when my non-cleared employee arrived, it was considered to be a security breach. That is when we were together with them for about fifteen minutes. We mostly talked about Maine and Walker's Point in Kennebunkport. That is where their Maine home was located, and my wife and I had visited there many times. Because of my Security Clearance, my contract work that I did for Special Services, or any communications or duties that I participated in can't be printed or told to anyone without a similar Security Clearance.... Sorry!

About a year later, Harcourt Brace Jovanovich Inc., HBJ for short had just moved their world headquarters from New York City to Orlando and had a staff of over 1,800 just in the Orlando office. They began chartering, on a regular basis, the management Lear Jet that we operated. They soon found out that they had a need for their own aircraft, so they purchased three Lear 35s, two Bell Long Ranger helicopters and a Gulfstream II, and I managed all of them. I was their point of contact person at the airport. They had offices in San Diego, Austin, Cleveland, and New York City. In addition to publishing, they also owned Sea Worlds, Boardwalk and Baseball, Insurance Companies and Consulting firms. They are best known for publishing textbooks, fiction and non-fiction books and over one hundred magazines. Look on the back spine of almost any of your textbooks, it will have "Harcourt Brace" printed on the bottom of it.

HBJ Office – Orlando

William Jovanovich, the Chairman and his personal assistant, Susan were my main contacts. I could contact him anytime I had a need to speak with him, however, I usually relayed messages through Susan. This really pissed off his Vice Presidents since they needed an appointment to meet with the Chairman and I could walk in or call him anytime, sometimes interrupting his meetings with one of them. The Chairman must have thought I was an important member of the team because he had a million-dollar life insurance policy on me, had a phone installed in my car and a cell phone to carry with me at all times; at that time, those cell phones were about the size and weight of a brick.

For insurance reasons, once a year our HBJ jet crews (both had to be captain rated) would go to Flight Safety for re-current training. On this particular training, during a final session, the instructor happened to mention a maneuver called the "Split S", in a Lear (it's a maneuver where you roll the plane over on its back and push it down and then pull out right side up just before you come in contact with the earth); the only way a Lear could recover was to lower the flaps and extend the landing gear to slow it down enough to pull it through. Well, one of our pilots tried this on his way back from school. It put so much stress on the aircraft that one of the flaps was damaged on its attachment point, and it stressed the wings so that we were never able to get all of the fuel leaks fixed. Needless to say, we no longer employed him. But he got a job flying another jet that was also based in Orlando, within a week. Go figure!

The Chairman had homes in Orlando, San Diego and one in Canada. When he went to the Canadian one, it was located deep in the woods. We found a private air strip and a Customs agent who agreed to meet the plane at the private air strip, within twenty-four-hour notice, that was just plain luck. The Chairman was also on the Board of Regents for Smith College located in Northampton, Massachusetts. The closest limo service was in Boston, so we contacted a local funeral home in Northampton, they agreed to rent their "Cadillac Limo" for his arrivals. They promised to take the identification plaques off when we used that vehicle, he didn't ever find out that it was funeral rolling stock. When he was in San Diego he would almost always fly up to Long Beach in the Gulfstream, each time it exceeded the noise threshold, and the captain would have to pay the city a hefty fine of $2,000.00. He would not go in one of the Lear Jets even though that would not have violated the decibel measurement. The city threatened to take action to get the captain's license suspended, but that turned out to just be an idle threat, furthermore, they didn't have the authority to suspend a pilot's license. I think the city wanted the cash they received from the noise violations more than they wanted to take any further action.

It was a very stressful job, for the Chairman had some unusual guidelines, such as no alcohol on any of their planes except when he was a passenger, then a bottle of Taittinger Champaign must be on board, he had purchased the entire 1983 vintage and had it shipped from France and we kept it in a locked refrigerated storage facility and we had to keep a log of the date and plane on which each bottle was placed. In addition, we had to have coffee, made from freshly ground beans from Kona, Hawaii, and Licorice Nibs for his trips. On the trips that the Vice Presidents were the passengers on, we would find empty miniatures stuffed between the seat cushions. On more than half of the flights that the Chairman was not on board, he would change their destinations while the planes were already in the air. We would have to determine the approximate location of the plane, locate the closest cell tower, and make an up call to the plane in order to turn it around. That kept one of our dispatchers busy most of the time. That dispatcher was able to create a program that would locate the proper cell tower.

Orcas, or killer whales, are the largest of the dolphin species and one of the world's most powerful predators. They feast on marine mammals such as seals, sea lions, and even whales. Puffins (birds) live at the top of the planet. The Arctic Penguins live at the bottom: the Antarctic. One of the trips we did for HBJ was to the North Pole, to count puffins and tag Orcas. As close as we could get a Lear Jet to the North Pole happened to be a gravel landing strip that was used by scientists, and even though the people at the airport promised that the strip was frozen, it had thawed by the time we got there. We took the Lear that had a gravel kit installed and still the flaps had several dents punched in them from the gravel that the wheels kicked up. We put the crew in the only "motel" that was available, which happened to be a dormitory and the only restaurant was a mess hall where everyone ate. The crew wasn't too happy with the accommodation. They even offered to go back to Moose Jaw, Wyoming, up to that point they thought it was the worst place I had sent them, until this trip. I'm not sure how true this is, but they told me that the hunters they took to Moose Jaw came back to the plane with a whole deer. When asked where the hunters thought they could put this carcass, they told the crew just to strap it over the plane's nose. I was not sure if that was really what they said, or if the crew made up that story. It was a good one anyway.

Then we went to the South Pole to gather penguin eggs for Sea World. On that trip, we used a Lear Jet whose interior could easily be converted to an ambulance, as the interior was designed to be quickly converted to transport patients. We used the electrical connections in the cabin for incubators. There was a Sea World veterinarian and an "egg gatherer", a National Geographic representative, and our crew on board. We flew the Lear as far south as possible, then transferred the equipment to a C-130, it went as far as it could go then the crew took helicopters the rest of the way to get to the nesting area. It was a two-day trip in the Lear.

Each female penguin lays two eggs, when the first one hatches, and it is in decent shape, the mother gets off the nest and abandons the second egg. Sea World would only take one egg from each nest. On the way back, several of the eggs hatched. We had an extra crew positioned in Columbia, as the first crew would run out of duty time before they could get back to California. When the plane got to San Diego, we arranged to have it met by Agriculture and Customs for a quick inspection of the "cargo", then get the newborns and eggs to Sea World as soon as possible.

For the original Penguin Encounters, they gathered their penguins after they had hatched, who were then uncomfortable with human contact. If you go to a Penguin Encounter, the original birds stay in the back of the display, while the hand raised ones will come to the glass windows. The ones that hatched in San Diego were raised by humans and were very comfortable around people. In fact, they trained six of those that had the best personalities, to follow red carpets; they would bring them to the airport, lay down a red carpet and they would follow it to the plane. Each one would jump into the Learjet and then jump up on the seat backs, so they could look out the windows. The reason for the flights was to take them to children's hospitals across America. They would get on the beds and let the kids pet them.

Signature at Orlando International got the management contract a year later, and two months after they got the contract, there was a take-over attempt by Rupert Murdoch, and to prevent the take-over the Chairman took the company deeply into debt. The take-over failed, and the creditors swarmed in on the company. One of the VPs jumped off the roof of the headquarters building, and basically all the physical assets were sold, including Sea World to Anheuser Busch. Of course, the planes were the first to go.

Many times, my wife and I would go to Southern California, Key West, New York and once even to Havana, as previously mentioned, when the opportunities came up. Our neighbors at the time would say they wished they could travel like we did, and we told them that usually we could take them along. Most of the time we would travel on deadhead legs (no passengers, just crew) on corporate jets, so there was room for at least two other couples, but it would almost always be a last-minute event. We would contact them when a trip came up, but none of them ever took us up on the offer.

On the morning the Challenger took off from Cape Canaveral, all our employees were on the ramp to witness the liftoff. We had an unobstructed view from out ramp of the liftoffs from the Cape and the Shuttles even flew over the airport on their return from space for their approach to landing, including the two sonic booms. Back to the Challenger, we all witnessed the explosion, and all ran into the terminal to watch the news to find out what had actually happened. That was a tragic day.

Goodyear awarded Prestige Jet the contract to be at the Shuttle Landing Strip for each shuttle return flight, to immediately take the brakes back to their testing facility in Akron, Ohio. As far as I know, our Learjet was the only civilian plane to use the landing strip at that time. For each flight, it was a real ordeal to get permission to land there, one would think that after one or two trips, it would become a regular thing, not so! The enormous amount of paperwork had to be submitted for each trip. However, it was neat to see our Learjet on TV parked on the ramp near the Assembly Building for each return trip. We would go for each return flight of the shuttle whether it was scheduled to land at Cape Canaveral or Edward's Airforce Base.

I am not sure if our association with Goodyear had anything to do with the blimp basing with us for the Citrus Bowl games or not. I was lucky enough to get a ride on it and it was really an experience. It's the only aircraft where you are not required to wear seat belts, it cannot make any violent moves that would require them. They explained how they maneuver this airship, they move the "air bags" forward and aft to climb and descend. An unusual fact about the blimp is that it gets every dog they fly over to bark non-stop. That took care of another line on my bucket list.

Across the street from the Prestige Jet facility was an

exceptionally good steak house, Al and Linda's La-Cantina, you would think Italian or Mexican, but beef was their specialty. This is where the "movers and shakers" in the area would hang out, including the Governor and past Governors. Linda caught Al with his young girlfriend, and in the divorce settlement, she got the restaurant. "Al and Linda's" was displayed on the fireplace chimney of the building. The day the divorce was final, Linda had "Al" changed to "All" Linda's La-Cantina". At least she still had her sense of humor.

One Friday afternoon, we had a Learjet in Orlando that had to be in Van Nuys, California by Saturday at eight in the morning, California time. The flight to El Paso, Texas was normal. It was just a fuel stop; it was winter, and there was quite a bit of snow on the ramps and taxiways in Texas. After a quick stop, we were off to Van Nuys. It started out as a boring flight, then Lynne had the idea that we should see how high a Lear 35 could go. As we passed 35,000 (51,000 feet was the max service ceiling that the FAA had certified for that model Lear) feet, there was a transponder failure (they turned it off so the Air Traffic Control Center could not get a reading of our altitude). As we climbed higher it was more than the heater could handle, so it started getting colder and colder in the cabin, on top of the fact that it was winter. Then, passing through 55,000 feet was really cold and the performance of the plane was fading fast. They pushed it up to 60,000 feet, which was the maximum altitude possible for the existing conditions. The engines were just barely getting enough oxygen to maintain power, and we were approaching the stall speed and the maximum speed at the same time.

The views from this altitude were magnificent, we could see the curvature of the earth, the lights down the California coast, then total darkness in Mexico with the exceptions of spots of light to the south. Stars were at eye level and below us; and it was jet black above us. Did I mention that it was colder than a well diggers ass in the Yukon?

Then they pitched the nose down just a couple of degrees and did not make any additional adjustments to it all the way to the California coast. We cleared the Rockies, no problem, when we got back to 35,000 feet the transponder magically started working again and glided the rest of the way into Van Nuys. What started out as just another uneventful trip, turned into one that I will never forget!

One of our jet co-pilots was a lady named Tweet; she is one of the most remarkable people I have ever had the pleasure to work with. She was a CFI (certified flight instructor), a radio talk show host, had a law degree and even a Learjet type rating. Her husband was in the Navy, and they moved a lot, he had a new base assignment in Guam. When she left Prestige Jet, she had also gotten a new job, co-pilot with Continental Air Lines, and was also going to be based in Guam, as it turned out she was a one half of an all-female flight crew.

Once every two weeks, we had a charter to pick up an author in Key West, fly him to New York for the weekend to be with his kids, and return him to Key West. From time-to-time, Lynne and I would go on the deadhead trips to Key West. On one of these trips Lynne and Earl were flying, Tweet and I were the only "passengers" on board. On about a five-mile straight in final to Key West, she rolled the Lear. It was a perfectly coordinated maneuver, the coffee didn't even spill out of my cup, but I was not a happy camper. When we landed, we used every inch of the runway to stop; the ground controller said he had never seen anything quite like that and told us to taxi to the ramp! Lynne's idea of flying was to do aerobatics, depending on the plane, spins, loops, rolls, Split S's or Cuban 8's, as many as possible between point A and B. My idea was to fly a straight line from point A to point B.

One of our hangar customers, Charlie Bradshaw owner of Hi-Acres Citrus Groves, was one of the largest in the country, but three freezes forced him to sell off part of his acreage. In 1981, he bought the historic Durango & Silverton Narrow Gauge Railroad in

Colorado, after taking the 47-mile train ride through mountains in the San Juan National Forest. Bradshaw restored the Durango-Silverton line, complete with the steam locomotive that was put back into service after 20 years in retirement. The antique railway, now 148 years old, has been named the top North American train trip by National Geographic Traveler. He invited Lynne and I to take a trip on the railroad any time we were in the area, instructing us to just call his secretary and she would take care of everything. As it would happen, we would be in Durango on July third with two other couples. I called and advised her of the date, and sked if it would be possible to get tickets for the trip? She told me that the train had been sold out for over a month, but she would see what she could do for us, to just check in at the station and they would let me know if she was successful in getting us on the train.

As it turned out she had arranged for all six of us to ride in the caboose, it had a pot belly stove, a bar and a hostess. It was in the low 70's when we left Durango and she would advise us every time a photo opportunity would be coming up, to get our cameras ready. There were about twenty cars on the train, several of which were wide open with park benches for seating. About halfway up to Silverton it started raining, which changed to sleet, then snow. When we arrived in Silverton, there was four inches of new snow on the ground. Many of the passengers that were on the open cars took a bus back down to Durango. The six of us had a very comfortable great trip!

The Orlando Symphony Orchestra contacted us to see if we could arrange a fund raiser using the British Airways Concord for an overnight trip to Bermuda. After much planning, it happened, the tickets were $1,000.00 each and it sold out in a matter of days. It was my only time on the Concord. I got a special tour of the plane, which was very narrow, the cockpit was extremely long and narrow. The bathroom door was a bi-fold, because there was not enough room in the isle for a regular door to fully open. The bathroom was also very narrow, you almost had to go in, in the direction you needed to do your business. The food/bar carts were specially designed to be narrow enough to get them down the aisle. The carpet in the cabin had elastic edges because at that speed and altitude the cabin would expand, and before they put elastic on the edges of the carpet it would tear apart. In take-off and landing configuration, the very pointed nose would drop down and at altitude it would be raised up. That was because when it was raised, the two windshields (one that did not move and the one that did) would create a telescope so the pilots could see far enough ahead to avoid a collision with another aircraft or maybe a mountain. It's really too bad that they were grounded, but they were very unprofitable to operate. I wish there had been a Concord 200, (the original Concorde was 100) to allow for more passengers and a chance to work out the technical problems with the aircraft. The noise level on the ground was deafening when it was taking off, that needed to be corrected as well.

Our most famous guest that would arrive unannounced, was Michael Jackson. He loved to go to Disney World. When he arrived, he would have roses for all the lady employees; he was really a great customer. When he got to Disney, they would take him around the park through the tunnels so he would not have to wait in lines, and if he had walked through the park, he would have gotten mobbed. One morning when he arrived, he wanted us to take him to Burdines Department Store. We all advised against it, but he said no one would recognize him because he was wearing sunglasses and a baseball cap. He said he would be in and out in a flash. Well guess what, he was recognized, and a rather large group of people swarmed around him. We got him out and led him safely to the car, then back to the airport. Whatever he went there to purchase, he didn't get it.

It was during this time that the movie "Top Gun" was released, and of course we had to go the theatre to see it, (many times). One of my standby pilots was the owner of a cocktail theatre just outside the front gate of the Orlando Naval Training Center. He had given me a stack of complimentary tickets to use whenever we chose to see a movie. Those tickets got a lot of use during the time "Top Gun" was playing. It was kind of fun, the Navy personnel filled the place, and along with them Lynne knew the entire script by heart. The Naval base entrance was located one block from the theater.

One weekend I had a rather large Top Gun party at our house. I had made a tape of the complete soundtrack, and it was playing in the living room along with a tape of the movie. In the den another TV was playing the movie also. A lot of liquor was consumed that night. (One of the original guests called when *Top Gun Maverick* was released and asked if I was having another Top Gun Party.)

I had another large party for friends, it was for a 50th Anniversary, for fifty guests (fiftieth anniversary and fifty invited guests) in our back yard under the blooming orange trees in Orlando. For that one, we hired a professional bar tender and our housecleaner Olean acted as a chambermaid to help with serving and with cleanup. Her only request was that we get her a maid's uniform. I had many other parties and dinners for private and airport functions and Olean was always an immense help.

During my time at Prestige, I met Don Moss (from New York) and John Winthrop (from Hollywood), both were charter operators, and we would share trips. If I needed a trip out of New York or the West Coast they would put Prestige Jet brochures, cocktail napkins on one of their planes and do the trip for me, and I would do the same for them for their Florida trips. During the Panama invasion, I needed a large aircraft for one of the major networks to use to get their equipment and reporters down there, their regular charter company, Hop-A-Jet was already there. Don had a Challenger available; it was owned by a company that Don had an agreement with to use for charter. On arrival in Panama, it came under fire by the Panamanian army, it so happened the owner saw his plane landing on TV, he was not a happy camper, that was the last time Don was able to use that plane. Just a note, the plane did not receive any damage.

Don expanded his business into flying sports teams around the country and then he got into providing air transportation for the music industry. He provided transportation for Sting, Metallica, The Beach Boys, Billy Joel, The Police, and Tina Turner among others. For Tina Turner's first world concert tour, the qualified flight attendant was still on a trip with Metallica for one more week, at the last minute we needed a fill-in until Barbara was available. So, I got Kim, who worked on our front desk, to take the first week. We told her not to do anything until the plane was twelve miles out of U.S. territory, so she would not be in violation of the Federal Aviation Regulations.

She called me on the sixth day of the trip and told me she wasn't coming back, I said Okay, but Barbara has her ticket to Brazil and one for you to return tomorrow. What will you be doing in Brazil? She said wait a minute and handed the phone to Tina who said "Bill, Please don't take Kim away from us, she is the best hostess we have ever had. I know that you have someone else lined up to replace her, so I will pay her until you can put her on another trip." What a great and thoughtful lady!

It just so happened that one of the salespeople that lived in Bryn Mar J. Scott Schloeser stopped by when I was mowing the yard one Saturday, and asked if the lady he had in the car could look at our house. Since I was president of the HOA, I thought he just wanted her to see a finished model, since they had sold the builder's model. He took her inside, and I continued mowing, he came out in a few minutes, and asked how much I wanted for the house, it's not for sale, he said it's already sold. I asked him how much this model had sold for, and he told me, I added $10,000.00 to that amount. She had been transferred by Walt Disney World and was preapproved for a loan, (she was moving from Marina Del Ray, so she had the money) and needed to move in within thirty days. Lynne was working for the same reality company on their next project, in other words she was not home. We went out to dinner that night so we would be in a public place when I told her that I had sold the house. When we were looking for a home to purchase in Orlando, it was between two, the one we purchased and a condo in the center of town. It just so happened that the models for the condo project were available for rent just when we needed to find a place to live. We rented the model that we had been interested in purchasing. We soon found out that we had made the right choice in purchasing the home in Bryn Mar. Fortunately, we were only in the condo for two months.

This was about half-way through my second term as President of the HOA, I had to resign because I sold our house and we soon moved to Ft. Lauderdale to work at Banyan. I went back about fifteen years later, and the trees had formed an arch over the streets, it was beautiful.

After we lost the HBJ contract, there really wasn't enough business for Mr. Harger to keep me on the payroll, so I offered my resignation. I had trained my assistant well enough so that he could take over the operation. I accepted a job in Ft. Lauderdale, at a small FBO, Banyan Air Service. Going back to Lauderdale made life easier for me, since Lynne wasn't at all pleased that I had sold the house without even talking it over with her, the good thing was that we both loved living in Ft. Lauderdale. Ah, lunch on the intra-coastal waterway, and the cruise ships in Port Everglades.

If you say no to adventure,
You say no to life.

CHAPTER NINE:
BANYAN AIR SERVICE
1986 - 1994

Banyan Air Service located at the Ft. Lauderdale Executive Airport is quite a success story; and is now recognized around the world as one of the best Fixed Base Operations. In its beginning, Don Campion and Brian Grothe started a maintenance operation for the small charter operators that could not afford to have a Chief of Maintenance on their staff, so Banyan Air Service met that requirement for them. I had previously worked with Brian at Miami Aviation Corporation. He witnessed how I could grow the corporate aviation business and saw how much it diminished after I left. He persuaded me to join the Banyan team. It didn't take much persuasion since I had resigned from Prestige Jet. By the time I came on the scene, they had moved from a single hangar to a rather small terminal area that was attached to a rather small hangar which housed an avionics repair company and one other medium sized hangar with enough space in a lean-to building that housed the parts department and two offices. But the main advantage was they now had fueling rights at the airport and a fuel farm. Don and Brian gave me the authority to do whatever I thought would increase their fuel business. Prior to my arrival, Banyan was run like a family operation; every employee was part of the "Banyan family". None of their current employees had a clue as to how an FBO needed to operate or what customer service was really about. Several members of the Customer Service team were not willing, at first, to accept the changes to their standard operating procedures that had been in place since the beginning, and I was implementing a whole new set of procedures. Before I accepted the job, Brian guaranteed Lynne a job in the Maintenance Department if we would join their team, which she accepted over my objections.

Their front ramp could only accommodate four medium sized jets or one Gulfstream and two other planes. The lobby area could seat maybe six people. It was from this that we grew the business from 30,000 gallons pumped to 300,000 gallons per month, when I left. Sheltair was their landlord, they had built many hangars on the field and Banyan rented them as the demand dictated.

Ft. Lauderdale Executive Airport is owned and operated by the city, and Ft. Lauderdale International Airport is owned and operated by Broward County. One of Brian and Don's first requests was for me to plan and host an open house to get the Airport Commission and City Council and Airport Manager to come to our facility. It started with an invitation-only 10:00 AM Saturday brunch for the city representatives, which I set up in the hangar adjacent to the lobby area. We hired a harpist for entertainment and did the full spread for the brunch that even included mimosas. Then the menu rolled over at 1:00 PM and we invited all airport employees for a BBQ that included brats, burgers, and beer. At 6:00 PM it became a Banyan employee event that went on for hours. Brian and Don were very pleased with the results, and I was pleased to hear that, since the Customer Service and Line employees had been making derogatory remarks to them about the new procedures that I had put in place. In the end, all but two of the original employees adapted to the new Banyan. As time went on, we hosted many themed parties, such as casino night complete with roulette, craps, blackjack tables with professional dealers, then we recreated Ricks Café from Casablanca including the upright piano with pianist, a casino, cafe and even had a Beech 18 in front of the hangar which was for airport employees and their guests. We had an estimated 700 in attendance for that event. The word had gotten out about Banyan's parties.

Once again, soon after I arrived, I started a direct mail program, targeting the aircraft that were using the competitors, going to the other operators on the field, and the users of Ft. Lauderdale International, Pompano Beach and even Boca Raton. One of the first to give us a try was Peavey Electronics (Peavey amplifiers and guitars), they had a King Air 200. Prior to their arrival, they had requested a Budget Rent-A-Car, it had to be a white Lincoln Town Car,. That was their only request, and it was for every future trip, that it had to be white. All went well on their arrival, and on their departure, I was getting ready to move the Lincoln to the parking lot and for some reason I happened to check under the passenger seat. There was a velvet-covered jewelry case under there, and I asked Melia (Mrs. Peavey) if it was hers. Her quote "Oh my God, those were my mother's pearls", after that, we had them.

Their home was in Palm Beach, yet they chose Banyan as their South Florida FBO. They would drive past three other airports on their way home. Ed, their pilot, told me they had tried all the other operators at those airports, but Banyan won hands down. Their only other request was that we should open a marina and provide the same service for their yacht that we offered for their plane. Melia said that's where their headaches begin when they get to the marina.

In 1987, my Uncle Bill (he was only 64) passed away after a long illness. His funeral was one of the three that I went back to attend. His was in Knoxville, Illinois, and we stayed in a motel there, not in Geneseo. The funeral was so large that the funeral home had placed loud speakers outside, there was a very large crowd of people standing in the street, for those who could not get into the funeral home. The Farkles were there, but we did not speak to each other. There was a potluck dinner after the service, again there was a mulitude of people in attendance, in excess of one hundred, to my best estimate. This was expected, so they had rented a large tent, tables and seating for the crowd. It allowed me keep my distance from the Farkles. Right after dinner Lynne and I headed back to Florida, As a side note, It was the first time Lynne had ever had "fresh" fried chicken – never refrigerated or frozen. If you've never tasted it, what a surprise - it's teriffic!

When they read his will, he had left me his eighty acre farm in Farmington, Illinois, one of many, most of which were adjacent to his base in Knoxville, The Mid-Road Farm. But there were certain conditions to my inheritance; I could not sell the farm for five years and I had to work it (not rent out the land to a neighbor). By this time, I was getting well established in the corporate aviation world and respectfully declined this unexpected gift. His gesture reaffirmed my belief that he knew exactly what I had endured. I have often wonderd what the Farkles thought of this, for they were not mentioned in his will, nor was Ken. I gave my inheritance to his wife, Marilyn, I'm sure she would put it up for sale, it was too far from their base in Knoxville and difficult to manage under those circumstances.

About two years later, Ed Boykin, Peavey's King Air 200 pilot, told me he was going to Gulfstream school. I asked if he was changing jobs, and he replied that Hartley had purchased one. I replied with a question in my voice, you are going from a King Air to a Gulfstream? He said yes. I asked if Hartley had studied what the annual costs would be for that large of a plane? He said that Gulfstream had guaranteed the operational costs that they had quoted, and under no circumstances would they be exceeded. That was a first for me, I had never heard of a manufacturer offering a guarantee like that. After Melia passed away, Hartley sold the plane and Ed went on to another Gulfstream job.

Triton Fuel Group was Banyan's fuel supplier, they operated in Ft. Lauderdale as a Texaco dealer and at a few other locations in the United States. Triton was branded at the rest of their dealers. Ed Blair was in charge of Triton's aviation fuel division. Ed selected five dealers from across the states, some large fuel users and other dealers that weren't as busy. I was selected as a medium size dealer. We were to meet and come up with a program that would be attractive to pilots, as opposed to owners of corporate aircrafts, which would encourage the pilots to seek out the Triton/Texaco branded dealers. We had several meetings, most of which were at Love Field in Dallas, but various other meetings were held at the King Ranch in Texas, Gaston's on the River in Arkansas, and Lake Geneva in Wisconsin. Ed had an outside company run a blind survey of pilots, what they came up with, among other things, is that most pilots did not stay with their employer long enough to qualify for that company's retirement program. What we produced was TRIP, Triton Retirement Incentive Program. Each jet fuel purchaser would get two points for each gallon purchased. When they reached 5,000 points, they would get a $25 dollar Savings Bond. If a 24-year-old pilot started purchasing 60% of their fuel at a participating Triton dealer, beginning with fuel for a turbo-prop aircraft such as a King Air and ending up at retirement age of 60, flying a large corporate jet, such as a Gulfstream. They would have over $1,000,000. for their retirement. This turned out to be the best incentive program out there, most other suppliers came up with various kinds of rewards for the owners, not the pilots. The other incentives came and went, none were nearly as successful as this one.

Then along came AvFuel, they purchased Triton Fuel Group, among other items TRIP became AvTrip, which was rumored to be one of the main reasons for their purchase. At the time of the purchase AvFuel did not have any large dealers, or the staff to support the large ones. In the beginning, it was not a smooth transition. In fact, all five of us who put together the retirement program were talking with other suppliers, we could not live with their lack of support. One afternoon, I decided to call the President of AvFuel and explain our problems with their service. I went into great detail with Craig Sincock about the problems, and that all five of us were talking with other fuel suppliers. Craig's response was that if we could give them 30 days to correct those items, and if they were unable to correct them, he would release all of us from our contracts. Much to my surprise, at 8:30 the next morning, Craig and his marketing manager Marci Ammerman were in my lobby with two whiteboards, one listing the problems and the other with how they were going to correct them. I was pleased that within one week they had managed to resolve all of the problems that I had pointed out. We had a great relationship from then on, we were known as "the premier AvFuel dealer".

Lynne was beginning to accept the fact that her illness was not going to be curable, one weekend our friends from Riverside, Eddy and Dorothy, were with us for a week or two. Lynne wanted to go to Maine, Greenville in particular. That is where she camped as a youngster, on the shore of Moosehead Lake. Eddy asked if there was room for them, he always wanted to go to Stowe, Vermont and Franklin Delano Roosevelt's summer white house on Campobello Island in New Brunswick, Canada. Eddy mentioned that was the only Roosevelt residence that Eleanor had been allowed to decorate. We said sure and packed up for the trip. Stowe is a beautiful small town. The hotel we stayed in was well over 100 years old, the floor in our room was so uneven that the bed had shims on three of the legs to make it level. When we got to the Canadian border, the Customs Agent said that I looked familiar to him, had I been through there recently? My smart-ass answer was that I had not been there in several years, but had he been to a U.S. Post Office, my picture was posted in the ten most wanted section. He didn't have a sense of humor; my comment delayed our entry into Canada by about thirty minutes.

Dick Armagost was already a customer at Banyan when I arrived. Lynne and I knew him from Opa-locka, where he had a flight school which specialized in Multi-Engine training. Now he was running a Lear Jet charter service. Lynne flew with him on many of his trips, she was able to arrange her schedule to accommodate Dick's trips. This is where she got most of her jet time, she was his co-pilot.

Soon after I arrived Don told me that they had a silent partner in the business, his name was Doug Jaworski, he was Canadian, as was Don. When I met Doug, he was very personable, rather young and had a profound sense of humor. Each time he arrived; he would be in a different aircraft. Sometimes he brought in a Turbo Commander, one time he was in a Lockheed Jetstar and at other times he would be in King Airs and assorted other aircraft. For each trip he would schedule maintenance, then purchase a life jacket and a two-man life raft which he would fuel up and depart, usually about 6:00 in the morning.

On one of his arrivals in the middle of the night, he was in a Turbo Commander. He paid the two third shift Linemen who were on duty $100.00 each to wash as much mud off the plane as possible, and to pay particular attention to getting as much out of the wheel wells as they could. When I got to work, the local DEA (who was a tenant of ours) was taking samples of the mud and were trying to look inside the plane. Doug showed up a couple of hours later, it was obvious that he had taken off from a dirt strip that was very muddy. I told him that DEA had been there, he told me not to worry about that. He opened a work order with maintenance to inspect the plane and gave him a report on its condition. Almost everything checked out except for both wings, they were slightly twisted, probably from jerking the plane out of the mud on take-off. We named that plane "Twisted Sister". The only way maintenance could get the wings straightened out was to replace them. So, Twisted Sister flew crooked from then on, it made several more trips.

Lynne and I were looking for a house that we could afford, and Doug's was for sale, we saw it with his realtor and had decided to submit an offer on it. I mentioned that to him, and he said that he would not sell it to us. I asked why and all he said was "I just will not sell it to you."

197

About this time, my wife and I took a motor trip to the Northeast and one of my Linemen suggested that we go to Princeton, Maine; where he grew up, and have dinner at a particular restaurant. We found the place, ordered dinner, which was very good. Our server asked if there was anything else she could do for us. I asked if she could make a reservation for us at a local motel. She left, and I thought she must have gone on vacation because she was gone for so long. When she returned, she told us that the only motel in town was sold out and both B&Bs were filled also; she said the closest motel with a vacancy was in Bangor, that was more than a two-hour drive. Then she offered a possible solution, one of the cooks had a cabin in the woods that we could rent for $50.00. We took it and he came out of the kitchen and gave us the directions to the cabin. It was so far out in the woods that I was sure I had missed the turn onto the dirt road. Then the road appeared just as I was going to turn around. It was a one lane dirt path through the woods, around some trees, then some lights came into view, and there were a half a dozen cabins around a larger building. A lady came out of the large building and asked if we were the folks who rented their last cabin. She led us down a path to a cabin. It had a pot-belly wood burning stove in one of the two rooms. You could see the stars through the roof, but it had two beds, a toilet, and a sink. Most important of all, it was warm; there was a fire in that pot-belly stove which the owner's wife had fired up. About every two hours, I would put more logs in it to keep the cabin "warm". When the sun came up, we were about fifteen feet from the shore of the most beautiful, large lake. No other structures were in sight, and the grounds around the cabins were very well maintained. The cabins were also in pretty good shape except for the holes in the roof and the cracks in between the logs which made up the exterior walls, I would have liked to stay there a few more days, if the owner would have placed a fishing pole by the door. I would have seriously considered it.

We loaded the car and headed back up the dirt road. When we got to the paved road and headed back to the interstate, about a mile from the camp's dirt road, there was an airport out there. There were no planes on the ramps, and we didn't see any people on the property. There were several large hangars and what appeared to be about a 7,000-foot concrete runway. I mentioned to Lynne that it was strange, it appeared to be in good condition, granted it was really out in the woods, but why had it been abandoned? Then on to Bangor on I-95, on our way to Moosehead Lake, it was the first time for me to see it. Upon approaching Greenville, there is a hill just past the Indian Hill Trading Post, (General Store/Gas Station), at the top of the hill you have your first opportunity to see the lake, what a beautiful sight! The lake is 40 miles long and 21 miles wide with many tree covered islands and one large island, Mount Kineo.

First View of Moosehead Lake

Mount Kineo

I didn't see Doug for about two months, then I learned what he had been doing. Doug was the purveyor of aircraft and helped smuggle cocaine for the Medellin Cartel. For some reason the cartel had threatened his parents, who had recently moved from Canada and were now living in Tortola, British Virgin Islands. The Cartel knew his parent's address and phone number, Doug did not trust the American DEA, so he turned himself in to the Canadian DEA. He then betrayed the Cartel, supplying information to the Canadians that made possible the biggest "sting" operation in Canadian police history. On his last trip south, he flew a swat team into the Cartel's compound. Then we found out why Doug would not sell us the house, he believed they might make a hit on the house believing he was the occupant.

Shortly after we returned from our trip, I mentioned to Doug that we saw this abandoned airport about ten miles outside of Princeton. At that time, he did not comment on it. This is the history of the mysterious airport, the Cartel had purchased it, raised all the rents and fees so the planes that were based there moved to other airports. It was extremely valuable to the Cartel because it was totally out of any radar coverage, and they used it as a fueling stop for the planes with their cargo on board going to various destinations in Canada. Doug had been using it but did not tell me about the abandoned airport until after the sting was completed. It was really strange how we just happened to find it.

Doug is under the Canadian witness protection program and is living under a different identity. However, I have seen him several times since, he was driving through the Executive Airport, and I have seen him walking on the beach in Ft. Lauderdale. When I called out to him, he did not answer, but I still gave him my message, get out of town, if they find you, they will kill you. I heard his new occupation was that of a bartender in Utah at a gay bar. There is a book written about Doug, "The Big Sting", written by Peter Edwards and published by Key Porter Books, a Canadian company.

On another house hunting trip to Greenville, Maine I decided to take the long way home, cross over to Montreal and take the Queen's Highway as far west as Sault St. Marie, Michigan to clear U.S. Customs. Another delay, the agent saw a fishing pole in the back of the SUV, and asked what I was fishing for. I told him whatever was biting, but I was catching mainly perch. He said they were his favorite fish, where were they? I said back in the lakes. He proceeded to take everything out of the back of the car to find "those fish", because it was illegal to import them. Another thirty-minute delay. The Mackinaw Bridge is quite long and very high, it sways in the wind, and they have valet drivers for those who are too uncomfortable to drive themselves. At the time of our crossing only one vehicle had been blown off, it was a Volkswagen. I called AvFuel and advised them that we had made it to Michigan. They said they had been trying to get in touch with us for two days. They had arranged a suite in The Grand Hotel on Mackinaw Island for that night. The only way over to the island was on a ferry, and we needed to take dressy attire for dinner at the Hotel. There are no vehicles on the island except for one fire truck. Bicycles and horse drawn carriages are the only transportation except, of course, for walking. The movie "Somewhere In Time" was filmed there, starring Christopher Reeve and Jane Seymour. The hotel is actually like stepping back in time, during dinner there are two orchestras, so there is no "dead" time, the porch is 385 feet long with bar and cigar carts serving the guests after dinner. No non-guests are allowed on the property after 6:00 PM and all gentlemen are required to be dressed in a coat and tie at that time. I was challenged, we had just returned from touring downtown, and it was after 6:00 PM and I wasn't wearing a dinner jacket.

The Grand Hotel

The next day AvFuel's King Air picked us up at the local airport and flew us to Minneapolis to their truck manufacturing facility. We got to the airport via a horse drawn carriage, the horse farted all the way. I had done so much complaining about the way the trucks were set up, they had arranged for the engineers to meet with me and discuss the changes I had proposed. None of the engineers had ever fueled an aircraft, let alone even driven a truck bigger than a Ford F-150; AvFuel approved most of my suggestions and implemented them on their future vehicles. That design was known as" Bill's Design" and many of my suggestions were implemented by other fuel truck suppliers.

The next items on the agenda were a tour of AvFuel's corporate offices, Michigan's huge Football Stadium, and the rest of Ann Arbor. Then dinner at Chops Steak House. The next morning, we were taken to Selene for the monthly "high end" huge flea market, mostly antiques. Then back to Ft. Lauderdale.

Tom Smith was a Banyan customer and had his plane based with us and was a successful auto salesman. He came in one afternoon and asked about what was bothering me, since I was not my usual happy self. I told him that we could not find a house to buy, that checked most of our boxes that we could afford, and our lease was about to expire on the townhouse we rented in Coconut Creek. He said his house was for sale in Coral Springs and he was sure that we could work out the price and a payment method that I could afford. He offered that after work he would show it to us. It was located on the original model row for the sales office, in what was the parking lot, it was a Westinghouse community. Tom's house was built by the main contractor on what was to be his residence. It was quite large, over 3,000 sq. ft. with four bedrooms, two bathrooms, a living room, a formal dining room, a large family room, the kitchen even had three ovens, and there was a breakfast dining area included in it as well. Outside, it was on a large lot, because it was model row the houses were a minimum of seventy-five feet apart. There was an Olympic size pool, a screened in back porch, and an attached two car garage. Lynne hated it, but I could see a lot of potential with the property.

Tom offered to sell it to me for the same price that he had paid for it, and if I would make his mortgage payments on a "lease to buy" contract, that would work for him. All of my rent payments went towards the purchase of the property. His kids had married and moved out and his wife was in ill health and could not do anything around the house. He wanted to get out of that large home and wanted to move into a two-bedroom condo. His wife hated that idea, much like Lynne hated his house. I agreed to the purchase agreement, we moved in on the last day of our lease in Coconut Creek. Tom's wife had not done anything toward getting ready to move out and Tom asked for an extension, I could not do that, my reply was that one of us was going to move two times and it wasn't going to be me. He hired movers to pack the house and put all their stuff in storage until he could find a place to move into.

He was using my monthly payments, not to pay the mortgage but for other expenses. Southeast Banks was going to foreclose on the property. I got with the vice-president of the bank, explained the situation, and worked out a payment schedule with them.

When I arrived at Banyan, there were six other FBOs at the airport, all pumping around 30,000 gallons of fuel a month. That number eventually dwindled to two other operators. Banyan's number of gallons pumped grew to 300,000 gallons a month at the "old" facility (and has grown to 900,000 gallons three years after they moved into their new facility Figure 9 - 1). They have taken over the entire south side of the airport, and have over one million square feet of hangar space and have recently taken over another facility on the north side of the airport, (Figure 9 – 2). That facility is just for private corporate jets with its own lobby, it is entirely sold out, and Banyan's fuel sales have risen to over 1,000,000 a month. There is even a corporate Boeing 737 based on the ramp there.

After living in the Ft. Lauderdale area, I learned a lot about the Seminole Indians. First that they live in the Everglades, I don't know how they can do that, but they do. Heat, humidity, and of course alligators. They have never signed a peace agreement with the United States. They made a considerable amount of money selling cigarettes along state route 441, out of two trailers. Chief Billy had a twin-engine plane; one of my friends was his pilot. He built a runway and hangar on the reservation. He soon purchased a rather large jet. His pilot told him about me, and he wondered if I would be interested in running a marina for him, if his plan to purchase the hotel complex on the beach was approved. He wanted to open a casino on the lower level but had no interest in managing the large marina that was part of the deal. The state said he could not open a casino in that location because it wasn't located on Indian land. He told them that when he purchased the property it would be Indian land. The state disagreed with him, and would not allow him to build a casino. Many years later, he opened the Hard Rock casino on

204

Indian property. Chief Billy was quite generous and well respected by all the members of the tribe.

The 1989 Super Bowl was held in Joe Robbie Stadium (in the North Miami area) and we were quite busy. The day before the game, Dave Thomas (Wendys) arrived, he was sitting on the porch enjoying the warm weather. Just a few minutes after Dave arrived, Tim Horton (Tim Horton Donuts - Canada) arrived and he also sat down with Dave, and they struck up a conversation. It was the first time they had met each other. Since they both think out of the box, Dave with fresh beef instead of frozen like his competitors, for his square burgers, and adding chili to his menu. Tim was the first donut store in Canada to offer a drive-up window and a lower one for snow mobiles. As the weekend went on, they negotiated a deal, Wendys bought Tim Horton Donuts for 400 million dollars. So those IRS agents who say that no business is conducted at Super Bowl, it can't be a business trip, they are wrong again.

I had a girl working on the ramp, which freed up line service, she would direct the planes on and off the ramp and take care of straightening up the aircraft's interior. She had concocted a mixture that would make their coffee jugs look like new, another plus. Her name was Tabitha, and she was extremely smart and could get along with all our customers, especially the ones from South America. Our crew cars were Chrysler Sebring convertibles, and she would drive it up to the plane after the passengers were taken care of; with her long blonde hair blowing in the wind, she soon had the crew's complete attention. Again, we had the tipping problem; many crews would gave her a large tip, usually $100.00 and an additional $20.00 for line service. That did not go over very well, as the other members of line service thought they should get half of what she received. That problem was not ever resolved to everyone's satisfaction.

Then one day, one of the Air Force's Gulfstreams from Andrews arrived with Barbara Bush on board. Tabitha directed it onto the ramp, placed the chocks, rolled out the red carpet and stood by the stairs to greet the passengers. When Barbara got off, she took Tabitha by the arm to the front of the plane and told her that she had watched from the cockpit and praised her for doing an excellent job. We couldn't get her attention for about a month; she would remind us that Barbara Bush said she was doing an "excellent job".

I relied on the skills from cooking at The Cellar, many times for Banyan's large parties; also, two close friends (both were Banyan employees) got married in our Ft. Lauderdale back yard, the theme for the wedding was "The Great Gatsby", and period dress was requested. The actual wedding service was held next to the pool under the palm trees, and after the service, dinner was served for seventy-five in our adjacent yard. I had set up an external sound system and made an endless tape of the music from that era. It was quite an event.

Bruce Green, Banyan's company lawyer and my personal lawyer, the one that I had a retainer with, had a C-182 based with us. One morning he had an early flight, and when he checked the oil, the engine was warm. As it turned out, one of my third shift employees had taken the plane for a local flight. Of course, he was immediately released of his duty. Within a month, he had another line service job at Ft. Lauderdale International Airport.

Another one of our line personnel was involved in an incident; the hitch broke off the tug that was towing an oil bowser (a 150-gallon oil tank on wheels) and it ran into a C-172, it hit just behind the back seats and did major damage to the plane; it was parked on one of our remote ramps. It was not his fault, however, according to company policy he was sent for drug testing, the results came back positive. We had no choice but to release him. Within a week, he had been hired by one of our competitors on the north side of the airport as their Line Manager.

Edward DeBartolo, Jr. arrived one day to pick up relatives for his father's funeral. A bit of Eddy's history is that most of his wealth comes from real estate, shopping malls; but he is best known as one of the most successful NFL owners, the San Francisco 49ers. Under his ownership, they won five championships during the 1980's and 1990's.

On his return trip, I had received a message for him, it was just a California phone number, after his relatives were in their cars and leaving, I handed him the note. He instantly became furious and asked if we had a secluded area where he could make a call. I took him into my office and started to leave when he asked me to remain and close the door. He said that he might need a witness. The person on the other end of the line turned out to be Joe Montana, the 49ers quarterback. To make this brief, after an exchange of a few nasty words, he told Joe that he was fired, and he (Eddy Jr.) would make a public statement explaining his actions in two weeks.

The first week of each New Year, General Electric would hold a meeting with the presidents of all of their various companies, the meeting was held at the Boca Raton Resort and Club. Boca's airport did not have an ILS (Instrument Landing System), so they scheduled their aircraft to come into Ft. Lauderdale Executive. They were thinking ahead, if there was bad weather in Boca and they were unable to land there, it would have really messed up their schedules. We were fortunate to get their business away from one of our competitors, Million Air.

Between GE's own planes and the chartered jets, that added up to 19 arrivals within about three hours. The planes came from the U.S., Europe, and the Far East. GE brought their own mechanics to handle any maintenance issues and their own Chef to supervise the food service at the resort for their meetings and catering for the aircraft's departures. We really looked forward to the plane that came in from Paris, the leftover catering that came off that plane was terrific. Being that time of year, high season, we were already busy, and their fleet pushed us to the maximum. We would rent a refrigerated truck and park it next to the terminal on the edge of the ramp just for their departure catering. We had to keep a large amount of catering separated by flight and keep it cold. It took a lot of planning and staging for their departures; but in the end we all had a good feeling about how well we handled it.

There was a long hallway, that ran from the auto parking area to the front of the terminal. The walls were covered with autographed photos of our "famous" customers. Our customers would spend quite a long time admiring those who had come through Banyan. Mariette Hartley was a frequent "guest", you might remember her from a series of Polaroid commercials that she did with James Garner, and she appeared in several episodes of Gunsmoke, Columbo and Love Boat just to name a few. We became friends and through our discussions, we discovered that we had almost identical childhoods. She was the first person besides my wife that I felt comfortable enough to go into the details about my early life. After many private discussions with her, I was able to begin to close that chapter of my past life, but it's not completely closed yet.

Then, along came hurricane Andrew, the only damage that happened at Banyan was a windsock that was mounted on top of the hangar was gone. There were a lot of trees, branches, and other stuff in the streets, but enough of our employees were able to make their way to the airport, so that we would be able to open when the FAA "cleared the airport. There was no significant damage at the airport and that allowed us to open so soon after the storm. We were the closest airport that was open to the actual path of the storm. Ft. Lauderdale International had some of their fencing knocked down and because it served the airlines, they could not re-open until the fences were repaired.

We opened at 3:00 in the afternoon right after the storm, and our competitors at Executive didn't re-open until 6:00 the next morning. We were overrun with traffic, FEMA, FP&L, all the major insurance companies, and a few of the banks. We had planes parked all over our end of the airport. For any flight coming in with supplies for the relief effort, I sold them fuel for $0.25 over cost. We donated one of our hangars to store the supplies until the Salvation Army and/or the Red Cross could make a pick-up. We had "stuff" stored for over a month, churches and other groups would run flights as soon as they accumulated enough supplies to fill their planes. The pilot for one of the church groups from Tampa told me much later that because of our low fuel price they were able to make two additional trips. After International opened, the major FBO there, AMR Combs, raised their posted fuel price by $0.50 a gallon. Word of that price gouging went across the country within hours; and we got even more business because of their pricing policy.

Our maintenance department had been doing the maintenance inspections and repairs on Manuel Noriega's Learjet. During the Panama invasion, our forces shot up the plane, so he couldn't use it to make an escape. Another tenant at the airport patched it up and flew it back to Executive Airport. They could not pressurize the plane, so they had to fly low and slow. During GE week one of the chartered Lear's was backed into a palm tree. It was raining very hard when we parked it, the line-man probably didn't even know that he had run into the tree. When the crew came out three hours early for their departure, they noticed damage on the trailing edge of the right tip tank. Anyway, their plane and Noriega's Lear were the same model, we got the trailing edge of the tank from Noriega's plane and installed it on the charter plane and had it ready to go for their scheduled departure. We were lucky. I saw the crew a year later at the NBAA (National Business Aircraft Association) Convention and told them where the part came from, they thought that was pretty funny.

One of our based charter companies had just gotten a new Challenger on a management agreement, and on its first departure, I was watching it take off. It had just gotten out of sight (behind buildings) and I heard a crash and almost immediately there was an explosion. I ran back to the terminal and immediately called the tower and asked if it was the Challenger, and they said no, that a train crashed into a fuel transport truck that was stuck on the tracks. Within about an hour my heart rate returned to normal.

The first Gulfstream that based with us had scheduled a major maintenance inspection in Van Nuys, (near Beverly Hills) California. The pilot asked Lynne and myself if we would like to ride along. Of course, we did, we left quite early, for us, and when we were about halfway there, Air Traffic Control requested that we reduce our speed to 300 knots and hold our present altitude and heading. About forty-five minutes later Center advised us that we had traffic at eleven o'clock, one hundred twenty-five miles out. "What the hell is going on, they are not talking to any other planes," then it appeared, the Shuttle passed right in front of us, and touched down on the salt flats. We could even see the contrails, quite impressive. Then Center told us to resume speed and asked if the slowdown was worth it? It sure was!

One of our semi-regular customers was Frank Sinatra, Don Moss had set him up on a hub and spoke plan for his tours. They would arrive in Ft. Lauderdale and settle in for about two weeks in a rental condo on the beach. He would limo to Miami for that concert and return that night to the condo. Two or three days later he would take his Gulfstream to Orlando for another performance and return to the condo that night and so on. The day after one of their trips, Barbara Sinatra's secretary called and told me that she wanted to go shopping, get their plane ready and notify their pilots. I told her that their plane went back to California for a major inspection and there would be a chartered plane for Frank's next concert date. I asked where Barbara wanted to go for her shopping trip, and she said Rodeo Drive in Beverly Hills of course. I told her that we could get a jet for her trip, but it would not be a Gulfstream, because there were none in the area for her pop-up trip. She said, "do the best you can" and hung up.

In about an hour and a half, Barbara showed up and asked where her plane was, since she didn't see it on the ramp. I said didn't your secretary tell you that it was in Van Nuys for major maintenance. I had arranged for a Lear 55 to take her shopping, she wasn't very understanding, and I told her that was the best we could do at such a short notice. For one passenger, you will find it to be very comfortable, and it had a private lavatory, so off to Beverly Hills she went. When she returned the next evening, she was very pleased with her flight, and asked what kind of plane we had got for her, because she was going to ask Frank to get her one just for her trips. After that she was very pleased, when they departed for Virginia, the next hub, she gave me her home address. When she got to the zip code, she said 90210 and I said now give me your real zip code, and she said that was theirs, that they actually lived in Beverly Hills. She also gave me their private home phone number.

After Frank collapsed during his concert in South Carolina, they got him stabilized and flew him home. Two or three days after he returned home, we were standing around the Front Desk, one of the Customer Service Representatives (CSR's) wondered how Frank was doing. I said let's call and find out, I have their home number. So, we put the phone on speaker so all could hear and placed the call. Nancy Sinatra answered, and we told her who we were and why we were calling. She handed the phone to Barbara, to paraphrase her words, Frank isn't doing very well, but your call means more to me and when I tell him about your call, I'm sure he will feel the same way. She said this house is full of flowers and fruit, but the people who sent it felt it was their obligation to do that, but your call really means that you care about how he is doing. Frank passed away shortly after we made the call.

The plane that picked Howard Hughes up at the end of his life on April 5, 1976, was now based with me at Banyan, and I knew the crew quite well. I asked them if he was still alive when they put him on board, and they did not answer that question. As for his physical appearance, the crew said they were so tired of the press asking what he looked like, that they actually made up the story that was published of his long hair and long fingernails.

It was during this time that I first met Jimmy Buffett (I'm not counting going to his concert at Bay Front Park in Miami), he was in Ft. Lauderdale taking instructions to obtain his Cessna Citation type rating (it's a medium size jet). The classes were held in an office complex adjacent to our property, and he would come over on his breaks. After having several brief discussions with him, I soon realized how down to earth he was. At our first meeting, he requested that I address him as Jimmy not Mr. Buffett. Over the next few years, I was able to serve Jimmy with his various planes, and we got to be better friends.

During my time at Banyan, I was fortunate enough to meet so many great people, some famous and some not so famous, and so many have become friends rather than just customers.

After eight years at Banyan, I was at the end of my rope. For all eight years, Don's wife did all she could to make life difficult for me. Don found out that I was looking for another job. He was very fair with his offer to let me resign, which I did. My parting remark to him were that I hoped he had a good buyout agreement with Brian because he (Brian) was happy with the current situation, he did not want to grow the business any more than what it already was. Don very much wanted to grow it as much as possible, with the possibility of opening Banyan South at Opa-locka. I made many lasting relationships while at Banyan: of course, Don Campion and Dale Meiler in the Maintenance Department, and in the Customer Service Department, Bobby Kiesz, Mike Sullivan, Eric Veal, Barbara Bauer and Lisa Stevens, they are still there since I hired them. When I get to Ft. Lauderdale, we still have dinner together, usually at Chuck's Steakhouse. It's been over thirty-five years since we started working together, time flies when you're enjoying your job and having fun.

My Wife on the Lear Jet She Flew

Banyan Air Service - Current Facility

Figure 9 – 1

Banyan North

Figure 9 - 2

Life is not about the destination,
It's about the journey.

CHAPTER TEN:
GMD AVIATION (Glen, Mike, and Dick)
1994 - 1997

My next adventure in aviation was at Atlanta Jet in Lawrenceville, Georgia, about thirty minutes northeast of Atlanta. It started out as Atlanta Jet, which was really an aircraft sales organization. The owner, Rick Steelman was considering purchasing the building next door, it was a charter operation, but could easily become an FBO. There was one other operator on the field, Hawthorn Aviation. Their facility was very much in need of a major facelift, while the one Rick was looking at was quite elegant and relatively new. It had six layers of crown molding, all counter tops were marble or granite, cloth hand towels in the bathrooms, you get the picture.

I met Rick while I was at Banyan. He had them do many pre-purchase inspections since they were not a competitor, Banyan did not have an aircraft sales department at that time. Rick was a typical used car salesman, but instead of cars, it was airplanes. I didn't realize how far his reputation was known throughout the industry, and the effect it would have on the proposed FBO.

I performed a due-diligence inspection and wrote a report on the possible purchase. I did a proposed profit and loss statement using a lot of incorrect information that was provided to me by Mr. Steelman. For example, I was told to include twenty King Air 200s for a new fractional ownership program that was in the planning stages, which, of course, did not materialize.

When the purchase of the building concluded, we opened a new FBO under the name of Atlanta Jet. Needless to say, my projections were off by a mile and Rick's new accountant did not want to hear that my numbers were based on the information that Rick gave to me. It was my fault that the FBO wasn't performing up to projections. They were actively looking for a new General Manager at that time, and it was okay with me. They didn't think I knew about their search, but corporate aviation is a small world. The same day that GMD Aviation entered the picture their "replacement manager" gave me a call and told me that he had turned down Rick's offer. He also knew about the pending sale of the FBO.

As fate would have it, when GMD Aviation, which was comprised of three owners: Glenn Collis, Mike Dahan and Dick Homa sold a Westwind Jet that was owned by GMD Aviation and was based at Peachtree-DeKalb (PDK) Airport, in Atlanta, and purchased a Challenge 600. There was no room at PDK for an aircraft of that size, so they purchased a hangar in Lawrenceville, which also had a lot of office space and a restaurant. It was located next door to the FBO, just to find out that I had a five-year lease on the hangar portion of the building. They had no choice but to purchase the FBO to get the hangar space they required. Money was not a problem for them.

Dick came into my office, introduced himself and told me that he was my new boss, that they had just completed the purchase of Atlanta Jet, the FBO. He said they had deposited $500,000.00 in the checking account and when we needed more, just let him know. He told me that Rick was going to terminate me on Friday of that week. As luck would have it, two days later our ramp was actually filled with jets. The Mall of Georgia had just been completed - Melvin Simon built it, and he was hosting a pre-grand-opening celebration. All the major mall tenants and both of Simon's Gulfstreams flew in for the festivities. Rick's personal attorney happened to be at the airport, and he came over to congratulate me on the amount of traffic we had and mentioned what a negative effect Rick's reputation had on our business. I questioned if Rick and his accountant had figured out what the problem had been, and he assured me they understood. That made my week. It is amazing how fast the word of the new ownership had traveled throughout the industry; however, the problems were just beginning.

As I mentioned earlier, the owners of GMD Aviation comprised of Glenn, Mike and Dick. Glenn had many Waffle House franchises, Mike and Dick owned several "Cash for Cars" locations, and other shell companies. As mentioned earlier, two days after Rick Steelman was out, we suddenly became busy. It was an enjoyable time; we had no outstanding bills to pay. Dick said that whatever equipment or supplies that would make life easier, I should just go ahead and get them. I gave him a list of those items and his reply was that our list wasn't long enough, and the maintenance department's list was too long. We even joined the ramps between the two hangars (ours and the one they purchased) creating a huge paved front ramp.

At this time, the Atlanta Olympics was underway, and my fuel supplier's representative Bill Cooper, who happened to be a long-time friend of mine took me and his wife to Olympic Park one evening, before my wife came to Lawrenceville, she stayed in Coral Springs until that house was sold. We wandered around the park for a few hours and decided to take a break and have a Coke. We found a vacant bench and sat down for a few minutes. As it happened, it was the bench where Eric Rudolph placed his bomb exactly twenty-four hours later. There was one death and eleven injured when the bomb went off. Avoided death one more time.,,

A few weeks later, we went to Turner Field for a Cubs-Braves game. We had seats behind home plate, it was the first professional baseball game that I had ever attended. His wife, Kat, took my ticket to the announcer's booth and had Harry, Skip and Chip Carey sign it; father, son and grandson's signatures on one ticket. Harry was the sportscaster for sixteen years for the Cubs, "Holy Cow – Cubs Win", Skip was a longtime sportscaster for the Braves and Chip was a television broadcaster for Fox Sports South and Fox Sports Southeast's coverage of the Atlanta Braves. One more memento, for my growing collection!

Another one of our based customers was Don and Nancy Panoz (Unfortunately, Don passed away in 2018). In 1961, Don Panoz founded Milan Pharmaceuticals, before moving on to create the Élan Corporation, where he developed a method of delivering medicine through a patch applied to the skin. Today, Panoz's transdermal technology is best known through the nicotine patch that helps people quit smoking. Ironically, Don was allergic to the patch. When he would come to the airport for a flight, he would invite me to go with him outside of the terminal and have a cigarette. He also founded Panoz Motorsports; currently his son Dan oversees that project. Paul Newman was one of Panoz's drivers. When he would fly in Don would always be on hand to greet him. I asked Don if it would be possible to get Paul to sign a photo that we had ready printed, to go with the others we had hanging on one of the walls in the terminal. On one of his arrivals, Don asked him to come inside and sign the photo that we had printed from the internet. Paul said he did not sign autographs, but obviously Paul detected Don's displeasure with that answer, so he agreed to sign some of his products on his next trip. When he arrived the next time, Don told him that we had a few of his products awaiting his signature. He once again refused to sign any autographs. Mr. Panoz told Paul Newman to get back on his jet and go home, he told Paul that since his word was no good, and he didn't want him to be associated in any way with Panoz Motor Sports. He reminded him that he said he would sign his products, and now his words were no good, that was totally unacceptable. Paul changed his mind, came into the terminal, and signed the products. I have one of those autographed jars of his salsa on my back bar. On a future trip, Paul even gave me a signed photograph.

Chateau Elan, a Luxury Resort, and winery that was located in Brazelton, Georgia also located northeast of Atlanta, it was another one of Panos's projects. It is an extremely luxurious resort with every amenity imaginable. That is where their vineyard is located; they produce their own wines. When they drilled the wells for irrigating the grape vines, they sent a sample of the water to the county health department, the results came back with a hand-written note that their wells were producing the purest water that they had ever tested. Hence, Elan Waters was born. Nancy purchased the house in Savannah where a substantial portion of the movie *"Midnight in The Garden of Good and Evil"* was filmed. She turned it into a B&B, known as Granite Steps. Over a brief period of time, she also purchased the adjacent homes around the square, creating a huge B&B. She went before the city to request that two of the houses become parking garages, leaving the facades intact. Her request was denied, so she closed the B&B's and sold all the properties. From our perspective, they were some of the most pleasant customers any company could ask for. Don also purchased several racetracks, including Road Atlanta and Sebring.

I didn't go back to Geneseo for 50 years; except for my parent's funerals, but there was one time when (Lynne and I) were on a road trip in the northeast. We had three days left before we needed to return to Georgia. We were at her godparents' home in southern Pennsylvania and were only a day's drive away from both Geneseo, Illinois and Geneseo, New York. So, we did a brief stop at the one located in New York, that was very interesting; and then on to Illinois. I did try to see the Farkles when we arrived in town; it was about 30 years after I left. We just arrived in Geneseo, Illinois in time to have a wonderful dinner at The Cellar and checked into the Deck Motel. We rang their doorbell early the next morning, my Dad answered the door. He made the comment that he was hoping it was my brother who had planned a trip to see them (I believe he lived in Austin, Texas at that time). Dad blocked the doorway and did not invite us in, Lynne asked if we could come in and he asked how long we were planning to stay. I said just a few minutes; I wanted to look in the storage room to pick up what I had left there. He said that anything that I had left was destroyed years ago. Then he said, "Don't you remember what I told you that if you left, that you could never come back." So we left immediately, and went to Chicago and had a late lunch in the Walnut Room at Marshall Fields. At least I had tried to make peace with them, no guilt feelings here. After that episode, my wife was totally convinced that the events I had relayed to her were actually the way it had been, not just the way I had perceived them to be.

When I was manager of the FBO in Lawrenceville, Ft. Lauderdale, Salt Lake and Destin I had barber shops set up at those locations at the airport. In Lawrenceville, we were an emergency maintenance facility for one of the major fractional carriers, Flex Jet, and when they had maintenance issues in the area their dispatchers would divert them to us. Over time, I developed a rather large following with several of their crews, they would always seem to have a maintenance issue about every two weeks, just when they needed to get their hair cut. Years later, when I was at other facilities, they would recognize me and request my services. To this day, I have a shop set up in my home.

Jay Sekulow, was another one of our tenants; he had a large-mid-size jet based with us. Jay has since become one of President Trump's personal lawyers. Prior to that, he was one of Pat Robertson's lawyers. When Jay was working for Pat, he argued thirteen cases before the Supreme Court. I certainly had some in-depth conversations with him. He always took the time to speak with all the employees who were on duty at that time. Now when I see him or his son on TV, I get a warm spot in my heart remembering the conversations that we had many years ago.

During my time at GMD Aviation, Ken, my brother, called me very late one evening. I was already in bed, and I had no idea how he found me or got my number. But the gist of his conversation was that "mom and dad" were probably going to outlive their retirement savings, and he wanted me to know that they were expecting me to come up with an unknown amount of money so they could maintain their current lifestyle (going to Las Vegas on a regular basis) since I was doing so well. My first verbal response was "You've got to be shitting me." When I calmed down a bit, I told him that I would gladly repay all the money they had contributed towards my college education, which was a twenty-dollar bill! I also told him that if I were choosing my friends that none of them would be included, including him. After the abuse I endured from them, there is no chance of me coming up with any more than the twenty dollars I had already told him about. I never sent the twenty dollars. As I pondered this request, the only thing that makes any sense is that Ken was broke. Because I spent almost three years fighting the State of Texas over the money that the Farkles still had in their three retirement accounts.

Not long after that phone call, there was no chance that they would outlive the retirement savings, first my mother passed, then my brother and then my father. I had not planned to attend any of their funerals, but Lynne absolutely insisted that we show up. Then the legal battles began, mom and dad's wills were written in Illinois, but they died in Texas. It finally went to the Illinois Supreme Court to rule on the distribution, by this time (about three years) there was not that much left. I made countless trips to Texas for hearings, and every time the State of Texas would grant an extension to further the delay in making a decision, as to how the remaining funds would be distributed. The state argued that I would get the $100.00 dollars that the will stated, and the State of Texas would get the remainder of the estate. The will stated that if anybody contested any of the provisions contained in the will, they would not receive any of the proceeds. I argued that there was no provision in the will stating that the State of Texas would receive the remainder of the proceeds. Finally, it was decided to get the Illinois Supreme Court's opinion on the distribution of the remaining funds and that would be the final decision. At least I got a lot of flight time going back and forth.

Except for the Farkles' two funerals, I stayed totally away from Geneseo. During the funerals, I planned it so that we would arrive right at the end of the evening visitation, then we would have dinner at The Cellar. The funeral was the next morning, out of town immediately after the burial which was in Farmington, Illinois (about 80 miles from Geneseo), I had to lead the way to the cemetery, because the Funeral Director did not know where it was located. Then, on to Florida. The funerals were for mom in 1995 and dad in 1999. I would not have gone to either one except Lynne insisted that I show up. We always stayed in a motel; I would not, or could not stay in their house, we decided not to push the issue. Just before my mother's funeral, my dad and brother showed up at the motel before we checked out. They had a large number of legal papers with them and said I had to sign them right then, before I left town. I told them that I would fax them to my attorney, Bruce Green, in Ft. Lauderdale. and I would get back to them after he had a chance to review them. They were astonished (and pissed) that I had a lawyer on retainer, and snatched up the papers and stormed out of the room. I have no idea what they contained. Shortly after, we arrived for my father's funeral visitation, late of course, the undertaker came up to me and said that he noticed that I had not said good-bye to my father and that in a few minutes the visitation would be over, and the casket would be closed. I told him that I had said goodbye to that bastard when I was sixteen! That really took him by surprise. I guess that was the first time he had ever heard such a comment.

My brother passed between my mother and my father's deaths in 1997. His passing was under questionable circumstances. It seems he hung himself in his garage with a chain, intentionally or not was never revealed to me.

Back to the airport, Mike and Dick made regular trips to Grand Cayman in the Cayman Islands and appeared to be living the "good" life. In particular, Mike who had a home on Lake Lanier, just north of Atlanta and another on the Intracoastal Waterway in Ft. Lauderdale. At the Lake Lanier home, he had full size royal palm trees planted every spring, because they could not survive the Georgia winters, he treated them like annual flowers. Their supposed income was derived from the tremendous success of the Cash for Cars venture. In fact, they went out to obtain additional cash from investors to have even more money to lend. For this they guaranteed a huge return for their investors; they charged just under 300% on their loans. Can you say Ponzi scheme? If it sounds too good to be true, it probably is. Mike, with a bible in his hand, targeted churches, their building funds, the retirement savings of the parishioners and anybody else who had heard about the incredible return on their investment.

Ultimately, Dick turned himself in to the Security and Exchange commission and filled them in on his operations, I don't think Mike followed suit. The SEC came into the operation at the airport and took it over until Glen was proven not to have any part in his partner's crimes. The takeover lasted for about six months. That was a very hard time for me, trying to hold the operation together. The attorneys for the SEC had seized the bank accounts, so we were unable to pay even the electric and phone bills, and they were always late in paying them. Just more problems, not to mention paychecks that ran two weeks behind! Most of our hourly employees were living paycheck to paycheck. When it was over, Glen appointed his longtime friend and maintenance director to take the operations over.

He changed the name of the FBO to match the name of his maintenance department, Aircraft Specialists and he decided that they could no longer afford to keep me on the payroll. The person he put in charge of Line Service among other things, didn't understand that fuel costs change every week, their posted price went unchanged for over a year without being adjusted for cost increases. AvFuel calculated they lost well over one hundred thousand dollars. I guess they could have afforded to keep me on after all. I found out much later that the Shell Aviation Supplier, Buddy Stallings had contacted Glen and told him that the only reason I chose AvFuel over Shell to be our supplier is that AvFuel gave me a car when I was able to make the switch. Long after I had been terminated, Glen called AvFuel and asked them if the story they had been told was true. Of course, it was false. I believed that Buddy would try this stunt again when I was hired to be President of Salt Lake Jet Center, my next aviation employer. This time I told the owners of Salt Lake Jet Center to expect this call from Buddy and they could verify with AvFuel that I had never received any kind of reward from them. I chose AvFuel because they were the best aviation fuel supplier out there.

After my ordeal with GMD / Aircraft Specialists, I decided it was time to move to Maine, into the house that we had purchased with the money that I received from the court settlement from the will. Lynne was getting worse, health wise, and this is where she wanted to be at the end, at Moosehead Lake. I contracted with a local "handy man" to begin the required repairs and remodeling to turn it into a Bed & Breakfast and it would be associated with The Lodge at Mooosehead. New metal roof, all new windows, new entrances with airlocks – front and back, all new siding, all new plumbing, updating the electrical wiring, and replacing all the major appliances. He did an outstanding job, but just one person doing the work, it took quite a long time, even though I was doing a lot of the finish work in the bedrooms and bathrooms, it was dragging on.

With the cost of the remodeling and Lynne's medical expenses, I found it necessary to find another job. There were no good paying employment options where we were in the Greenville area, so I contacted several networking partners to seek employment.

Then an AvFuel representative in the west suggested that I contact Rocky Mountain Jet Centers located just outside of Denver. They were looking for a President for their Salt Lake facility, and we worked out an employment agreement for one year, with options for additional time if all parties were happy with the arrangement. I was hired as President of Salt Lake JetCenters.

GMD's Ramp after Purchase from Atlanta Jet

Figure 10 – 1

Don't ever feel like you have failed.
You either win, or you learn.

The more you learn,
The closer to success you become.

Believe it!

CHAPTER ELEVEN:
SALT LAKE JETCENTER
1997 – 1998

As I just mentioned, Rocky Mountain JetCenters got in touch with me through AvFuel, because they had purchased one of the competing FBOs in Salt Lake, Global Aero, and the current President at Salt Lake JetCenter who was about to retire had no intention of combining the two operations. My main project was to merge the two companies into one. The former President was running them as two individual companies. Each had their own Line and Customer Service employees, their own accounting departments, and their own standard operating procedures. Soon after I arrived, it became obvious that neither one was profitable. They were competing against a very powerful Million Air franchise. Million Air, was much larger than the combined operations and had much larger and better facilities.

When I accepted the position in Salt Lake, we rented a house in Bountiful, just north of Salt Lake City. The owner was a psychologist, and we became friends. At dinner one evening, my wife mentioned how my early life had been. She asked me some rather pointed questions and then said that I was in the top 10 to 15% of those who came from similar backgrounds that had survived and have become a success in their chosen fields. The other 85 to 90% made a choice to turn to alcohol, drugs or suicide. It doesn't matter where you came from, but what you are made of, and the choices you have made. That made me feel pretty good about the way my life has turned out, at least up to that point.

A week before Lynne's drastic downturn, I was mowing the yard and a neighbor stopped by and introduced herself as Ruth Oyler. I told her it was a pleasure to meet a neighbor and that Lynne was inside but not able to come out, and I explained the situation. Ruth all but begged me to let her go in and meet her, and she did go in. When she came out, I was just finishing up with the yard and she said that we really needed help, and she was just the person to handle it, if that was okay with me. I told her to go for it. This was my first encounter with someone of the Mormon faith. Did I mention that we were one of only two houses in the entire neighborhood that were not Mormons? I gave her a key so she could get in while I was at work. She arranged with a few others in the neighborhood to go in and check on Lynne every hour while I was at the airport. Another neighbor from across the street, soon came over and introduced herself, and wanted to meet Lynne. Upon entering, she met Duchess, our Akita, and asked where we kept the ribbons and trophies. I explained she was just a pet, and we hadn't ever entered her in a competition. She told me that she had been a judge for the Westminster Dog Show, and that Duchess would take best in class, if not the best in the show; she went on in and introduced herself to Lynne. Then another neighbor lady came by, introduced herself, and said that she owned a beauty salon and when Lynne was up to riding in a car she would come over after she closed her shop and take Lynne and shampoo and set her hair; she would not accept any form of remuneration for services. She said she was just doing what neighbors do for each other. We were new to the area, and were not Mormon, these acts of kindness just blew me away.

Shortly after we arrived in Utah, Lynne got much worse health-wise, leukemia was advancing quite rapidly. Then one evening, she was unable to get off the couch or walk without assistance, and I took her to the LDS hospital in Salt Lake. In the emergency room, there were four attending physicians on duty, it was a very large trauma center. Three of the four doctors' diagnoses were that she was having a stroke. The fourth doctor came to me and said she didn't have enough of the symptoms for a heart attack or stroke, she had a high fever and an extreme headache. He had already contacted the CDC in Atlanta and they concluded that she was probably coming down with encephalitis. He said he wanted to administer a combination of drugs that CDC had suggested, and they would do no harm if it turned out to be a heart attack or stroke, but if, in fact it was encephalitis, these drugs were her only chance of survival. Of course, I told him to go ahead with the drug treatment. She was getting worse rapidly and they admitted her to the Intensive Care unit, where she would remain for several weeks.

I didn't go to the hospital on Halloween night, it was pretty late in the evening, about 8:30, when a man knocked on the door for trick-or-treat, he had two children with him. He introduced himself, another neighbor and explained that Ruth had told him about Lynne, and he asked if it would be okay if he would stop by her room when he was at the hospital, which was three times a week. I said sure, and he said he would include her in his prayers. I had a rather large canoe leaning against the wall which he saw, and he asked if we were from Minnesota or Michigan or somewhere, and I told him Maine. He asked where in Maine, and I said way up north on a large lake. He said, "Not Moosehead Lake?" I was really taken aback, that somebody in Utah would know about Moosehead Lake, and I replied, "Yes. Let me formally introduce myself, I'm Lee Groberg and I make movies for the LDS Church and National Geographic"; he went to Greenville, Maine to do a documentary on the expanding moose population. I asked where they stayed in Greenville, he didn't remember the name of the place, but described it in detail. It was The Lodge at Moosehead, across the road from our B&B (Inn). He then proceeded to describe my house. What a coincidence that he stayed across the road from my house and remembered it in detail. As it turned out, he was the leader of the 11th Ward in Bountiful, as well as being a Counselor in the State Presidency, then he became a Bishop in the Mormon Church. As a side note, he made a movie about his close relative John H. Groberg's struggles when he was a missionary in Tonga. As I mentioned, Lee made the original movie on VHS and DVD, it has now been released in theaters: "The Other Side of Heaven, Two".

The Groberg's often had cookouts and potlucks in their back yard, when Lynne was well enough, we were often included as the neighbors who weren't yet Mormons. A lot of good-hearted comments were made when Lee introduced us. Comments like "you are not doing your job; they are not Mormons yet" we all had a good laugh. Actually, all the neighbors told us that if we had any questions about their religion, they would gladly answer them, if they didn't know the answer, they would find out for us. That was the only time they mentioned their religion to us.

When Lynne was transferred to a regular room from the intensive care unit, she wanted to see Duchess, and the hospital agreed that it would be a good thing. So, every Friday evening, I would take Duchess to the hospital with me. The only request the hospital made was that I use the service elevator in the rear of that section of the hospital. The hospital was huge; it covered a city block and even had a four-story parking garage across the street. Quite a place! When we got off the elevator, if there were anybody in the halls, most of them freaked out at the sight of my large dog. Anyway, Duchess soon became a "hospital dog", she would go into every room on the way to Lynne's room and let the patients pet her. Then one evening, a mother was pushing her daughter in a wheelchair down the hall. Duchess headed for the little girl, but she pulled away from her, and I told her that Duchess would like some pets. She didn't want anything to do with that, so we went on our way. The next week we passed her room, and she cried out, "Duchess is back" so we went in her room, she gave Duchess a few pats on her head and kissed her nose. By now her mother was crying and she motioned us to the hall and told me that those were the first words her daughter had spoken in weeks. The next Friday when we passed her room, it was empty, the nurse told me that the little girl had passed away from cancer. That was one of those real heart-breaking moments, it still gets to me each time I think about it.

When I would get home after a snowstorm the driveway would be plowed, and the sidewalks shoveled. I asked Ruth who was doing that for me, she replied don't worry about that, you have more important things to think about. Some days when I came home to let Duchess out and change clothes, before I went to the hospital, there would be a note on the door. Look in the refrigerator before you go out for a burger, there would be a meal in there. She never would tell me who was doing these things. This was absolutely incredible to me, we weren't Mormons, we were new to the neighborhood, and the entire neighborhood pitched in to help us!

Temple Square – Salt Lake City

LDS Hospital

This is why, after Lynne passed, I have sought out the Mormon Missionaries, wherever I was living, and invite them in, and have a satisfying meal and just relax. No religion is discussed, we usually talk about their life before they went on their Mission. I have formed some long-lasting relationships with a few of them. And for Ruth, we still email each other several times a year. Ruth sent me a book, "Mormonism for Dummies", almost every time the Elders come over, they look something up in that book. When I was in Destin, two of the Elders requested that I prepare a dinner for their parents who came to Destin when they concluded their Mission. They even requested what they hoped would be on the menu. Both sets of parents went into great detail about how pleased they were that I had "taken in" their boys. Some evening the Elders would call me and ask if they could come over, they were having a dreadful day and just wanted to come to a friendly place where they could relax and calm down. Of course, they could come over.

When Lynne got a little stronger, she had to re-learn the most basic functions like, writing, speaking and even using a fork and spoon. After several weeks of therapy, she was well enough to be transferred to an assisted living facility. Her first night there she woke up and thought she was home and headed for the bathroom, but there was a wheelchair in her path, she fell over it and broke her hip. She went back to the hospital to have it replaced and the room she was in also included physical therapy, but she was too weak to get any therapy. For just the room, the rate was eleven thousand dollars a day! I requested that she be transferred back to her old room, I was advised that her surgeon would not check up on her progress anywhere in the hospital except for this one particular recovery area. The bill for that room for six days was sixty-six thousand dollars. Now I understand how major hospital administrators can be paid over a million dollars a year!

Back to the airport. The current Line Manager was more interested in playing golf or going out for lunch rather than tending to the daily operations. Not to mention, getting the two operations operating as one. Every morning he would read the paper and send one of the line crew out to get his breakfast. His golf games left the crew to be in charge of running the operation, things such as maintaining the fuel supply, snow removal, resolving problems with the based customers and quoting our rates for potential customers. When a storm was approaching, transient aircraft would often request to be hangared, but that meant Line Service would have to open and possibly re-stack a hangar to accommodate the request. It was easier just to stay warm in the Line Room and not honor the request, that is what they did. There was no incentive to generate as much revenue as possible. The Line Manager was soon doing even less since he was no longer employed by Salt Lake JetCenter.

The Customer Service Manager had her own domain at the front desk, and she was also the bookkeeper. She did not want to integrate with the other company, because that would increase her workload and she would have less time to socialize. She also enjoyed going to Las Vegas for a long weekend and going to England and Hawaii a couple times a year. In the end, she got a real surprise when her workload doubled.

It was almost unbelievable the attitude that the Jet Center employees had toward the former Global employees. I heard comments like; "those bastards will never be allowed to come into our line room" and "those counter girls aren't smart enough to work here". The Line Manager from Global was a great employee and filled the leadership vacancy in JetCenter's staff. Some of the front desk employees from Global left by natural attrition and the rest were absorbed into JetCenter's operations. It took me about three months to close the Global operation. The former Global employees were profit and customer service oriented, and for the first time, JetCenter's bottom line was printed in black instead of red ink. I turned the Global facility into a storage hangar, and we used their lobby area for large aircraft arrivals and departures, such as when the Russian Antonov An-22, a Russian built cargo aircraft came in. By the way it took over 30,000 gallons of fuel on departure, it took two trucks all night to fuel the plane. It transported an entire oil drilling rig to Saudi Arabia, non-stop. The semi-trailer trucks actually drove through the plane. There was an internal crane system that could unload the trucks while they were inside the aircraft. (Figure 11 – 1)

The building maintenance man was very good at making phone calls to various service companies, who would change the air filters, change light bulbs, and polish the floors; you get the idea. He did almost nothing for forty hours a week. That changed too, I cancelled all the contracted service people who were doing his job. He got the picture and started to earn his paycheck.

Ultimately, only four JetCenter employees were terminated, under my leadership they soon figured out that there were new rules and policies and if they were not followed, they would no longer be employed.

Shortly before my contract ended, discussions were underway with Million Air to purchase the Jet Center's lease. I decided not to extend my contract. I was already in discussions with Ranger Jet

Center in Kissimmee, FL to manage their facility with the possibility of part ownership. When I left, Salt Lake JetCenters the former President was brought back to hold it together until the sale was completed with Million Air.

Just to bring you up to date, Million Air ultimately purchased the JetCenter's lease hold, which included the former Global hangar; then Million Air was taken over by TAC Air. The county would not re-new the lease of the former Salt Lake JetCenter, it went out for bid, and it is now an Atlantic Aviation location, because the county wanted to reinstate competition on the field.

Antonov Stock Photo

Figure 11 – 1

Richard Zimmerman, 6'4" Line Manager, On the ramp with the
Antonov

Figure 11 - 2

Your life is the same as boiling water, it softens potatoes and hardens eggs.
It's about what you're made of and your circumstances that determine which it will be.

CHAPTER TWELVE:
RANGER JET CENTER
1998 – 1999

During my last month in Salt Lake, Bill Cooper, (the longtime friend of mine from Lawrenceville, GA.) put me in touch with the owners of Ranger Jet Center, which was located at the Kissimmee Gateway Airport, which is located just southwest of Orlando International and is the closest airport to Walt Disney World and Sea World. Bill Cooper was their fuel supplier, and he believed that I would be able to turn this company around and ultimately have ownership of it.

There were two owners of the facility; one was a general contractor whose expertise was building hospitals and schools. The other was a traveling evangelist. They had big plans for Ranger Jet, even had artist conceptions of the completed facility. However, after phase one there was no more construction of the needed hangars and most of all, a free-standing terminal. The current terminal was a modified corporate aviation department's office which was just part of a storage hangar, totally inadequate. The accounting and President's offices were upstairs, and President's office was four times larger than the lobby area downstairs.

With no aviation business experience, other than the contactor previously owning a plane, or a reasonable understanding of generally accepted accounting procedures, they did not understand their P&L's. One example of this was they had their accountant book an outside investment in the company as income, not a liability. They believed they were profitable when they were running in the red since day one. When I pointed this out to them, they doubted my accounting knowledge. Based on the number of gallons of fuel they were selling, it was impossible to show a profit. Another time, with a hurricane approaching I asked them what insurance coverage they had, and they said they had complete coverage including the hurricane coverage which included a rider that would keep their payroll funded until normal operations could resume. Totally false! They carried only the basic minimum insurance required to keep their lease with the county in good standing.

One of our line employees had a very good relationship with John Travolta, and we were the provider of his fuel at Jumble Air, that was John's home just outside of Ocala. There was a long-paved runway on the property and John built his home to accommodate two of his planes, a Gulfstream and a Quantis Boeing 707, plus there were ramp areas for additional planes. Originally, the runway was built on the property where the founder of Nautilus exercise equipment, Arthur Jones, had his home and had the runway built in order to handle Nautilus's 707, which Arthurs's wife was a qualified pilot and was the Chief Pilot of. After Arthur's death in 2007, the property around the runway was divided into building lots and John purchased one of them. I actually watched the movie *Grease* with him in his media room.

Working with the owners was difficult based on their lack of experience in the ownership of an FBO. One of the owners took pleasure in walking around the facility dropping candy wrappers on the ground to see how long it would take line service to picked them up. Not a very good use of his or the employee's time! Also, the traveling evangelist kept his large motor home in the hangar, taking up valuable rental space.

We did have the NetJets contract, one of the three major

fractional companies, and occasionally we would have one of their jets scheduled. The Kansas City Royals had their spring training camp at Boardwalk and Baseball, a theme park owned by Harcourt Brace Jovanovich, about thirty minutes from the airport. When the Yankees played the Royals, Andy Pettitt and Derek Jeter would arrive on a NetJets Lear. They graciously autographed baseballs, and had autographed photos for our employees; they were very considerate.

A few months after I arrived, Hurricane Charley was the first of three hurricanes to impact the Orlando area during 2004. The other two were Frances and Ivan. All three hit Kissimmee Airport with varying effects. Charley did the most damage, totaling the largest hangar and doing major damage to several aircraft in the hangar. Other hangars sustained lesser amounts of damage. Neither of the owners bothered to come to the airport to check for damage. There was no phone service, so I sent a line man to the home of the President to inform him of the damage that had been done to the facility. When he did finally arrive and several days after the first storm, he was running from building to building making unreasonable demands of the employees concerning the clean-up. It was at this time, that I learned that what I was told about our insurance coverage was not true. Their coverage was far from adequate to cover all the physical damage and there was no provision to cover the employees' payroll.

The morning after the storm passed, there was a strange station wagon parked in front of the terminal, filled with bottled water. I asked where that came from, and much to my surprise, John Travolta had one of his people drive it down from Ocala. We were to keep the car for as long as we needed it, and of course the water was a welcome sight.

By the time that Ivan was approaching, Lynne wanted to evacuate and we headed for our home in Maine. That was the first time we had ever encountered the traffic involved with the evacuation, the first hour on the Florida Turnpike we went three miles. It was basically bumper to bumper, all the way to Atlanta. Then we headed east on I-85 and ran into another evacuation from another storm heading for South Carolina. It was several more hours of heavy traffic, then pretty good the rest of the way to Maine. A few days after being back in Maine we decided that I would not continue my employment with Ranger. It just wasn't worth the stress involved in working with them. Lynne was not doing very well, and I really needed to spend more time caring for her. Hence, I returned to Florida, officially resigned, packed up the house and then off to Maine.

Ranger Jet Center has been sold two times since I left and is currently owned by Odyssey Aviation, who happen to be a group of former Million Air franchise owners who decided to start their own chain of FBO's. They have done a considerable amount of re-modeling, creating a workable lobby area.

Ranger Jet Center

Figure 12 – 1

John Travolta's Jumble Air Home

Figure 12 - 2

*Life's journey is not to
arrive at the grave safely
in a well-preserved body,
but rather to skid in sideways,
totally used up and worn out, shouting
'...man, what a ride!'*

CHAPTER THIRTEEN: CAREGIVER 1999 - 2006

Lynne was diagnosed with leukemia while I was working for GMD Aviation and went on for seven years. So, this chapter will span those seven years. The day our household furnishings arrived in Maine was 09-11-2001. Bruce, the owner of The Lodge at Moosehead kept us up to date as to what was happening in New York City until our TV was unloaded and connected to the cable. As I mentioned earlier, The Lodge was just across the road from our home.

We met Bruce and Sonda the first time we went to Greenville, at that time they owned the Evergreen Lodge B&B and have been good friends since then. The day we closed on our home; they closed on The Lodge. The Lodge was a Five Star – Four Diamond Inn, at that time it was the only B&B/Inn in Maine to have both of those top ratings.

We went to the Moosehead Lake region because Lynne had vacationed (camped) at the lake when she was young, and it was on her bucket list that it was where she wanted to be at the end. The lake is over forty miles long and twenty-one miles wide, to give you some idea of how cold it gets in Greenville, the frost point is forty-eight inches deep and so is the ice on the lake. We went to Greenville several times before we found the house that we ended up purchasing. Each time we stayed at Bruce and Sonda's Evergreen Lodge. The first time we stayed there, it was over the fourth of July weekend, and they invited us to be with them on their boat for the fireworks display, the fireworks were specular. Sonda had even stopped in town, and picked up sandwiches for us. They really made us feel welcome. By the way, we were the only one of their guests that were invited to join them on the lake. On another day, Bruce, who was also a Certified Maine Guide, invited us to evaluate his first moose sighting adventure tour, he was the only moose-sighting guide to use a boat. We saw a lot of moose that day and came within twenty-five feet of one of them who was grazing on "Moose Muck" at the water's edge.

On one of the trips to look for a Maine house, we stopped in Kennebunkport. It was Memorial Day weekend, and we left the motel rather early and walked a few blocks to the center of town. There was a bit of a crowd gathering on the sidewalk in front of us, and it turned out it was President George H. W. Bush with two Secret Service men. When we were a few feet away from him I said, "Good Morning Mr., President" and he replied "Good morning. . .. Oh, I know you." We chatted for a bit and the Secret Service was getting rather nervous because a crowd was gathering. They asked him to go into the bakery and pick up his order. He asked us to follow him into a bakery to pick up some sweet rolls that Barbara had ordered. As he reached for his billfold, the clerk said, "Oh no, Mr. President, it's on the house." but he insisted on paying for them. He took out his American Express Card and presented it to her and explained to us that he loves to use it. He went on that there were only six of those cards in existence, the name imprinted on the card was "The President". There is much more to this story, but it would not be appropriate to go into the details about our lunch, which consisted of lobster rolls, at his home on Walker's Point.

The house we purchased had been vacant for several years and needed a lot of TLC and a lot of remodeling to make it into a B&B.

Much of this work had been completed when we were in Salt Lake and Kissimmee. The remainder of the work, was completed by Moosehead Building, Inc. Kyle Pellitier's company and his crew. I put it on the "fast track" so we could get the B&B open. Then, we were ready for the state inspector to grant a license for a B&B and a commercial kitchen, so we could serve dinners as well as breakfasts and be an "Inn" instead of a "B&B". We had planned to work closely with The Lodge across the road to handle their overflow. Our B&B/Inn did not open because Lynne was getting worse by the day, and it wouldn't be fair to our guests to be subjected to someone in her condition.

Every year the town of Greenville, which is located on the south end of Moosehead Lake in the northwestern part of the state, hosts the "International Seaplane Fly In". The Fly-In Association is a non-profit organization whose focus is to provide aviation education scholarships for the local high school students, and it was a whole lot of fun for the participants and the spectators alike. The Fly-In brings thousands of participants and spectators to the Moosehead Region on the weekend after Labor Day.

One of the members of the steering committee was Kyle Pellitier who was doing the work for me on our soon to be an "Inn". I asked him if he thought that the committee would allow me to join the planning of the event; he was closely related to the organizer. Since I was from "away", I wasn't sure if they would want or appreciate my participation. He said sure and told me when the next meeting was scheduled. During the meeting, one of the members mentioned they needed something special to kick off the event; it was a three-day happening. By the way, it drew about 300 seaplanes along with thousands of tourists. Anyway, I asked them if they would like to have John Travolta's Boeing 707 do a flyby, they all looked at me like I was crazy. They half-heartedly said sure, so I called John and explained the event. John had a home on an exclusive island just outside of Portland, Maine. As luck would have it, he was filming a movie in Toronto and said he planned to fly to Portland on the opening day of the event. He would be more than happy to do the flight. At exactly noon, during the opening ceremony, John's Qantas 707 flew the entire length of Pratham Avenue (the main street in town) at 500 feet. My stature was elevated, at least a little bit, even though I was still from "away". If your grandparents weren't born in that county, you were not considered to be a native, so you were from "away", and for the most part you were treated as such.

I volunteered to work at the airport and was asked to direct the arriving planes to the tie down areas. That was quite a job since most of the pilots were not used to having someone direct them; they wanted to go wherever they chose to go. Some did not even understand international hand signals, at least that's what they told me when I asked them to move their plane to one of the proper areas. The airport didn't even have tie-down ropes or chocks for transient planes. After the event, I wrote a several page report on my suggestions for the future fly-ins. I don't know whether they took any of my suggestions seriously or if they even read it. Jimmy Buffett brought his Albatross (Figure 13 -5) to the annual Sea Plane fly-in. After that, he returned to go fishing and invited me to go along.

Remember our hospital dog, Duchess; she was Lynne's dog, and stayed beside her almost all of the time. One evening when I was sleeping on the couch near Lynne, Duchess woke me up and licked my face, then went into the kitchen and laid down in front of the refrigerator. About an hour later, I went into the kitchen and found that she had passed away. That was a very hard morning for me, but Lynne believed that she would be reunited with her in the very near future. I had Bruce come over and help me get Duchess into the car, and took her body to the vet and had her cremated. It was Lynne's request that both of their ashes be placed into Moosehead Lake when the time came. Lynne passed over on October 12, 2006. It was on our anniversary, Christmas Eve, that I placed both of their ashes into the Lake. I found an area where the lake had not yet frozen over. That was the first Christmas that I was alone in thirty-three years, it was a hard one, one of many hard ones to come.

Soon after Duchess passed away, both of us wanted another dog to fill the void that we both felt. We went to the shelter in Bangor and chose Dex. A rather large, older black dog that had been there for quite some time. I did the paperwork and as we were walking out to the car, Dex led us to it. He jumped into the back seat, and it was off to Greenville. Dex was extremely protective of Lynne, so much so that any male that came to the door, he would challenge them. I had to place a jar of milk bones in the airlock so they could bribe him and get in. He would stay between the guest and Lynne until they left or if we went to the basement where I had located the barbershop. After her passing, he would let anybody into the house, unchallenged!

I worked part-time for the Watts, they owned The Indian Hill Trading Post on edge of town, which included a gas station and in the main store, souvenirs, household items, groceries, men's and women's clothing, shoes, and a large sporting goods department. They also had another smaller grocery store and the trading post in the business district, the trading post had everything from yarn to animal mounts and shed antlers to furniture, Christmas ornaments, Stone Wall jams and jellies, and a lot in-between. They were so good to me, granting time off whenever I needed to take Lynne to her appointments, or when I felt I needed to stay home and tend to her needs.

There were no "box" stores or chain restaurants in Greenville, it was an hour and a half drive to Bangor to find them, such stores as Home Depot, KFC, Pizza Hut, and even a dry cleaner; you get the picture. That was one of the real downsides to living in Greenville.

When Lynne passed away, she wanted to be in the house until the end, and it was close, I was able to keep her there until the day before she passed. The lady from the Hospice, Kay Johnson, came to the house that morning and determined that I was no longer able to handle the situation, and she called the ambulance and Lynne was admitted to the local hospital. They administered hourly injections to keep the pain under control. But as long as Kay and I were in the room, she would not give up. Kay had to leave and go to Bangor, and I needed to leave to feed and let Dex out. As I was leaving the hospital, I told her that she was on the runway, had her take off clearance and it was time to add full power and take off. Then I left for home and as I was walking through the door, the phone was ringing. It was the hospital telling me to come right back, when Lynne was alone, she crossed over. The hospital called Bruce and Sonda to be there since I had no other family to be with me.

I had a Memorial service at the house for Lynne a week later. As it happened, another Greenville resident had passed on the same day as Lynne, and there was a church service for her. Her ashes were taken to the family farm, and when they opened the container to spread her ashes, they were labeled Lynne's ashes. The funeral director that we both used, and a member of the other family came to the door and asked if I had opened my container, I had not. The crematory had placed the two sets of ashes in the wrong boxes. We exchanged the contents and both families continued with their services. The crematory refunded the cost of their service for the mental anguish they had caused.

Unless you have been in the position of full-time caregiver, you cannot appreciate the stress that it puts on that person twenty-four hours a day. One day, during the next to the last month, Kay (the hospice representative) asked if I would like to get out of the house for the afternoon? I requested that she take Lynne out, for the afternoon, even if it was just to their room at the hospital, so I could get some things done around the house without the constant interruption of having to keep checking in on the patient, to just be alone for a few hours. She told me that was the first time that she had heard that request. She thought for a moment, bundled Lynne up and off they went. I cherished that afternoon, to be alone and get so many things handled around the house. Kay told me later that she had made the same offer to other caregivers, and every one of them had taken her up on it.

Irving Litchfield, an AvFuel district manager was in contact with Jay Odom in Destin Florida. He was going to build a world class FBO and was checking with all the fuel suppliers to find out what they had to offer. Irving asked Jay who was going to manage the facility for him, and he responded that his pilots would handle that. Irving went on to explain and gave him several examples of other FBO's that had done just that, and every one of them had all failed. He told Jay that he needed to find someone who was experienced in the business if he wanted it to be successful. Jay asked how he could find such a person. He told him about me, and the success that I had accomplished in other FBO's, but that my wife had just passed away and he didn't know if I would be interested; but he would find out and if I was interested, he would have me get in contact with Crystal Beach Development in Destin Florida, Jay's parent company. The rest is history.

Moosehead Lake –40 Miles Long 21 Miles Wide, (View from our front window, the third row of mountains is in Canada)

Figure 13 – 1

Fixed Wing Aircraft and Campers at the Airport

Figure 13 – 2

A few of the 300 Seaplanes

Figure 13 - 3

Arts and Crafts Area

Figure 13 – 4

Albatross

The same model as Jimmy Buffets, now located at

Universal Studios Theme Park in Orlando

Figure 13 – 5

Own Who You Are,
Believe in yourself!, and
Don't be afraid to chase your dreams!

CHAPTER FOURTEEN:
DESTIN JET
2007 - 2016

Jay had previously met with the three owners of Miracle Strip Aviation and offered to purchase their facility, the only FBO at Destin Airport. It was owned by three old men who looked at the facility as a cash cow, not a customer service operation. He made a very fair offer, so I have heard. When they turned him down, then he told them that he was going to build a new facility and go into competition with them. One of the owners told him that he would never be able to build a facility at his airport. That's all it took – seven years later we opened, after overcoming all the obstacles that were thrown at him. Jay said that he would have given up on the project years ago, if it had not been for that challenge. Miracle Strip was one of those "turnpike gas stations for aircraft", gouging their customers and offering no extra services.

A month after Lynne's death, I received a call from Irving Litchfield. He inquired as to how I was doing, and would I be interested in going back to Florida. I told him that it was really cold, and I was still adjusting to being alone. He had just met with Jay Odom who was building a new FBO in Destin and really needed someone who could handle the start-up and then run it. He told Jay that I had just lost my wife and he had no idea if I would be interested, if I was, that I would give him a call. I called; we spoke for over an hour; then we planned to meet just before Thanksgiving.

I flew to Destin to meet with him and get the "feel" of the town. I stayed five days in a Gulf front condo, and the first thing I did when I got into my room was to open the sliders and enjoy the warm weather and the sounds and smell of the Gulf. I only met with him two times in five days, and I agreed to work with his architects who were in Birmingham; via phone conferences and he would determine how it was working out. It was difficult working with those architects, they didn't have a clue as to what was needed to handle private-corporate aviation, they only understood commercial aviation. They refused to go to the airport in Birmingham and visit the FBO's and see for themselves how the private facilities operated. They were more interested in creating a logo instead of understanding the flow that is required for private aircraft and the passengers' needs.

I found out years later that Jay had continued the search for his General Manager, but he believed that I was the only one who had the necessary experience to take over the project. The following March one of his emails contained an attachment with an employment contract, we hadn't even discussed that. I made a few changes and returned it, he agreed to the changes, and I would begin on the first of June. In the meantime, I returned to Destin and rented a townhouse adjacent to the airport. It overlooked Miracle Strip Aviation, our soon to be competitor.

On my first day working for Jay, I learned there was no room in his offices, so I began working out of the Club House at Hammock Bay. It is a three hundred acre planned community, that Jay was developing thirty minutes north of Destin in Freeport. I was the "hall monitor" there, but it gave me the space and time to develop a list of required equipment and supplies that would be needed and write a policy manual and the guides for how we were going to deal with our customers. For example, no front-line employee could tell a customer "No", they were to refer them to a supervisor. For example, if a customer requested hangar space and there was none available, we would offer to put their request on a list and should space become available we would hangar their aircraft. We didn't tell them no but did not actually tell them yes either; most would leave with a positive feeling about the way they were handled. Also, I developed job descriptions for every position and appearance standards, which I had created (and had made very few changes) based on my history with RCA at Miami Aviation so many years before.

Two of the people who worked at the Club House and the Sales Center at Hammock Bay, were Wanda and James Bird, wonderful people. Wanda thought I should be dating somebody, so I told her what my conditions were: she had to be rich, single with no children, older than me, and in poor health. About a week later Wanda brought the first of two qualified candidates in to meet me, God they were old.

Soon after I arrived in Destin, Jay fired the architects that I had been working with via the conference calls. They never understood how private aviation is not like the airlines, for example, the lobby is not street-side but needs to be air-side. We started again, but with a local firm, and the learning curve began once again. We created an incredible terminal, but it took a long time to get it built. It was designed to withstand Category 5 hurricane winds as were our hangars, which were already in place. The interior finishing was a complicated and time-consuming process, it took over a week just to install the tile and finish the men's rest room. There were four different tiles, that went halfway up the walls and two different finishes of the same color paint, flat and semi-gloss, to finish the upper portion of the walls.

We finally opened at the end of April, it was a slow start because of many construction delays. However, once the word got around that we were actually open for business (about three weeks) the influx of aircraft was incredible, very similar to what occurred at GMD Aviation. During those first two weeks, Jay was very concerned about the lack of traffic, and I just kept giving him assurance that when our potential customers saw that we were finally open, we would have them for their next trip. When he drove into the airport the Friday evening of Memorial Day weekend, he was disappointed in the lack of traffic on Miracle Strip's ramp, believing we would not have many customers either. To get to our location you had to drive past Miracle Strip and you could not see our south ramp until you got into our parking lot and the north ramp was totally obscure. One could only see the tails of the large aircraft over the eight-foot sound barrier fence on the south ramp. There were three of those large tails backed up to the fence and both of our ramps were covered with jets, he became a believer! . . . And so did Miracle Strip.

Before we opened, it was very useful for me to witness how poorly Miracle Strip was handling their customers. I also witnessed who were "good" workers and those who just showed up to collect a paycheck. Before anyone knew who I was, I toured their facilities three times. Not one time was I greeted as I came into their lobby and walked past their "front desk" or challenged me as I walked around the terminal and out onto the ramp. Most of the employees on duty were just too busy texting to notice me. About a month before we opened, they (Miracle Strip) released their General Manager, his assistant and two members of their accounting department for mishandling company funds and doing some creative accounting to cover it. They interviewed several candidates for the GM position, some of them called me and told me about their meeting with the owners of Miracle Strip; when they found out that I would be their competition, they chose not to accept the position, and that is how Laverne became the manager.

The owners of Miracle Strip appointed Laverne Brigman, who was the wife of one of the three elderly owners, to be General Manager. She called just before we opened Destin Jet and asked me how many of her employees I had hired so she would know how many she needed to replace, my reply to her was, "Not nearly as many as have filled out our application. At the first meeting Laverne made some very derogatory remarks toward me, I told the Director that I wasn't going to put up with that and was halfway out the door when he asked me to return and gave Laverne a lecture on how these meetings were going to be conducted in the future. At that moment, I decided I would do everything possible to put them into bankruptcy as soon as I possibly could. Our second airport meeting, which had been requested by the Aviation Director, was in our facility. I asked Laverne if she would like to see the rest of the facility, she firmly declined my offer. That was a preview of how our relationship would continue. On my back balcony, which overlooked Miracle Strip's large ramp where they parked the few jets that still went there, I hung a full-length banner that said "Destin Jet" and had a large arrow pointing to our facility. Also, I had it illuminated for night viewing. It was also visible from the taxiway. Jay's marketing department had it made for our grand opening that we never had. Miracle Strip contacted the manager of the townhouses to come over and demand that I take the banner down. I refused, stating that it was not facing any city street and there was nothing in my lease that prevented me from having it located on my balcony. I left it up until it began to fade, after about six months. That was the end of that!

We were such a successful competitor, Laverne had to reduce their payroll by cutting wages and putting all their employees on a thirty-hour work week. Soon after that, they were forced to close their Maintenance Department. Due to Laverne's health issues, she had stage four leukemia, she had to retire, so they chose a daughter-in-law of another one of the owners whose aviation experience was working in a bank as a teller, then in the Miracle Strip's accounting department to be their General Manager. A year later, she moved back to the Cacaos Islands, then they chose another accounting person to run the company, Brian Cherry.

A few years after Destin Jet opened, I had not taken any time off, and things were running well. I decided that I should "get out" again and continue to do things that were on my "Bucket List". I booked a two-week trip to Alaska, the first week was touring the Fairbanks area, including the North Pole – actually it is a small town just outside of Fairbanks. While in the Fairbanks area I took a chartered Navajo to Fort Yukon inside the Arctic Circle, and on to Anwar over the proposed oil fields. Where the test wells have been drilled, it is a vast quicksand area and totally void of any vegetation, contrary to what the tree-huggers have told us; the national park is over one hundred miles from the drilling area. They only need to build eighty miles of pipeline to connect to the existing one, a one-year project; not the five years that we were told and used to put off the approval for drilling. Then on to the Yukon Territories in Canada, the vastness of the mountains and forests in Alaska is breath taking. There are scattered home-sites dotting the landscape, most have a landing strip in their yard, there are no roads to these sites. In fact, only 20% of Alaska is accessible by road. Then we were just Northeast of Fairbanks and flew over a huge gold mine, it was the same size and appearance as the copper mines in Utah. When I got back from the flight, I went to the hotel, showered, and decided to get something to eat. It was still light outside, but nothing was open – it was one-thirty in the morning! Got a Snickers and a Coke out of the machines in the hotel. The Coke was $3.75 for a 16-ounce bottle! Then I spent the next night in Denali National Park, the following day we took the train from Danali National Park to Anchorage. It happened to make a stop in Wasilla, Sarah Palin's Alaska home, then on to Anchorage.

My hotel room in Anchorage was on the fourteenth floor (it was actually the thirteenth), from there I had an unobstructed view of the airport, mainly the wide-body aircraft arriving and departing, like one about every ten minutes around the clock. Of course, I was thinking about the fuel loads they must have been taking. On another train to Seward (another one-hundred-twenty miles to the seaport) on the way we passed close to the Boeing Dreamlifter, which was parked on the ramp in Anchorage, it was built to transport parts for the 787 Dreamliner. At that time, it was the largest cargo plane in the world. On to the seaport, it was the fourth of July and 71 degrees; where I boarded a Holland America cruise ship for the trip to Vancouver, British Columbia. It was a large, beautiful city.

I chose Holland America because they cater to older adults, not families with children. They sure do, I had to be one of the youngest passengers on board. The ship's food and service were horrible. No coffee was available until breakfast was served and none until after dinner was served. I was seated at a table with three other men who were traveling together. By the time I would get to the table for dinner, they would have eaten all the rolls. When I requested more, the waiter would take the roll basket and not return until he delivered a meager portion of food, they called dinner. I requested to have coffee with dinner, and it was denied, could only have one cup after dinner. The plates and cups were cracked or chipped, I truly thought they were about to go into bankruptcy. However, the ports of call were very interesting; such as Hubbard Glacier (Figure 14 - 6), the capital of Alaska, Juneau has no roads leading into it, the only way to get there is to fly or take a boat, it is surrounded by mountains similar to the Tetons at Jackson Hole. On one of the stops, we were taken to see the totem poles. (Figure 14 – 7). It was in a wooded area with a countless number of totems, very interesting.

For Destin Jet's seventh anniversary celebration and our placing as the third best FBO in the Americas, as chosen by the readers of Aviation International News, we put together a "Props – Wings – and Wheels" event. We had over two hundred million dollars' worth of equipment and jewels on display. Jets, Motorcycles, Boats, luxury autos and diamonds, there were games of chance, raffles for a champagne ride in a jet, for a sunset Helicopter tour and Resort Accommodations at the Emerald Grand, as well as a silent auction. There was an admission charge, and all profits were donated to the

Wounded Warriors Project. The paid admission count was over four hundred fifty, it was the most unusual event that Destin had ever seen. Most of the ladies were dressed to the hilt and most of the men were in dress slacks and sport coats. There were two bands for continuous listening and dancing, heavy finger food served by a variety of caterers, and tours through some of the luxury boats and planes. Yes, we did hire off-duty Deputy Sheriff's Officers to maintain order with this much of high value equipment in one location. The jewelry store had their own armed security people, they brought over $1,000,000 worth of diamonds. We even provided valet parking since almost all parking had to be located on a remote ramp.

Paula Dean and her husband Michael Groover arrived just as we were doing the final setting up for the event. They came to town for another function, and they took the time to look at all the equipment as it was arriving. Michael was most interested in the motorcycles that were on display in the lobby. While he was doing his thing, Paula sat down with the linemen and myself and asked if it would be okay to have a cigarette (we were in the outside line area). I reached into my pocket and pulled mine out and she said she had her own, dumped her purse out on the table, found her cigarettes, and lit up. She also had a couple cups of coffee and a cupcake with us. She was one of our most gracious guests ever, she chatted with us for at least a half an hour, like we had known her for years.

About this time, more of the national awards for our service started coming in. Then Aviation International News conducted a survey of their subscribers, and Destin Jet was voted third best FBO in the Americas. Shortly after that, Business Jet Traveler did an international survey, we came in fourth in the world. This was unbelievable to me, we were competing with every FBO in the world, there are approximately 5,000 FBOs just in the U.S. Every customer we had would have had to vote for us to receive these honors. Several other surveys listed us in their top ten operations in the United States.

In keeping with my decision to get out of my shell and do things, I accepted an invitation from Butch and Russ Smith to attend the Reno Air Race as a guest of Southwest Airlines and the River Rats, a group of fighter pilots that have attended the race for many years, a distinguished group of pilots. This race will be known as the "The Crash of the P-51 - Galloping Ghost" September 23, 2011. I am extremely grateful to still be here to write about this. Yeah, it was close – very close. We were in a reserved VIP box – it was two boxes located on the ramp area in front the permanent grandstand. The boxes are divided with convention style three-foot rails and drapes; each one has twelve padded folding chairs and room for coolers and such. It is a very comfortable way to view the races.

Friday, the Gold Race, all the biggies from last year's final (that was cancelled due to high winds) with a lot of bragging rights on the table, not to mention that this would be the first time since that cancelled race that they would race each other or anyone else. Strega qualified first position, then Voodoo, Rare Bear, Galloping Ghost, Dreadnaught, and Sawbones, in this order. The order stretches out a little but stays that way to Lap #3 when Jimmy Leeward in the Ghost makes his move on Rare Bear on the back straightaway. Galloping Ghost passed him cleanly on the outside. Pylons 7, 8, and 9 are next as the racers come to the Home Pylon past the Grandstand – Ghost doesn't make the turn, he pulled to the outside and straight up HARD. I thought he was pulling out of the race, but strange it was so abrupt. Straightening out, but going straight up, now rolling slightly right. I sensed that something very bad was about to happen. After climbing 1,500 to 2,000 feet his direction now changed; the Ghost was now coming straight towards me, it seemed like no one was flying the plane. The engine wound up and was howling. Ghost on its way down and pointing directly at me with literally seconds to go, and I basically frozen in my tracks, trying to decide which way to go, I dove toward the front of the Grandstand next to a short concrete staircase.

There was a lady next to me, I threw her down and dropped on top of her. This all happened extremely fast; in my mind I was sure that this was the end as the aircraft was heading straight towards us. The noise reminded me of what we've all heard in the movies when a propeller driven fighter goes in. Then a really LOUD boom! It hit box 105 about 50 feet from us – we were in boxes 108 and 109.

The impact rattled us right down to our core, however no explosion, just debris raining down on us and heaviness. I smelled the atomized fuel as it settled down upon us and the odor of burnt metal. When I felt the debris had settled, I got up and then realized we were all covered with very high-octane fuel mist, I once again thought this was the end; couldn't believe there was no expulsion. Everyone's nerves were pretty well shot at this point. I pulled a small piece of shrapnel out of my right calf, that is the sum total of my injuries. As the people were milling around us, we took an inventory of the people in our group – all accounted for, except for one, turns out Butch was in the porta potty, behind the grandstands at the time. All the people in our group just had relatively minor scrapes and cuts. At this point, we knew many didn't make it. There were two doctors in our group, and they immediately went into action. A lady immediately in front of us didn't make it and a man next to our booth lost his leg, just above his knee. My belt was used for a tourniquet for him. A triage unit was set up between us and the crash site within a few minutes – incredible response – the PA announcer (after a soft "Oh My God") requested that any medical personnel come forward and give their assistance. Then he immediately requested that the crowd move away from the site and leave the area. I was dazed and in shock, it took a while for me to regain my composure and follow their requests. It took the security and the police to bring me back to my senses and move me back and then out of the grandstand area to the midway. Almost everyone remained very calm – shaken for sure and we departed the area within 10 to 15 minutes.

The debris field was spread over 300 yards, the engine block slid down the ramp at least 300 yards, however, its path was just outside of the VIP area or there would have been many more injuries and possible deaths. As it was, there were 19 deaths and over 45 amputations. Right beside me there was a tennis shoe with a foot still in it. Photos show the left elevator trim tab separated from the rest of the tail section. NTSB findings indicate that this is what caused the violent upward pitch creating over 11 G's on the pilot, causing him to immediately lose consciousness. Once that happened, he was no longer in control of his aircraft, contrary to what the news media said about him not crashing into the stands, but rather into a less concentrated area, the VIP seating section. Once again, I avoided death! This time it was really close.

My next annual trip was another check off the Bucket List, Fiji, Australia, and New Zealand. That was my Christmas trip, no more being home alone on my Anniversary and on Christmas Day. That was a great trip! I flew on Air Pacific, which now has restructured into Fiji Airways, from Los Angeles to Fiji. I got off in Fiji for two days and then on to Sydney. I knew one of the mechanics who worked for Island Hoppers, a helicopter tour operator in Fiji. He worked for Vertol Systems, the parent company of Island Hoppers, who was based with us in Destin. We toured the island, both the exclusive and beautiful, the island and the homes and resorts, then on to the native sides. The most unusual thing was there are no supermarkets, instead only canned goods are sold in the grocery stores. You must get your meat at a meat market, bread items at a bakery, and produce, usually at roadside stands. The island itself is very much like the Windward Islands.

Then on to Sydney. It was the first time I was met by a chauffeur holding a sign with my name on it. At the hotel, I met the rest of the group who were on the land and sea program with Royal Caribbean Cruise Lines. On the first evening at the hotel, we had a get to know each other meeting, it was a small group that were on that program, a family of four from Columbus Ohio, an older couple from Philadelphia, and an "odd" couple, from White Plains, Westchester County, New York, however only the husband attended the meeting, and myself. The family of four and the older couple and I immediately liked each other. After that meeting, the family and I walked around Sydney to find a reasonably priced place to have dinner. The Australian version of Golden Corral was $99.00 per person for dinner. We found an Italian restaurant just a few blocks from the hotel where we had dinner and got to know each other a bit better. Walking around the streets of Sydney we felt very safe, there was even a free Michael Bublé Christmas concert in a public park. Near the park, there was a Cathedral that was used as the base structure for projected images, an incredible continuous running program. There were even bleachers, so everyone had an unobstructed view of the show. As the tour progressed, I became much better friends with the family from Columbus Ohio. It was a two-and-a-half-week cruise tour.

(Getting a bit ahead of myself, the family from Ohio have become traveling buddies, the "gang of five" – sometimes a "gang of seven", we have taken twelve cruises together, so far. They have taken many more cruises than I have, they were Diamond Plus on Royal Caribbean Cruise Lines, and before I became a Diamond member, they included me with some of the perks that go with the Diamond and Diamond Plus designation.) The odd couple stayed to themselves for the entire trip. He said that he was becoming a monk and when he did speak to us, he tried to impress us with his education and their home in Westchester County, (White Plaines, New York). I wasn't impressed!

The RCL trip included flying to Cairns, Australia, it was about a three-hour flight; then a bus to Port Douglas where we stayed overnight. The next morning, we took a hydrofoil out to the Great Barrier Reef. That was about a two-hour trip out to an anchored, huge structure (raft), (Figure 14 – 7). It contained a seating area, a post Office, snack bar and an area where they rented wet suits for diving in the reef. Also, from there I took a helicopter that was on another nearby anchored raft that served as a landing site. The flight took me over the reef, at a very low altitude. Then we took the hydrofoil back to Port Douglas.

From there we had another three-hour flight to Alice Springs, another overnight; it is the closest town to Ayres Rock, (Figure 14 – 8) that is the place where the dingoes eat babies. The next morning, we boarded a large van and did a full tour of the area which is basically a desert. There are many rock formations similar to Ayres Rock. We could climb on them, and on our way over to the main event, we saw a camel lying near the edge of the road. Our driver told us that many years ago, a person tried to form a settlement in the area and imported camels. When the settlement failed, he just turned them loose. We had a full tour of the rock; the various areas of interest were explained to us.

Later that evening, we had cocktails to the tunes of a dirigible, then dinner was served. It was served open air (no tent) just flying insects, thousands of them. After dinner, we were given an explanation of the star formation in the Southern Hemisphere. The next morning, we went back to the rock to see the color change at sunrise. The rock is located near the center of Australia; then we flew back to Sydney, another three-hour fight.

When we got back to the hotel, our luggage that we had left at the hotel was delivered to our rooms, we could only take one bag with us on the first part of the tour. Since this was about a three-week trip, we all had more than one piece of luggage. We re-packed and checked out of the hotel and had a tour of the city that lasted more than three hours. (We couldn't board the ship until after noon.) The cruise ship was docked in the downtown harbor adjacent to the famous Opera House, which was on the tour, but we were not allowed to take any pictures of the interior. It is actually comprised of several theaters. The famous Sydney bridge was on the other side of the ship. The tour included going past many of the Hollywood star's residences, the harbor, and a stop at Bondi Beach, where the Speedo was invented. Then onto the ship for a twelve-day circuit of New Zealand.

Bondi Beach – Sydney
Cruise Ship Terminal – Sydney

Our "odd couple" refused to turn over their luggage over to the ship's porters causing quite a scene. Eventually they were taken into a room at the rear of the baggage building, we were never informed what was in the baggage, but they were ultimately allowed to carry their bags to their cabin, it had to go through another screening before it was distributed to the cabins. That was the last time we were together with them; we didn't even see them for the rest of the trip.

Before we got to the first port in New Zealand, a teenager was playing on an antique pin-ball machine and could not get a very high score, so he knocked it over and smashed it. It happened to be the Captain's personal pinball machine. When we arrived in Dunedin the ship's Captain threw the whole family off the ship, and charged them $6,000.00 dollars for the damages.

Dunedin, New Zealand

The twelve-day cruise sailed around New Zealand, both islands. While anchored in Wellington, there was an earthquake. I was back on the ship, at first the Captain thought that a generator had exploded, it really shook the ship, it was at anchor in the harbor, not on a dock. The other four were on a tour and happened to be in a mountain town and took shelter in doorways. There was no major damage, but it was quite an experience for someone who had never encountered an earthquake and its aftershocks.

In Auckland, there is a tower similar to the Space Needle in

Seattle, but this one had a glass floor at the top viewing level. "Pitt", one of the four, and I just spent a very few minutes up there, just long enough to take some pictures and take the elevator back down. The tower was designed to sway in the wind, and it did just that.

Auckland, New Zealand

Then on New Years' Eve we were back in the Sydney harbor. Sydney (and Salt Lake City) are the cleanest cities I have ever visited, but Sydney is so expensive, almost everything must be flown in, similar to Alaska. To park your car downtown for the day it was $74.00 U.S dollars. Food, clothing, and apartment rents are just as expensive.

They drive on the wrong side of the road; and downtown they have painted on the street "Look Right" at every corner. On New Year's Day, the family of four took the "tour" of climbing over the Sydney bridge, while I flew back to Fiji.

New Years Eve – Sydney

New Year Day - Climbers at top of Sydney Bridge

Back to Destin. Governor Mike Huckabee was a regular customer. His home is just east of Destin on the beach on 30A for those of you who know the area. His Fox News TV show originated in New York. Many evenings his private flight was ahead of schedule and his wife, Janet would not be there to pick him up until the time of his scheduled arrival. Many times, the Governor would spend the time in my office, and we would have some very interesting discussions. He autographed several books for me and one for my neighbor; she didn't believe that I was having "regular" discussions with the Governor. For that matter, she didn't believe many of the stories of my life experiences.

The Governor would use our conference room for some of his video press releases before the studio was built in his new home.

As time went on, Jimmy (Buffett) "accidentally" met my traveling companions, the ones I met in Sydney Australia. My friends are true Parrot-Heads. Leanne has been to fifty+ concerts and John her son has been to seventy-five+ concerts. Jimmy was performing in Paris. Yes, Leanne and John did fly to Paris for one of Jimmy's concerts, they have done this twice, fly to Paris for his concert, that is. He actually sat down in the hotel lobby and chatted with them for about fifteen minutes, after Leanne mentioned that we have a friend in common. He told them that he had just seen me in Destin the week before. That verified my credibility somewhat and Jimmy verified that we knew each other.

A year later, John met Jimmy at the gym in Las Vegas, and Jimmy asked where his mother was. John told him that she had been diagnosed with breast cancer, had surgery, and was recovering in the hospital in Clearwater. He asked for John's phone and recorded a song just for her, so John would be able to play it later for her.

That's Jimmy!

Like we had at Banyan, we had a rather long hallway; on one side were framed survey results and commendations for our service. On the other side of the hall were autographed photos of our "famous" guests. Like Banyan's wall-of-fame, customers would spend quite a bit of time checking them out.

I was invited to attend a private gathering with Dakota Meyer, a Medal of Honor recipient for his heroism. His talk was inspiring, and we were presented with his book, which was personalized and autographed. This was in conjunction with the annual convention of the National Business Aircraft Association (NBAA). The gathering was held in a true ice bar in Orlando. Upon entry, you are given a parka and gloves, the bar is all ice, and the glasses are made of ice also. The gathering was held in a room where the temperature was 72 degrees. They did not want to freeze us out.

For my 50th high school class reunion in 2014, I stayed In Geneseo for two days, it was most enlightening. The town itself has changed very little, same buildings downtown, just different tenants. The population has only increased by less than one thousand. But of course, I had dinner at The Cellar; it is still just as I remembered, it was as good as it was 50 years ago, the menu has hardly changed.

Don't know how so many of my classmates have gone through life without a lens on the world but a lot of them have. I just had to show off, so I used the company jet (Figure 14 – 8), to get there and let the members of my class find out that I lived in Destin Florida and had a log cabin lodge in the Appalachian Mountains. By the time the word got around the room, I had arrived in my personal jet, and I had a large home on the water in Florida and a lodge in the mountains, I decided not to correct them. It was like coming home for the first time. It was great to not be the odd ball out, but a respected member of my class. I was the only one who arrived in a private jet, had been in all fifty states, been on five continents and have touched down in over ninety countries and actually toured fifty-six of them.

Quite honestly, the success that I have enjoyed has been beyond all odds. One of my former classmates asked what my favorite place was that I had visited, I thought for a minute and said, "My favorite Island is Barbados, and my favorite city is Sydney, Australia". The response was: "Oh, the United States isn't good enough for you anymore". Need I say more. One couple said their highlight was they had gone to Chicago (150 miles) to Wrigley Field to see a Cubs game! As a side note, my pilot rented a car and went to a Cubs game while I was in Geneseo.

The evening before the actual reunion, there was an informal get together. It was very interesting, most of the attendees I did not recognize at all, a very few I could recognize from my high school days, but then there were three girls that had not changed at all. I have no idea how much they must have invested with cosmetic surgeons. I had dated one of them, Terri Morland, she recognized me as soon as she came into the room and jumped into my lap. I thought this would be a great evening, then she said, "Bill, I want you to meet my husband". So much for those thoughts! For the most part, I felt like I was in a room full of old people, wheelchairs, oxygen tanks, walkers, canes, you get the idea. Most of the remaining members of my class have never moved away from Geneseo, while I could not wait to get the hell out of there since I was not a very popular member of my class and of course the Farkles. Unfortunately, several of my classmates that I really wanted to chat with and see how they were doing had passed away or just didn't show up for the reunion. I estimate that about one third of my classmates are no longer with us. That was a sobering thought. They just aren't doing well; I believe the many years I spent in south Florida with the high oxygen content has a lot to do with my good health. The pollution just blows across the state into the Gulf and the vegetation in the Everglades creates a high oxygen content. It's been proven that our bodies slow down because of that, heart rates slow down and breathing also slows down because of that high oxygen content. Your body doesn't have to work as hard to get the oxygen it requires.

Before I went, I was speaking with my friend who owns AvFuel (my fuel supplier for many years) and he told me that he always schedules some kind of meeting for later in the evening when he attends this type of function, so he had a reason to leave early. With that in mind, I arranged for my departure flight to be at 10:00 PM, the celebration was not far from the Moline airport, only about 10 minutes away. I had to leave by 9:45, I was kind of sorry that I had done that, I would have liked to stay a little longer, however I can only imagine the conversations about my "good fortunes" after I left.

Speaking of the airport, it became obvious that the reason why so many customers were so impressed with Destin Jet and the other operations that I managed, was the lack of service that was provided by Elliott Aviation in Moline, the only FBO on the field. Nobody met the plane, we found a parking place, got our own chocks, and carried our luggage into the terminal. Inside, the "counter girl" had no idea who we were, even though we had made reservations for the plane and for cars. When she got the paperwork finished for my rental car, I asked her where the car was, her reply was, "Out in the back-parking lot. . . do you want it pulled up?" I asked why it wasn't delivered planeside, she just gave me a blank stare. I said I would appreciate it being delivered to the door. A few minutes later a line man pulled it up. On departure, the line man (who was called in for a $100.00 overtime charge) unlocked the entrance door and the door to the ramp, turned on one light, and sat behind the counter the whole time we were getting the plane ready. No offer to pull it up, connect a power cart, get ice and coffee, or direct us off the ramp. For that "service" they charged the call out fee, their regular closing time was 5:00 PM not the usual 10:00PM!

278

Back to Destin, we had a based ramp customer that had a twin-engine Cessna 421. He installed, and did some maintenance work on our computer's server, our terminals, our internet systems, and our sound systems. He replaced a major component and when Jay's IT person tried to register it for warranty purposes, she found out that that part had already been registered a year earlier by another company. Needless to say, we did not use his services any longer. But we had more of a relationship with him because of his work than we would have had if he had just been a based customer.

He had a lot of maintenance issues with his plane, typical for the Cessna 421's, and it was in the shop quite often. One evening, as he was taxiing onto the ramp, one of his engines just shut down for no apparent reason. He fiddled with it for a while and finally got it started. The next morning, he loaded up his entire family, his wife and five kids, and flew to St. Louis for a family gathering. On his return trip, he once again loaded up the entire family except for one daughter who lived in St. Louis. They were cruising at 15,000 feet over Alabama when both engines quit running. They were five miles from the nearest airport. They crashed one mile short of the runway, the plane exploded, and all were killed. I cannot understand how he could not make it to the airport, only five miles away from 15,000 feet. I have had thoughts about that but will not put them into writing. Just like the accident in Opa-locka with the McCabe vehicle in the parking lot, for a long time after their fatal accident, both of their cars were in the first two spaces in our parking lot. They were there for weeks; it was a constant reminder for our employees and some of our customers who recognized their cars.

After several years of competing with Miracle Strip Aviation, Jay arranged through a distant relative to purchase the facility on his behalf. They were virtually bankrupt, severely behind in their rent, and their asking price was much more realistic, most of their transient business was now using us, and their permanent tie down customers had been driven off by an unrealistic rate that had been instituted. A payment plan was worked out with the county aviation department to handle the large amount of unpaid back rent. The terminal was remodeled and refurbished to the style of Destin Jet. The actual ownership was not made public for about a year, then the Destin Jet South sign went up on the building.

Soon after, we started receiving the national and international awards; several national chain FBO's started inquiring if we were for sale. My response was that everything is for sale if the price is right. Jay received a firm offer from a chain operation with earnest money and it contained a date in which they had to complete their due diligence, if they were satisfied with their findings to proceed with the closing. They let the agreed upon date pass without an answer either way, so Jay terminated the negotiations and kept the earnest money.

Not long after, two other chain operations, Lynx and Sheltair expressed an interest in purchasing the operation, Lynx was next in line; they got their act together and completed the sale. I was seventy by this time, had my cabin in Blue Ridge, and decided not to go with the new owner and retired. This brought me to the end of my aviation career. I must say that Jay Odom was a very generous person and took good care of me throughout my employment and upon my retirement.

A very interesting fact just turned up. The Farkles claimed that we were all German, however "23 and Me" found that I was of Scandinavian and British decent, not German. Very interesting, and my closest relative that "23 and Me" could find was a fourth cousin in Europe. When I asked if I had been adopted they always avoided giving me a straight answer, "Why would you ask such a question/" was their response, but one time they did come up with what they said was my birth certificate. However, with their position politically and in Geneseo, I believe one could have been easily created for them. They were unable to produce a baby book of my early years and had no pictures of me before I was four. I have no memories before I was in kindergarden, and those are sketchy at best. Appearantly I was adopted at birth and taken home as their child.

I have since learned that when WWII was about over, the Catholic chuch would find many babies on their front steps most mornings. They had so many that the finally had to put them on a train and it headed west. The train would stop in towns along the way west and ask the local citizens if they wanted a baby or knew of someone who did. No actual adoption process was used, they just needed to find homes for all these babies. I undestand they came with blank birth certificates that a local doctor could fill out. I truly believe that is how I came into this world. That fits with my dad's unreasonable attitude toward all Catholics that I may have dated and the Catholic church.

Destin Jet's South Ramp, Memorial Day Weekend
Figure 14 – 1

Front Ramp
Figure 14 – 2

Reno Air Race Crash of P-51- Figures 14 – 3 & 4

Dreamlifter on Ramp in Anchorage
Figure 14 - 5

Hubbard Glacier

Figure 14 - 6

Figure 14 – 6

Great Barrier Reef floating raft

14 - 7

Ayres Rock

Figure 14 - 8

Arrival in Moline for 50th Class Reunion

Figure 14 - 9

I chose the skies.
That few have known
To follow where
The winds have blown.

I battle storms.
That none have seen
I find seas of gold.
To find seas of green

And if someday
I don't return.
Don't cry for me
Don't be concerned.

For high above
The clouds I will sing.
For a world I loved
And for silent wings.

Author Unknown

CHAPTER FIFTEEN:
FINAL THOUGHTS

Here I sit at my computer seven years after I retired, doing a lot of recollecting on the many adventures of my life so far; reflecting on how gratifying it has been since I left Geneseo. Sometimes, now that I have retired, it takes me all day to get nothing done and on other days it is just the opposite. I have been coming to terms with how my early years had such an impact on my actions and beliefs.

At a very early age I made the decision not to have any children, because there is no schooling required for people to take a course in child rearing, the only way one learns how to be a parent is from their own parents. An abused child becomes an abusive parent, and I chose not to bring a child into this world because I did not want to repeat how another person had treated me. I was fortunate enough to find my wife, she didn't want to have any children, however, for very different reasons. It all boils down to the choices I have made, and how they influenced my life and very few others close to me.

In writing this book, I learned just how driven I had become. There was something inside me that had to come out; but my life up to a point, while still living in Geneseo, was influenced by constantly being told by my parents, teachers, and classmates, how inferior I was. We all know people who speak fluent shit, unfortunately a lot of those people were an influence on my life. I had been surrounded by people who can look you dead in the face and not hear a damn thing you are saying. I had to learn how to sort these folks out and totally disregard their comments. You must believe in something, before you can become something. In my case, it was believing that I could become a pilot and then it became managing the best Fixed Base Operation on the field, if not one of the best in the country. Granted, it was a large learning curve for me, but soon I learned to listen to my customers: they were asking for what they wanted and expected, all I had to do was to listen.

I remember the first time I was given the actual responsibility for managing other people and achieving a specific goal. Instinctively I knew I could do it. In looking back, I was probably a terrible leader, but in my head, I was the best boss that they had ever had, but more importantly, at long last I was successful in achieving my assigned tasks. Many times, I took the long road just to go a short distance. Difficult roads often lead to great destinations. You can't direct the wind, but you can adjust your sails. So far, I've been able to go to all 50 states, touched down on five continents, and touched down over 90 countries and toured through 56 of them.

Instead of thinking and worrying about the worst things that could possibly happen – I learned to keep thinking about the positive good things that were happening in my life. During my early years, I had to keep my emotions and feelings to myself, I wasn't allowed to express them in any way; then with my wife's help I was somewhat able to develop "normal" feelings and emotions more closely. Since her passing, most of the time I haven't been able to suppress any of those emotions and feelings. If you don't know where you want to go, you may never get there.

At the last NBAA (National Business Aircraft Association) convention that I attended, it would take me over thirty minutes to get to the washroom from our booth because so many people recognized me and wanted to chat. I was totally amazed by the number of people that have made a special effort to thank me for the help and advice I have given them over the years; that I was responsible for their success. Recently, even more gratifying was that two people have told me that I was directly responsible for saving their lives, literally. Unknowingly I had prevented two suicides because of the discussions we had. I was totally blindsided by their confessions and had absolutely no idea that I had such an effect on their lives.

In looking back, especially in the weeks before attending my 50th class reunion, recalling the experiences that I have had, the people I have met and the friends, both famous and not so famous, that I have made, and the places that I have had the chance to see, it has been a marvelous experience. A few days before the reunion, I decided that I would not bring up most of my experiences because I thought they would not believe most of the experiences that I could have shared with them. After all, I was told throughout my school years that I would never amount to anything, never be able to accomplish anything. However, while attending Flight Training and working with their staff; it had a profound influence on me. For the first time in my life, I realized that I could actually succeed at something. I was given real responsibilities, included in their social activities, and I was invited to be a member of their group. That experience had a profound effect on me and completely changed my outlook on life. My life has been an adventure, never knowing in advance where it would lead me.

In the end, as far as the reunion was concerned, I was the only one who arrived in a private jet! Yes, I was showing off, and it felt great! I was living in Florida, had a lodge in the Appalachian Mountains and was riding around on a private jet. This was the only class reunion that I have attended, and it will probably be the last. I was in a room with a lot of really old people, who for the most part, were not recognizable to me, and I had absolutely nothing in common with almost all of them.

My mission in life has been not merely surviving, but thriving by taking chances, with passion, compassion, humor, and style. I hope that I will die before I get old. I have gotten older (that beats the alternative) but I haven't grown up. It isn't about the age in years, but the age in your brain. I have met many people in their eighties who have a young attitude about life and their brains are incredibly sharp. And I know forty-year old's who are old – really old, with one foot in the grave and the other on a banana peel.

"I have traveled to 96 countries on 5 continents so far and have learned things about every place. I visited and learned things about almost every person I have met along the way. If you're scared to travel, as I was at first, just take a deep breath and go anyway. Go everywhere. Go where you don't speak the language, where you're out of your comfort zone."

Along my journey in life, I finally concluded that my competition was not with other people, but my own procrastination, my ego and the knowledge I neglected to learn. Also, there were those negative thoughts that I had been nurturing. I had been competing against myself.

As Henry Ford once said: "Failure is simply the opportunity to begin again, this time more intelligently".

Just remember that the choices you have made is your life, you are taking charge of your destiny.

You may think that you are completely insignificant to this world, but someone drinks coffee every morning from their favorite cup that you gave them. Someone heard a song on the radio that reminded them of you, someone remembered your joke and smiled as they were returning home from work in the evening. Someone loves himself a little more because you gave them a compliment. Never think that you have no influence whatsoever; your words and actions, which you leave behind with even a few virtuous deeds, cannot be erased.

As a final thought: Don't chase people, be yourself, do your own thing and work hard. The right people – the ones who really belong in your life - will come to you and stay.

"If I've impacted on one heart, one mind, one soul, and brought to that individual a greater truth than that individual came into a relationship with me having, then I would say that I was in the right place at the right time."

Do not let your past control your future,

Live the life you have dreamed of.

You can have what you want.

As long as you believe you can have it.

You never get over hard (bad) times –

You just get through them.

"The saddest aspect of life right now is that science gathers knowledge faster than society gathers wisdom." Dr. David Agus, American physician and author

"I'm not telling you to make the world better, because I don't think that progress is necessarily part of the package. I'm just telling you to live in it. Not just to endure it, not just to suffer it, not just to pass through it, but to live in it. To look at it. To try to get the picture. To live recklessly. To take chances. To make your own work and take pride in it. To seize the moment.

The further you get from where you started, the closer you get to where you belong; even though for some, it may be back to where they began. But at least, you have taken the trip.

MORE
ACKNOWLEDGEMENT'S

I would like to acknowledge the following individuals that helped me along the way to get through my early years and into the life that I loved.

Doctor Watters, who diagnosed me, actually saved my life.

Jerry Roesner, was one of my few friends in High School and helped me overcome being the "odd man out".

Bob Minter hired me the second day I was in Flight Training and worked closely with me to become a true salesman for the school, that was a real confidence builder.

David Vaughn was an Eastern Aviation employee who really helped me to become a true leader in Customer Service.

Marty Sinker, my boss at Hangar One and turned the Customer Service Department over to me, as well as becoming my best friend. He stuck with me through the good times as well as the tough times, when I really needed a friend.

Ed Blair worked for Triton Fuel Group, and had enough faith in me to select me as one of the organizing members of the TRIP program. That was a real boost to my ego.

Craig Sincock, President, and CEO of AvFuel, he had enough confidence in my ideas to incorporate them into his company.

Jay Odom, owner of Crystal Beach Development, and Destin Jet, he had enough confidence in my abilities to turn the entire operation over to me, from the very beginning, and never questioned my decisions.

Lea and Stuart Watt, Moosehead Traders – were so helpful and kind to me when I needed it most. A great big Thank You!

Bruce and Sonda Hamilton, were there for me in Greenville, especially at the time of Lynne's death.

I needed these people's input throughout my life since I didn't receive any of it at home.